WOMEN AND PROPERTY: WOMEN AS PROPERTY

WOMEN AND PROPERTY - WOMEN AS PROPERTY

Edited by
RENÉE HIRSCHON

CROOM HELM
London & Canberra
ST. MARTIN'S PRESS
New York

© 1984 Renée Hirschon
Croom Helm Ltd, Provident House, Burrell Row,
Beckenham, Kent BR3 1AT
Croom Helm Australia, PO Box 391, Manuka,
ACT 2603, Australia

British Library Cataloguing in Publication Data

Women and property.
    1. Women – Social conditions
    I. Hirschon, Renée
    305.4'2   HQ.1121

    ISBN 0-7099-1233-1
    ISBN 0-7099-1258-7 Pbk

Library of Congress Cataloging in Publication Data
Main entry under title:

Women and property.

    1. Women – Legal status, laws, etc. 2. Married
women. 3. Property. I. Hirschon, Renée.
K644.W65   1984   346.04   83-11029
ISBN 0-312-88730-2   342.64

Printed and bound in Great Britain

CONTENTS

Preface

PREFACE

Over the past seven years the Oxford Women's Studies Committee has organised a regular series of lectures covering a wide range of topics. A number of books have resulted from this activity; the present volume is the seventh and others are planned. Queen Elizabeth House, Oxford, provides administrative facilities and a pleasant venue and this support for the Committee's work is gratefully acknowledged. Thanks are also due to the Ford Foundation for a grant to the Committee which helped to fund the lectures on which this book is based.

I wish to thank the contributors for their hard work and for waiving part of their royalties in support of the Committee's continuing activities. I am also grateful to members of the Women's Studies Committee for their support and to those who attended and enlivened discussions at the lecture series. In addition to the many people who helped me in preparing this book for publication, I thank Chris Storrar for editorial assistance and Maureen Beck who word-processed the text. My deepest personal debt is to Manolis and Nicolas Philippakis for their encouragement and help at all stages.

1 INTRODUCTION: PROPERTY, POWER AND GENDER RELATIONS

Renée Hirschon

Property and Power

Much feminist writing is in essence an attempt to grapple with issues of power in the relative positions of women and men. Whether expressed in terms of patriarchy, sexual asymmetry, female subordination or male dominance, questions regarding power lie at the heart of many discussions of gender relations. The issues related to power involve the ability to act autonomously, to command compliance from others or to control their actions.

In this respect 'property', however it is approached and whatever its constituents, is a crucial indicator of the balance of power between women and men. Although the significance of property is a commonplace in class analysis and basic to a materialist interpretation of social phenomena, little systematic attention has been directed to this factor in the analysis of women's position. This omission is even more striking in view of Engels' profound influence on feminist thought and his thesis that women's subordination developed through the private ownership of property together with monogamous marriage [1]. But ideas of this kind were not unique to Engels. In the general climate of nineteenth century opinion regarding social evolution, there was a widespread interest in the relationship between property institutions, marriage and women's position [2]. This intellectual preoccupation of the Victorian period has continued in some anthropological writing (see e.g. Goody, 1976) with differences in orientation. Since this book is based on the assumption that 'property' would illuminate important dimensions of gender relations, it follows this broad tradition. But the present endeavour is differently conceived. By placing women and property as the central focus, it seeks to explore wider dimensions of the topic and to open it up for further investigation.

The questions to be addressed are: In what ways have relationships between women and men been structured by access to, control over and transmission of property? To what extent and in what respects do women themselves or their offspring constitute property? Other points considered are ideological constructs, the effect of plural legal systems, and changes in types of property.

1

These apparently straightforward questions touch on issues of considerable complexity. This is because these papers cover a wide range of economic, political and social forms (but they do not purport to be specifically representative of any particular type). We have examples from old-world literate civilisations, post-colonial nations, socialist countries, capitalist and subsistence economies, from the urban as well as the rural sectors of society. Significant common features exist, however: all are today part of modern centralised states and all are integrated, to varying degrees, into the world economy. Some are closer to previous subsistence modes of production (East Africa, northern Ghana, New Guinea), others have been longer penetrated by capitalism (Portugal, India, Accra, South Africa), while some have undergone more radical conscious transformation of the traditional social and economic order (Turkey, China). Given the diversity of societies and the different perspectives of the authors, an overall synthesis is not possible. Some of the common themes which emerge are worth further research and consideration, however, and the introduction will indicate these briefly.

Conceptualising Property and Women

The most serious single source of misinterpretation of the concepts of alien cultures is inadequate mastery of the concepts of one's own culture (Finnegan and Horton, 1973, p.34).

While it can indeed be seen as a key dimension in gender relations, it soon becomes evident that 'property' as a category for analysis requires examination. The first confrontation is with our own notions of property. Inevitably for us as westerners these are rooted in our own particular historical experience. Broadly speaking, our attitudes to property are associated with the development of capitalism and with the notion of the commodity. Property for us is based on the idea of 'private ownership' which confers on the individual the right to use and to disposal. Property is thus seen as valued goods/objects which can be transferred between legally-constructed individuals. But what we take for granted – the idea of an individual actor having defined rights vis-à-vis others, and the notion of property as consisting in objects or things – is far from being universal. On the contrary these concepts are historically and culturally situated in the western tradition [3]. This very familiarity may blind us to fundamental differences in concepts of 'property' and 'persons' in other social groups.

Persons and Things; Subjects or Objects?

These issues are directly confronted in papers by Strathern (ch.9) and Whitehead (ch.10). In both, the western approach to property is shown to be characterised by the radical disjunction between

2

'persons' and 'things', between 'subject' and 'object'. Strathern's instructive analysis demonstrates clearly how inappropriate this framework is for interpreting systems of exchange in areas such as Melanesia where the notion of the gift (and not the commodity) prevails. She concentrates on explicating indigenous notions of wealth and personhood in Highlands New Guinea.

Women in Highlands New Guinea society are often equated with wealth, they are exchanged on marriage between patrilineal clans, and in some places the product of their labour is appropriated by men. Are they therefore to be seen as property? If they are viewed as wealth in these societies, are they being equated with things? Strathern argues that they are neither 'objects' nor 'property' if these terms imply objectification. In these societies, the notion of the person does not involve the manipulation of 'things' nor does the concept of wealth involve 'objects' in the western sense. Precious things may have a dual nature; although they may look like 'things', wealth items at the symbolic level always retain a reference to the person (either metaphorically or metonymically). In the latter case, wealth may be 'detachable' from the person but it is never alienated. Women and things are exchanged as inalienable gifts, but not as disposable property. This quality of 'detachability' is what makes women and wealth items in New Guinea systems appear as 'objects' to us. Thus women may be equated with wealth, but wealth is not equivalent to our notion of property. Strathern's analysis reminds us forcefully of the importance of understanding a society in its own terms and of taking seriously the indigenous categories of thought.

Taking a different perspective, Whitehead explores these and other issues. In discussing how Marx dealt with notions of the person through a contrast between feudal and capitalist society, she emphasises the social character of property. Bound up with our own notion of property is the abstract notion of the 'individual' having specific 'rights'. It is this jural construction of the person which, she argues, is absent in kin-based societies such as the Kusasi of Ghana. She analyses here the unequal access to and control of resources in a nominally egalitarian society, and concludes that women in most social groups are not granted the status of fully acting subjects.

These two papers reflect then what has been called 'the tension between specificity and universality' (Young et al., 1981, viii) which I see as inherent in current feminist discourse. Indeed, all the studies presented in this book disclose the specificity of property relationships while touching also on themes of wider, universal significance.

Women Divided

A similar set of conceptual issues must be faced with 'women' as a focus for analysis. As a number of writers have stressed, women cannot be treated as an undifferentiated group (see Edholm et al., 1977; Bujra, 1978; Harris and Young, 1981). Women's biological characteristics present a deceptively 'natural' set of criteria around which social distinctions are marked, but even these are culturally specific (cf. Ardener, 1978). Although 'women' as a category provides a convenient catch-all term (as the proliferation of women's studies literature shows), 'women' like 'property' should be subjected to analytical scrutiny. In some societies the most socially-significant distinctions are based on class, in others on kinship, while in all, women's life-cycle changes are marked in different ways.

Several cases presented here show how, by focusing on 'property', these divisions between women are revealed with sharp clarity. Inequality in private ownership of land emerges clearly in Pina-Cabral's account of two Portuguese rural parishes (ch.5). Women of the landed peasantry marry and enjoy an elevated position, being called 'female bosses'. By contrast, landless women rarely married in the past, they produced children out of wedlock and were dependent upon the wealthy for their livelihood. Even greater cleavages exist among women in South Africa (Burman, ch. 7). In addition to class and the State's policy of apartheid which divides Whites from other population groups, in Cape Town a job preference policy favours the Coloured population. This further exacerbates the plight of African women whose permitted presence in the towns depends only upon their legal employment or on marriage. Economic power and wealth also divide the urban Ga women in Accra (Westwood, ch. 8), as does land ownership in the nascent class-system of Bodrum region, Turkey (Starr, ch. 6). But in Sharma's discussion of dowry in North India (ch.4), it is a woman's life-cycle changes which determine her access to property. While a bride has little if any control over her own dowry goods, older married women do, either as givers of dowry (mothers of brides) or as receivers (mothers of grooms). This kind of differentiation can also be inferred from Croll's account of rural Chinese marriage transactions (ch.3).

At the outset, therefore, the cross-cultural scope of this book requires some conceptual groundwork. Assumptions which we hold self-evident as members of our own culture may be an impediment to a more complete understanding of the topic. In short, the book challenges a commonsense, simplistic approach to the topic and it does so on two fronts. We are forced to consider not only what constitutes 'property' in any society but also what is involved in the notion of the 'person'. By examining this topic in a range of different societies and through the historical process, we are given much data on the specificity of property forms and its consequences for gender relations. While the relative and specific nature of 'property' emerges clearly, it is also possible to move to a more general analytical level and consider the wider significance of these studies.

The Significance of Property

In addition to its intrinsic interest, 'property' as an analytical category can be seen to link several conceptually-distinct levels of social organisation. This may have considerable significance since it may help to overcome a limitation in much feminist theory. There has been a prevalent tendency in many studies of women to treat as conceptually separate the 'public' and 'private' domains (for example, Rosaldo and Lamphere, 1974). Attention tends to be directed to either one of these, conceptualised as women's activities in social and biological reproduction versus those in the sphere of production. This analytical separation may result in theoretical problems and is increasingly subject to critique. As Beechey suggests, it is essential to treat the interrelationship of production and reproduction as a 'single process' (1978; see also Harris, 1981). I would suggest that in its very nature, property as a conceptual focus helps us to do so. This is because property relations entail social mechanisms of transmission. Resources, whether productive assets or personal valuables, are transmitted through inheritance and marriage transactions (cf. Stolcke, 1981), as well as in purely economic exchanges.

In the first instance, therefore, property as the social construction of resources is an integral aspect of both domestic-group organisation and of forces in the wider sphere of social life (economic, political, legal, ideological). Consequently, whether by theoretical intent or not, all the papers consider these two dimensions of the social order. The interplay of the kinship and domestic realm with the economic order is developed in Caplan's analysis of the East African coastal region, in Burman's examination of economic, legal and social pressures which beset urban African women in Cape Town (South Africa) and in Westwood's account of Accra. Croll's analysis of marriage in contemporary rural China shows how the peasant household copes with contradictory demands on it posed by partial but radical reforms in the social and economic order. In arguing against simplistic materialist interpretations, Whitehead emphasises the significance of kinship in defining property relations and women's capacities to act as autonomous subjects in pre-state agrarian societies.

In the second place, the nature of 'property' requires that we consider linking two other features of the social order, conceptually distinguished as the material and the ideological (cf. M. Bloch, 1975, pp.205, 211). In any environment given the level of technology, the material resources potentially available to the group far exceed what is sought after or actually used. What is construed as a valued resource, whether personal or productive, is an expression of the material conditions of existence in terms of values and perceptions pertaining at that time. Thus, culturally-specific evaluations are intrinsic to the definition of what constitutes property or wealth, given the constraints of technology, expertise and of historical circumstance. Crude oil, for example, was known to have various uses, including lighting, for centuries in classical and Hellenistic times (Pliny, 1968). It did not, however, have today's value since mechanised forms of energy production did not employ fossil fuels at that time.

Thirdly, the nature of 'property' as a category is essentially dynamic. Its form depends on a combination of interacting forces, political, legal as well as economic and cultural and these change through time. The values attached to various resources, objects, things in any group respond to changing circumstances. It is essential, therefore, to take an historical perspective. In each paper the dimension of change is considered, though the time-span varies depending on the specific circumstances of the case study.

Longer historical perspectives are given, for example, in the chapters by Caplan (ch.2), Pina-Cabral (ch.5) and Starr (ch.6). Caplan outlines how, over nearly 1,000 years, the East African coastal region has experienced significant changes in mode of production (kin-based, capitalist, socialist), in political organisation and administration (Islamic state, western colony, post-colonial independence). The co-existence of these different forms and influences has had marked effects on women's autonomy and property relations. In Pina-Cabral's study of two Portuguese parishes, changing rates of migration over 100 years, together with recent capitalist penetration in the local economy are noted. These are associated with the decreasing rate of illegitimate births and of average age of marriage over the period; also, these demographic features are directly related to the distribution of property, particularly land-ownership by women. In Bodrum region, Turkey, there has been a marked change over 60 years in mode of production, together with the increased use of the state's secular legal code. Starr shows that its provisions for legal equality can be effectively used by women to exert their rights to property and personal justice.

Changes over the last thirty years are included in two papers. Croll analyses women's access to property in post-revolutionary China (ch.3) and assesses the uneven effects of radical political reforms on social and economic organisation in the rural sector. In Highlands New Guinea the introduction of coffee as a cash crop in the 1950s has had markedly different effects on women in separate communities contrasted by Strathern (ch.9). Although cash circulates widely throughout the region, its use has been subsumed into traditional modes of exchange and has varied in response to particular local notions of wealth and valuables.

The New Guinea example makes an additional point regarding the changing nature of 'property'. We are reminded that the existence and use of cash does not in itself indicate a commodity-exchange system, nor the notion of the commodity (Strathern, this volume; A. Strathern, 1979). Although wealth and property in different societies may take similar forms and parallel kinds of change may occur, their significance in the women/property relationship may vary greatly, even within the same society (as Strathern shows, ch.9).

While recognising the dynamic and critical nature of property, therefore, we should not jump to conclusions about patterns of change, or assume a level of universality. Each social situation reveals the specific historical circumstances in which women's access to resources affects their relationships to one another, to men, and to their children.

Property: Material and Cultural Variations

Case studies from widely dispersed geographical areas, not surprisingly, refer to very different kinds of resources. What is culturally and materially construed as 'property' shows great variation: privately-owned coconut trees and usufruct rights to land (East Africa); trucks, pigs, and shell valuables (New Guinea); orchards, houses and reputation (Turkey); bridewealth cattle, rights to urban housing and employment (South Africa); capital, market-trading positions and arcane knowledge (Accra). Everywhere and increasingly, however, cash is becoming predominant. In some cases 'property' may be best thought of in terms of labour (in parts of Africa, rural China, for example). Despite this diversity some general features can be noted which emerge as themes running through the case studies.

Land and Labour

In agrarian societies where, even alongside cash cropping, a subsistence type of agriculture continues, the importance of women's labour is evident (for an analytical approach to women's labour, see Harris and Young, 1981). Women may play a central role in production, but the degree to which they control the product of their labour or act as autonomous persons varies (East African coast, ch.2, Highlands New Guinea, ch. 9, Kusasi of Ghana, ch.10). Though land in a kin-based society provides livelihood for all by virtue of their kinship affiliations, Whitehead points out that inequalities do exist. Differentiation on the basis of age seniority and gender may be marked. Indeed, as Whitehead suggests, the differential capacity to recruit labour in such societies is a crucial aspect of inequality in gender relationships. Despite the ideology of sharing, it is women who tend to get the smaller share.

It is particularly interesting, therefore, that in contemporary rural China, a socialist society where land was formerly the major form of property, it is now labour, especially that of women, which achieves prime importance in social and economic differentiation. Croll argues that household strategies are directed to recruiting women's labour through marriage, since labour cannot be hired. But women's access to dowry goods, inheritance and even cash earned outside the household has apparently become restricted.

In the other rural examples, Turkey and Portugal, private ownership of land is associated with a clearer definition of women's rights. Here, the notion of persons as legal entities has developed: both are societies where a formal legal system, bureaucracy and literacy (in short, the state) are long established.

Cash Earnings

Several papers suggest that in changing circumstances (where cash crops are introduced or where wage labour becomes available), women may suffer distinct disadvantages in relation to men. Even where they earn considerable cash sums in commodity production, as in Highlands New Guinea, women do not necessarily control their cash earnings and they may even accede to its appropriation by men (Strathern, ch.9). In the mixed systems of ownership in Mafia Island, East Africa, women have limited access to cash earnings because they do not own as many coconut trees as men nor do they have the capital assets (boats, vehicles).

Everywhere wage labour is generally more accessible for men. This is so in Accra, in South African cities, and also holds for employment opportunities in the case of India and Portugal. Chances for migration, abroad in the case of Portugal and to urban centres from the impoverished rural areas of South Africa, are also more readily taken up by men. As successive studies since Boserup (1970) have shown, the processes of change may have detrimental consequences for women.

Houses, Households and Women's Power

The composition of the household group and the organisation of its functions have a direct bearing on the degree of independence which a woman may have. Within it she may enjoy considerable authority in the allocation of resources. Thus the definition of roles within residential groups is a major factor in gender relations [4].

The importance for women of residential arrangements is brought out in Caplan's study (ch.2). In Mafia Island, the contractual basis of marriage and of household organisation contributes to women's autonomy. House form permits flexible living arrangements, an additional factor which promotes women's ability to act independently. Among the urban Ga of Accra (ch.8), the residential separation of men and women promotes solidarity among women. Houses are capital assets and can be owned by wealthy market women. In contrast, freehold ownership of houses is not available for Africans in South African cities (ch.7). Everywhere there is an acute shortage of housing so that families who are not tenants of the local authority are forced to live in squatter settlements. Consequently, housing rights are a major issue in marital disputes and divorce settlements; it is divorced women whose position is most precarious.

An additional factor, the pattern of post-marital residence, is of great significance for women's rights to property and to their general status. Where brides leave their natal homes on marriage to live with the husband's group (virilocal residence) they may cease to exercise their rights to inheritance. They may be isolated, even ill-treated (as in the notorious Indian dowry deaths), since they lack the support of nearby kinsfolk (India, New Guinea, Kusasi of

Ghana, China, Bodrum). Where women continue to reside in the natal home or near it after marriage (uxorilocal residence), they may enjoy a position of authority (Alto Minho, Portugal), or at least a greater degree of emotional security. A change of this kind has been occurring in some villages of the Bodrum region with demonstrably beneficial effects on women's position (Starr).

Though uxorilocal residence may have an ameliorating effect, it should not be assumed to invert the situation and confer unconditional power on women. The husbands who marry in as 'strangers' do not necessarily become subordinate to the wife's kin (contra van Baal, 1975, pp.83-4). In urban Greece, for example, wives are provided with houses as dowry which, in some areas, may result in residential clusters of kin related through women. The in-marrying grooms in urban areas, however, do not lose prestige. The ideology of male superordination prevails and each conjugal household is accorded autonomy under its male head (Hirschon, in press; Zatz, in press; cf. du Boulay, 1974, pp.126-8).

Intangible Property

'Property' as a socially valued resource may take a non-material form. What Lowie called 'incorporeal property' has been documented by anthropologists in many societies. It includes certain privileges which constitute wealth, or the proprietorship of songs and legends, special skills or knowledge of rituals (Lowie, 1929, pp.225ff). The skills in interpretation and knowledge of mysteries of certain Ga women who earn their living as priestesses comprise their 'cultural capital' in Westwood's analysis. Starr's account of changes in the legal and social position of Turkish women in the Bodrum region includes also the notion of honour and reputation as property (although intangible) together with the movable and immovable items. Reputation also enters the traditional assessment of a bride's marriageability in India along with the dowry goods (Sharma).

The Transmission of Property for Women

At this point it is useful to reiterate some key points. I have already noted that the investigation of property relationships takes us beyond the specific into more general issues of theoretical interest in feminist studies. This is because the conceptualisation of property and its character as a socially defined category directs attention both to the overall and wider social forces and to the domestic/household locus. Property as a conceptual category thus links these two analytically separate spheres and it does so through various mechanisms of property transmission, particularly at the time of marriage and as inheritance [5]. Inheritance is the transfer of property (either as a set of rights or as access to use) down the generations through time, while marriage payments (dowry or bridewealth) are the transfer of property or wealth across kinship groups, in effect through space.

Giving Girls Away

Marriage is a theme common to all the papers. In many societies it marks a turning point for the transmission of socially valued resources. In some analyses, this includes the transfer of women themselves (South Africa, Ghana, China), although we are cautioned not to assume that they are therefore 'objectified' (New Guinea) [6]. The significance of marriage can be stated in more general terms. Marriage regulates in a socially-recognised form the women's capacity to produce new life through childbearing, to maintain it through her domestic services, and through those in productive activities. In other words, through marriage the woman takes on a full role in social and biological reproduction; she may be the conserver and processer of resources and even the producer (as in the cases where essential labour is provided by women) [7]. In regulating the woman's capacities to produce and reproduce, marriage is marked socially by the transfer - the detachment by some and appropriation by others - of valued resources.

These transactions associated with marriage are conventionally distinguished as bridewealth and dowry, indicating broadly the transfer of goods from the groom's side to the bride's and vice versa. Great differences exist, however, in the recipients of the transfers, the social persons involved, the form and value of the items, as in the meaning of the payments [8]. Indeed, variability within the categories of bridewealth and dowry is almost as striking as between them. Sharma reminds us that, taking the woman's position as the reference point, the differences in direction and form of these transfers are less significant for a woman than the control which she herself may exercise.

Dowry, Inheritance and Women's Control

This point can be illustrated with regard to the dowry. This term covers a wide range of transactions whose only common feature appears to be that property is offered by the bride's side of the union [9]. Dowry has long been interpreted as the pre-mortem transmission of inheritance (e.g. Goody and Tambiah, 1973). Though it may appear, in its various forms, as an institution which devolves property to women, in fact the critical questions are seldom clarified. How much actual control do women have over this property? At what points do ownership rights, if any, devolve (marriage, on parents' death, on husband's death)? Over what kinds of property do women gain full control?

The examples of dowry provision in these papers are suggestive. Firstly it appears that a woman's full control of dowry on marriage involves household and personal goods, but not of productive resources. Such valuables, controlled by the wife and retained in the case of divorce, are given in Mafia Island (East Africa), Alto Minho (Portugal), Bodrum (Turkey) and among Ga (Accra). In urban South Africa, these dowry goods are apparently increasing as bridewealth changes its functions and significance. In rural China, however, daughters' dowries appear to be losing out to the provision of betrothal gifts for sons' marriages.

Secondly, where women do have rights to land ownership, this most often takes the form of inheritance, and therefore only devolves fully after the parent's death. The cases of Bodrum (Turkey) and Alto Minho (Portugal) illustrate this. The modern Turkish legal code ensures equal portions of the patrimony for all children. Women are given movables at the time of marriage and are also assessed in the marriage stakes by the amount of productive land they will eventually inherit. In Alto Minho, arable land is made available for daughters of landed families at marriage. Although it is called dote, literally 'dowry', it is actually held in trust and only later devolves fully as inheritance (in the pattern Goody 1973, 1976, calls 'diverging devolution'). Productive resources (in these cases, land) are not handed over to women on their marriages. Here, parental control continues in effect until their death, suggesting that the intergenerational link is maintained. Possibly, notions defining 'adulthood' (and the 'person') play a part in this, as would the construction of the household and its relative autonomy. Both these factors, as I have already noted, are key elements associated with women's property relationships.

Greece and India: Dowry Comparisons and Contrasts

For the purposes of illuminating further some of these points, the Greek institution of dowry provides a useful example. In several respects it contrasts with that of India, though in both, dowry is a central concern in family life. Despite the ideology and precepts of Hindu law, dowry in North India does not provide wealth for the bride as Sharma's analysis reveals. The woman's dowry cash is administered by her father-in-law, household and other goods are controlled by her mother-in-law. Thus the bride is a vehicle for the passage of valuables from her own kin to those of her husband. Although dowry is held to be a woman's inheritance given at marriage, it is not easily recoverable at the time when the joint household divides. In practice, Sharma notes, it is not the bride nor her husband but her husband's family who may gain most out of this wealth. Also, the bride's family has a continuing obligation to provide gifts, an expectation of the unceasing reaffirmation of the affinal (in-law) relationship (cf. Comaroff, 1980, pp.37-9; Tambiah, 1973). In structural terms, Indian dowry is associated clearly with female hypergamy (lower status women marry into higher status families).

In the Greek case, the provision of dowry is a legally-stipulated obligation on the part of the bride's father (Greek Civil Code, 1946, article 1495) [10]. Its purpose is to 'alleviate the burdens of marriage' (art.1406) which fall on the husband who is solely responsible for the family's economic support. The dowry constitutes the inheritance portion of a daughter; it is not held in trust but devolves at marriage. There is no clear association with hypergamy. Individual family strategies may work on this basis, but marriage is usually conceived of in terms of matching the status of potential spouses. Also, in contrast with the North Indian institution, there is no further obligation to provide for the married woman on the part of her family. This reflects the autonomy of the conjugal unit [11]. Brothers may help contribute to a sister's dowry but once this is accomplished they have no further obligation towards her. Only where a sister suffers considerable hardship through an unsuccessful match would a brother be concerned to help in material matters.

The specification of ownership rights is clear for dowry property in Greece. There is a separate legal contract, the dowry agreement (proikosymphono), whereby the wife remains the legal owner of the dowry property but her husband is accorded rights to its management and usufruct. The wife has 'restricted rights' (termed psili kyriotita) which limit her full autonomous management of the property. However, there are safeguards: dowry property can only be sold with her formal consent (she appears independently in court) and, should the marriage end in divorce or on the husband's death, the property is retained by her. If she dies, her husband and children are the heirs to the dowry property in accordance with normal inheritance laws.

Thus, dowry property in Greece is given to the wife in the custodianship of her husband in accordance with her subordinate status in the family. The dowry has been under attack by feminists in Greece who see it as demeaning to women. In the sense that the law restricts a woman's rights to control the property given in her name, dowry reflects the inequality of Greek gender relations. However, the dowry contract does provide a woman with security of property ownership in the case of divorce or widowhood (although social norms mean that she may defer to a male kinsman's authority in these matters [12]). The security provided is considerable especially since, as is now common, dowry usually takes the form of the family home.

The Greek institution of dowry is one of considerable antiquity and it has shown great regional variation [13]. Associated with the accelerating rural exodus since the Second World War, there is now a countrywide emphasis on urban real estate as the most acceptable dowry. The provision of a dwelling, whether house or apartment, by the bride's family has had interesting effects on family relationships. It may possibly reflect demographic factors (the availability of marriageable men, cf. Loizos, 1975), and certainly has had wider economic repercussions, particularly for the construction industry.

This change in the form of the dowry is associated with its ever-increasing cost. Nowadays the provision of dowry commands the major portion of a family's wealth. Girls may be seen as liabilities and are sometimes called 'mortgages' (grammatia, literally 'promissory note'). Dowry inflation is also a feature of contemporary marriage in India for reasons indicated by Sharma. In both the Greek and Indian situations, there is noticeably a greater emphasis nowadays on material wealth over other qualities, such as reputation, virtue, skills (what might be viewed as 'intangible property'). At the same time, education is entering as a factor in women's marriageability in both places [14].

Dowry obviously represents a number of different property forms. For women, it seems that full control of resources is limited to the goods and personal valuables which equip her for her marital status together with personal valuables. In societies where individual ownership of productive resources is legally recognised, two patterns may be suggested. These rights are kept in trust to devolve with the division of the patrimony later in the woman's life cycle and not on marriage (Alto Minho, Bodrum). Otherwise, as in the Greek case, dowry devolves at marriage in the form of productive resources as well as movables. The woman has full control over the latter, but legal restrictions circumscribe her control of the former. Both situations deny women full, autonomous rights to dispose of the resources which generate wealth. A woman's independent legal person, although a potential status, is not recognised in the property transactions which accompany marriage. Death of the parent is the point of devolution in the Portuguese and Turkish cases. In the Greek case, although transfer takes place at marriage, full ownership only occurs with the loss of a husband (either through divorce or death, and remarriage is unusual). Whitehead's remarks on kinship and gender inequality are pertinent here. It is the primacy of a woman's kinship status as daughter or wife which apparently weighs against the application of full legal ownership rights at this point in her life. And in kinship terms, women are subordinate, defined as 'less than fully acting subjects' (Whitehead, this volume).

Bridewealth and Abduction

In most systems denoted as bridewealth, property transactions at marriage involve men who deal in and profit by these exchanges. (I consider the Islamic mahari an exception, since the groom presents personal gifts and cash to the bride herself.) In effect, bridewealth is exchanged for women or, as some have preferred to say, for rights in them [15]. The notion that women are somehow 'property' or 'objectified' is suggested in a number of papers. Strathern tackles this problem directly and answers it in terms of the indigenous categories of thought. Her paper reminds us to be cautious in our interpretations. None the less, in bridewealth systems, women do not have the power to conduct marriage transactions as freely as men. This is so even with regard to a woman's control of her own person. Reflecting this and associated with bridewealth is the institution of the 'levirate' (Whitehead, Westwood, Burman). In this a widow is taken over on her husband's death by his male kinsman, usually a brother, in a sense as part of the deceased's estate.

Another practice associated with bridewealth systems is marriage by abduction. It is a socially-recognised institution in the Bodrum region of Turkey (ch.6) and in the African population of Burman's study (ch.7). Indications exist that abduction becomes institutionalised where men must produce wealth to obtain a wife. In terms of a 'cost-benefit' type of interpretation (see Comaroff, 1980, pp.4-6; Sharma, ch.4) the temptation for men must be strong since full bridewealth payments are thereby circumvented [16]. Abduction by connivance between the couple is also socially recognised (marriage by elopement in Turkey), and again it has a similar effect: the material transactions are restricted or suspended. In the African case, social acceptance of marriage by abduction is reinforced since the contributions to the marriage by the woman's kin are waived. In both cases the ideology of sexual purity for women is associated with the reduction of bridewealth payments. Virginity, it seems, has its price. Should it, therefore, be considered a valued resource in the stakes of marriage? As a consequence, in bridewealth areas women may be more exposed to the risk of violence against themselves, and to forced marriages [17]. By contrast, in dowry systems it is not in a man's interest to pre-empt the formalities of marriage and thereby forfeit or severely reduce any claim the woman may have to her dowry property. Sanctions of violent retaliation together with female chastity provide a specific 'safeguard' against this kind of forcibly-contracted union. None the less, abduction and elopement may take place even in the societies where the penalties involve vengeance killings (cf. Campbell, 1964, pp.199ff).

Rights conferred by the transfer of bridewealth valuables are often linked with the social recognition of children (cf. Caplan, Westwood, Burman). These issues stand out more clearly when marriages break down. Custody of children and rights to property are associated social phenomena (descent and inheritance). Interestingly, where men's and women's independence is maintained in marriages, as in the East African case described by Caplan, children are not 'owned' by their parents but can be claimed by other cognatic kin and fostering is very common. In the South African example, custody of children in African divorce cases is of supreme importance since possession of a house (in critical demand) may depend upon it (Burman).

Divorce

The prevalence of property transfers on marriage has its corollary. Divorce is characterised by negotiations and transactions over valued resources. In bridewealth systems, the reluctance (or inability) of a woman's kin to return the valuables means that they often pressurise her to accept an unsatisfactory marriage (Burman). Exchanging a wife for wealth had an interesting history for a long period in Britain. Menefee (1981) has documented a form of popular divorce, the sale or auction of a wife, much as Hardy described it in The

Mayor of Casterbridge.

In the contemporary situation, notions of individual ownership are part of the legal definition of marital rights in property. Where marriages are in 'community of property', then the spouses have equal shares in the marital property (Alto Minho, South Africa; see Burman, note 7). But in Bodrum, divorce settlements recognise separate claims to property and these are upheld. This accords with the definition of equality for women and men in the modern Turkish legal code. The management and allocation of property has this public dimension, therefore, in the contemporary world. All the societies considered here are today part of modern centralised states; the legal norms encoded in state law reveal further interesting aspects of woman/property relationships.

The Law and The State

Situations of Legal Pluralism

In many societies today the legal dimension of property relations is far from simple. This is because different legal traditions (both written and unwritten) may coexist. This creates complex situations so that women's (and men's) access to property may be subject to contradictory norms. Situations like these are characteristic of post-colonial states. The chapters on East, West and South Africa indicate these complications with sharp clarity.

In Ghana, indigenous, customary law coexists with an imported western legal code. For Ga women, the inequities of the traditional system are rooted in patrilineal kinship forms which have cognatic elements. Westwood notes that some women prefer to contract western marriages in the hope of securing better economic support and a share in the husband's property.

In South Africa the apartheid system interacts with a dual legal code to produce an acute predicament for African women in towns. 'Customary law unions' are recognised by the state. But a civil law marriage supersedes a marriage previously contracted by customary law. Obviously this leaves a woman who married by customary law in a vulnerable position. However, civil law marriage does not necessarily secure a woman's position either. Rights to property are defined at marriage by particular contractual forms, the ante-nuptial contract or community property. The form to be used must be decided before the marriage; should the husband die without making specific provision for his wife, inheritance follows customary law so that property reverts to the husband's male kin.

Property rights in the East African coast are governed by customary, Islamic and contemporary state laws. Women have rights to land as members of cognatic kinship groups. As individuals they own personal and household goods, coconut trees, as well as the mahari payments which accompany marriage. In addition they also command the product of their labour. Caplan points out that recent state policy changes in the name of African socialism may erode the basis of women's autonomy by reorganising access to land (villagisation policy) and by redefining the household in terms of a new word, the famīlia (apparently a notion derived from western forms, since it presupposes a male-headed household).

State Intervention

The state's policy may intervene at many points, in some cases with the conscious intention to ameliorate the disabilities which women suffer. An instructive case where legal reforms have been instituted is that of Turkey. In the 1920s secular legal codes based on western models were introduced as part of the effort to create a modern nation state out of the disintegrating Ottoman Empire. In the late 1960s there were signs that women in one region of western Turkey were exercising their full legal rights to sue for divorce, to protect their personal reputations and their claims to property. Although a number of factors specific to this region have played their part in the use of law courts, Starr emphasises that it is provisions in the legal code which provide the basis for women to act as autonomous persons.

Attempts to rectify the inequities women suffer are not often successful. The dowry system in India has been banned for some years but it continues to dominate the concerns of families with marriageable daughters. Results from a 1982 survey indicated that over 60 per cent of young people approved of the dowry and nearly 95 per cent acknowledged that the payment of money as dowry was on the increase (The Guardian, 29th April 1982). Starr's interpretation of the successful use of the law in Bodrum region notes that a longer time span, in this case at least 50 years, may be required for reforms to take root.

This view might be applied to China. In the post-revolutionary period there has been an explicit commitment to create an egalitarian social order. Concerted efforts have been made to promote radical reforms of marriage where previously women's subordination had been most apparent. However, despite the provisions of the Marriage Law of 1950 and widespread educational programmes, marriages negotiated by the older generation continue to prevail in rural China, and women are even being deprived of the property traditionally passed at marriage as dowry. Through virilocal residence, they may also lose out on their inherited portion of the family estate. Possibly the time period of 30 years may be a limiting factor since the older generation upholds certain traditional values regarding parental authority. Croll shows clearly how problems result because reforms in rural social organisation have not been carried through consistently and she indicates various tensions caused by conflicting demands made on the household within the communal structure of rural society. Thus, although remarkable changes have been implemented in many areas of social and economic life, some of the goals set for women's emancipation in this socialist society have not yet been achieved.

Women in Court

Women's use of the courts is another significant variable. Since disputes over property resources are usually subject to formal adjudication, women's rights can only be protected when they are able to enter and participate fully in the procedures of the courts. Significantly, in many societies women are defined as legal minors, under the tutelage of males. In others, legal provisions may exist for their protection, yet they fail to bring their grievances forward or cannot support them adequately.

India provides an example of the latter situation. Although women have in law equal rights to inherited land in the patrimony, they seldom contest for land to which they might be legally entitled and tacitly waive their inheritance in favour of male kin. The contrast with the women of Bodrum is striking. Starr shows that Turkish women in this region are successfully using the courts in cases against men, in defence of their property interests.

In South Africa, women are not exercising their full rights in law, for example, in pursuing maintenance claims after divorce. Here the reasons which Burman notes are family pressure, mistrust of the state and ignorance of various aspects of the law. Indeed in a modern bureaucratic society ignorance of the law is understandable, all the more so in the case of the complexities of South African policy regarding Africans. In India, too, ignorance of the law may be a possible reason for the continuing pressure on providing a dowry, especially in rural areas, despite the laws which prohibit it.

In the example of a kin-based society, the Kusasi of Ghana, women are legal minors and have restricted access to the courts, which are run by male elders and chiefs. Yet the majority of cases regarding marriage, its breakdown and child custody concern them directly. In short, examination of the legal system and its application reveals certain inequities in women's jurally defined postion. Their general incapacity to exercise existing rights is also noteworthy. As Starr emphasises, however, as a first step the law must provide the basis for rectifying the disadvantages women may suffer.

Anthropological Insights and Women's Subordination

Anthropological research has made a considerable contribution to feminist studies (see Lamphere, 1977; Quinn, 1977; Rapp, 1979; Rosaldo, 1980). Besides demonstrating the range of variation in gender attributes and roles, in its best form anthropological analysis may counteract two stumbling blocks to theory.

On the one hand, it can provide a viewpoint to counteract reductionism (conclusions or explanation based on single-factor causes), a tendency apparent in some feminist literature. On the other, by widening the scope of the analysis and by its particular commitment to a holistic approach, anthropology can inhibit ethnocentric assessments (the imposition of preconceived notions inherent in our own culture). Many assumptions exist about the position of women which must be challenged and examined, for effective feminist action requires a deep understanding of the situation of women of other societies as well as our own. One valuable task therefore is the detailed and systematic examination of specific social forms.

The case studies presented here do provide a great deal of information. By assessing concepts of property and of persons, and the different ways in which resources are deployed, the book challenges the assumptions which westerners may hold about the nature of property and of access to it. The complexity of the topic and of the issues it raises are clear. In addition, the perspectives adopted by the authors are different. They can be distinguished in the degree of emphasis given to the indigenous or folk model (the emic approach) or the observer's or analytical model (the etic approach). But these models are all intellectual constructs, in essence constituting the anthropologists' 'professional models' (Scholte, 1981; Asad, 1979), and they cannot be treated as mutually exclusive types.

Ideology and Contradiction

The indigenous view is essential for the understanding of a culture in its own terms and to represent another view of social reality. When such a folk model is placed in relation to political and economic structures, as in some papers, acute contradictions may be revealed. Interestingly, in two cases where women have established economic power and even authority, as in Alto Minho and Accra, they are devalued and denigrated by the prevailing ideology. Portuguese peasant women may own and are closely associated with the land, the most important productive resource, yet they are held to be morally weak, sensuous, greedy and polluting. Similar contradictions exist among the Ga of Accra. Market women control much of Ghana's trade; as a group they command considerable economic wealth and potential power, shown by the increasing attacks to which they have been subjected in recent political changeovers. Yet the ideology characterises women as deceitful, irrational and inferior. They are jural minors in the society and cannot hold political offices. Similarly, Whitehead considers the characterisation of Kusasi society as egalitarian, but goes on to point out practical inequities which women suffer, and which may be expressed in other aspects of their ideology.

The contradiction between ideology and practice is one fascinating aspect of this topic. Another, brought out by Strathern, is the influence of ideological factors in constraining or fostering women's ability to act independently with regard to wealth. She does this by contrasting the notions of 'persons' and of 'things' in two communities in Highlands New Guinea, referring also to the wider region. Hagen women are cast as spendthrifts and give up their cash savings for men's enterprises but in Daoulo, the men are cast as irresponsible. Here women's groups have developed to manage their cash earnings which are saved and chanelled into investment projects.

In the other studies where less attention is paid to contradictions associated with ideology, valuable insights are provided on the structural characteristics of the woman/property relationship. In the wider debate on universals, these papers remind us of the variety which must be taken into account before reaching for overall generalisations.

Women's Subordination: Outstanding Issues

It is clear from this limited range of papers that property relationships in these contemporary societies are asymmetrical, that men and women have differential access to resources and distinct degrees of control over property. In feminist anthropology two broad positions can be distinguished: there are those who argue that women's subordination is a universal social fact and those who hold that some forms of social organisation were fully egalitarian [18]. There is no scope for entering the findings of this book into that debate. But it should not be concluded that the differentials in access and control of property documented here provide yet another demonstration of the universality of women's subordination. The analysis and conclusions must be more finely tuned, I feel, to pick up the particularity of subordination.

We have been shown that women are not necessarily 'objects' even if they are not fully 'subjects'. Similarly, if the issue revolves at heart around the relationships of women and men and their relative power, we should examine how 'power' is conceptualised (see Lukes, 1974). In western terms, power is assessed in terms of the pervasive dichotomy of 'private' and 'public', so deeply entrenched in its historical tradition. For us, power is usually associated with the public realm and it involves primarily economic and political action. It may be acknowledged as a dimension of relationships in the household or private domain. But the domestic/household sphere has been greatly devalued in the western view, as feminists have long recognised. I would argue therefore that it is difficult for us to concede any pre-eminence to the activities in this realm, or indeed to that of the metaphysical/religious realm. It seems likely that, unless revised, our own preconceptions regarding power and its proper locus in the public domain hinder us from appreciating its different expressions in other societies.

The subordination of women as a total equation, therefore, requires the addition of more flexible terms since subordination in one sphere may be offset by power in another. The picture can only be complex. Its completion necessitates a more detailed examination of women's roles in domestic, economic as well as ritual and religious spheres of action. In doing so, we need also to consider the evaluations made in terms of indigenous categories of thought.

Although this book provides no definitive answers, it offers more than simply another set of interesting ethnographic detail on women cross-culturally (as cautioned by Rosaldo, 1980, pp.389-

90). 'Property' as a category for analysis raises interesting questions: some of the common themes have been indicated and the papers now knit together somewhat like an unfinished cross-word puzzle.

Anthropology as a discipline reveals humankind's great ingenuity in constructing varieties of social and cultural forms. And it is the variations in the asymmetries of gender relations which become increasingly apparent with further investigation. Yet without considering the subtleties within these differences, our attempts to build an adequate theory will suffer. In the process of working towards more general schemes this dimension must be retained so as not to distort too much the very reality we seek to understand.

Notes

1. Engels' theory is the explicit point of reference for a number of studies; among these are contributions in Reiter, 1975; Critique of Anthropology, 1977; Sacks, 1979; Leacock, 1981.

2. McLennan posited a connection between monogamous marriage and private property (1865), predating Engels' Origins by two decades. He also asserted that individual property rights marked a great advance over previous periods when ownership was vested in family estates, clans and tribes: 'The history of property is the history of the development of proprietary rights' (p.67); in this he includes all other personal rights including 'rights in offspring'. There was also much interest in 'wife-capture' and whether women themselves constituted property. Lubbock's best-seller (1870) supported the idea that women in primitive society were reduced to chattels: 'Among low races the wife is literally the property of the husband' (1978 ed. p.68). But J.S. Mill, an early feminist, brought the argument closer to home, asserting that 'the wife's position under the common law of England is worse than that of slaves in the laws of many countries' (1869, 1970 ed., p.31). Related points of interest in Victorian anthropology are raised by Fee, 1974.

3. These notions are deeply entrenched and   influenced in some respects by Roman law (cf. Maine, 1861). Even a technical source, the International Encyclopaedia of the Social Sciences (1968) defines property narrowly in terms of 'scarce objects of value', competition and individual ownership. The conceptual approach taken in this volume emphasises 'property' as essentially a relationship between persons. As Gray and Symes note, in a useful exposition (1981, pp.1-14), 'property' identifies socially valued resources and 'exposes' relationships of dependence' (p.5).

4. The need for critical attention to residential group organisation is increasingly recognised in the literature. See for example Yanagisako, 1979; Verdon, 1980; Harris, 1981. Creighton, 1980, indicates some aspects of the debate over European household and family organisation in past periods.

5. Stolcke argues that inheritance rules and heredity, control of

female sexuality and class stratification are correlated (1981). In this collection of papers, inheritance receives less attention than property transactions at marriage; its significance for women could be explored more fully. I am grateful to Verena Stolcke whose comments on an earlier version of this paper stimulated me into considering property transmission more carefully.

6. For a feminist view on the 'traffic in women' see Rubin, 1975.

7. The concept of reproduction is the subject of recent critical attention, see Harris and Young, 1981; also articles in Critique of Anthropology, 1977.

8. Anthropological literature on the subject of marriage payments is extensive and represents contrasting approaches; see for example Goody and Tambiah, 1973 and Comaroff's edited collection, 1980.

9. Dowry most often consists of personal and household items, sometimes with cash, but it may also include productive resources such as land and houses. Sometimes it is provided by the girl's father aided possibly by her brothers, sometimes by her mother, together with other kin in various combinations. The bride herself may contribute in degrees which vary depending on the kind of property and its overall value.

10. Extensive and radical proposals to reform Greek family law are contained in a bill currently before the Greek Parliament (December 1982). Its provisions to establish full sexual equality in law include the abolition of the parental obligation to provide dowry (The Times, 1st Dec., 1982).

11. This applies in most parts of Greece. But among Sarakatsani shepherds, there is a joint family household. It is a rather short lived phase and here too the bride's family's obligation to provide for her terminates on marriage (Campbell, 1964).

12. June Starr (personal communication) noted the parallel with wealthy American widows who allow their considerable assets to be managed by professional men (bankers, accountants, lawyers).

13. The ethnographic literature on Greece is full of information on the dowry, indicating its varied form. See, for example, Friedl 1962, 1976; Campbell, 1964; du Boulay, 1974, in press; Loizos, 1975; Kenna, 1976; Skouteri-Didaskalou, 1976, Symeonidou-Alatopoulou, 1979; Piault, in preparation.

14. A perceptive analysis of qualitative changes in rural Greek dowry caused by 'inflation' together with other factors is presented in du Boulay, in press.

15. See comments in Caplan, Whitehead and Strathern, this volume. The limitations of the jurisprudential approach to marriage prestations are discussed in Comaroff's introduction (1980) and illustrated in several papers in that volume.

16. Sandra Burman (personal communication) suggested the possible link between abduction and bridewealth.

17. A new twist to kidnapping girls is at present occurring among Turkish migrants in the Netherlands. A few males who do not have work permits have abducted young Turkish girls who have

residence rights in order to marry them and obtain these rights for themselves (Starr, personal communication).

18. For stimulating discussions of these two positions and other issues in feminist anthropology, see review articles by Lamphere, 1977; Quinn, 1977; Rapp, 1979; Rosaldo, 1980. The question of 'power' is touched on in these discussions, as it is in Schlegel, 1977 and Sanday, 1981. But it remains to be tackled directly as a major conceptual and empirical issue in feminist anthropology. This would be a fruitful direction for possible future enquiry.

Acknowledgements

This introduction has benefitted greatly from many people's comments. I am especially grateful to Helen Callaway for her encouragement and many constructive criticisms throughout this endeavour. Helpful suggestions have also come from Dimitris Tsaoussis, Andrew Schuller, June Starr, Verena Stolcke, Sallie Westwood and Ann Whitehead. Thanks are due to Shirley Ardener, Debbie Bryceson, Judith Hendricks, Lidia Sciama, Crispin Shore and to members of Oxford Women's Anthropology Group for commenting on various aspects of the work.

2 COGNATIC DESCENT, ISLAMIC LAW AND WOMEN'S PROPERTY ON THE EAST AFRICAN COAST

Patricia Caplan

Engels suggests that women's subordination is historically specific, that it arises out of the development of private property and the notion of a specific kind of 'family' entity in which women are oppressed, both contained within a developed state structure. In a recent work, Karen Sacks has examined this thesis in the light of historical and ethnographic material from Africa. She concludes that in societies where 'kin corporations' (i.e. descent groups) are strong, and where women as 'sisters' (or descent group members) have full rights, then women are relatively equal to men. However, with the development of the state, the power of kin corporations lessens, and we see the emergence of families headed by males, in which women's roles as wives (rather than sisters) are dominant (Sacks, 1979).

This article looks at an area – the East Coast of Africa – where communal forms of property held by descent groups, and private property, held by individuals, both exist, and have done so for some time. One of the aims of the paper is to examine the articulation of these two forms of property-holding. In the process of doing this, kinship and descent, inheritance patterns and the economy are all examined. There then follows a discussion of the term 'family' and 'household' in the context of property-holding. I seek to show that it is precisely because such units are not corporate property-owning groups, but rather property is owned by individuals, both women and men, that women have a fair degree of autonomy in this society. In this context, I also examine the extent to which women and children are themselves considered forms of property. In the final section, some recent state-directed changes in the area of property-holding in Tanzania are considered, together with their possible implications for women. Also examined are the unspoken assumptions behind the implementation of such policies, and particularly the premises that 'households' are occupied by 'families' with male heads. It is argued that paradoxically, although it is the intention of these policies to bring about a more egalitarian form of society, their effect may well be to lessen the autonomy of women, and increase their dependence upon men.

23

The Area and its History

Most of the data presented in this paper is based upon field-work which I carried out on Mafia Island, Tanzania, between 1965 and 1967, and again in 1976 [1]. However, I shall also be making use of the considerable amount of sociological research which has been carried out in recent years on the Tanzanian and Kenyan coasts, as well as some important historical material.

Mafia is a large island, lying off the Rufiji Delta, some 80 miles to the south of Dar es Salaam. It occupies about 200 square miles, which is half the size of Zanzibar Island to the north. Culturally, the island forms part of a Swahili-speaking, Islamic belt which runs from Mozambique north into Somalia. This area has for centuries been a part of the Indian Ocean littoral, and subject to various outside influences, particularly as a result of the monsoon winds which made possible a vigorous trade with the Persian Gulf area. Over the past millenium, various city-states rose and fell in this coastal area, but Mafia Island itself never appears to have formed an independent polity. In earlier days it was subject to Kilwa, lying to the south, while later it came under the suzerainty of Zanzibar. Although the coast region has been Islamic and literate since the twelfth or thirteenth centuries AD, important changes did take place early in the nineteenth century when the Sultan of Oman, Seyyid Said, took control of the islands of Zanzibar and Pemba, and most of the mainly coastal belt of Kenya and Tanzania. Many Arabs from Oman and the Hadhramaut settled on the coast and island, and developed the clove plantations in Zanzibar and Pemba and coconut plantations on the mainland, using primarily slave labour (cf. Cooper, 1977). In the middle of the nineteenth century, the Omani Sultan Seyyid Said decided to move his capital to Zanzibar. Some of the local Arabs already settled there fell foul of the court, and fled to Mafia Island, where they established large coconut and cashewnut plantations in the sandy southern half of the island.

The next Sultan, Seyyid Barghash, consolidated the power of Zanzibar. He set up Islamic <u>kadhis'</u> courts along the coast, and also managed to get rid of any remaining local rulers (cf. Gray, 1962). For the next half century, the predominantly Arab-owned plantations flourished. However, with the takeover of Kenya by the British just before the turn of the century, and of Tanganyika by the Germans, as well as the abolition of slavery in both these territories and in Zanzibar itself, most of them went into decline. Many plantations were sold or mortgaged (often to Indian immigrants). In those areas where plantations had not been set up however, the local Muslim Swahili-speaking inhabitants [2] continued to cultivate subsistence crops, primarily millet and rice. Many of these areas were relatively remote from towns or <u>kadhis'</u> courts, and here <u>mila</u> (customary law) continued to be important.

In such areas then, two broad categories of property-holding, of law, and of belief and ritual are distinguished by the people themselves. On the one hand is <u>mila</u> (custom) which includes in its complex cognatic descent groups, communal property-holding,

24

egalitarian social relations, and relative equality for women and men; mila is articulated clearly in ritual (cf. Caplan, 1976). On the other hand, there exists the sharia (Islamic law) [3] which includes notions of private property, of social stratification based on ethnic affiliation (e.g. Arabs being superior to non-Arabs, and 'free-born' to descendants of slaves), and on the superiority of men to women; all of this is made explicit in a corpus of written theology (for a fuller discussion cf. Caplan, 1982). Although there are contradictions between these two categories as legal forms, in most social situations people draw from either or both, without necessarily always distinguishing between them.

One such area where mila and sharia co-exist is northern Mafia Island, which consists of six large villages, each surrounded by an extensive belt of bush land. Most field work was carried out in a village which I have named 'Minazini', but frequent visits were paid to two other villages. In this area, subsistence crops are grown, mainly on the bush land, which is cultivated on a shifting system. This land is held by named cognatic descent groups, and people must be members of a group in order to obtain access to its land. In and around the villages, land has been planted up with coconut trees which are owned by individuals, can be bought and sold, and are inherited according to Islamic law; these provide copra which is sold as a cash crop. In short, then, the bush land is communal property, while the coconut trees are private property.

Communal Property: Bush Land

Cognatic descent means that a person traces his or her descent through both male and female ancestors. Among anthropologists, who for many years thought that descent had either to be patrilineal or matrilineal, there is still relatively little understanding of how cognatic societies work, although there are now ethnographies of several such societies (cf. Scheffler, 1965; Hanson, 1970; Hoben, 1973; see also Westwood, this volume). Not all societies which recognise a cognatic descent principle use it to form groups, but several do, including the Wambwera of northern Mafia, the Wahadimu of Zanzibar, and several other East Coastal peoples (cf. Middleton, 1961; Caplan, 1975; Landberg, 1977).

The cognatic descent groups here operate in a very similar way to unilineal descent groups elsewhere; they segment into small units (here termed matumbo) which are the units through which land is actually allocated. Children inherit their land rights and their descent group membership through their fathers and mothers, which may well mean that they have access to the land of more than one group in a village, or even in several villages. What is even more important for the purposes of this discussion is that both women and men hold membership in their own right, and so both have access to land.

Descent group membership in this situation is not restricted either by a unilineal principle, nor, as in some other cognatic societies, by residence or some other form of social interaction.

People can and do choose to cultivate with different groups in different years.

In agriculture there is a recognised sexual division of labour for certain tasks. Men cut down the bush and fire it to clear the land, while women do most of the hoeing and planting. Men also build the stout fences around the fields to keep out pests such as wild pig. Both women and men may work at weeding, guarding the standing crop, and later at harvesting. It is thus rather difficult for a woman to work this kind of land alone, but widows and divorcees can usually get a brother or a son to 'cut' a field for them. Similarly, men who are currently without a wife may call a planting party of female relatives.

People are entitled to as much bush land as they can cultivate. For a married couple, this generally means at least an acre, with less for an individual or an older couple. Everyone works their own fields, except that sometimes people exchange labour on a reciprocal basis; this is particularly likely to be in fence-building (for men) and planting (for women). People who are cultivating bush fields usually build small huts in them and live there for several months to guard the crop and complete the harvesting. During this time, some women arrange with their female relatives or friends to form cooking groups for themselves, their husbands and children, so that each takes it in turn and frees the others for horticultural tasks.

There is a second area of bush land set aside by the government agricultural office for the cultivation of cassava, a hardy crop which needs little attention. The cassava land is in an area which was formerly under the control of the descent groups, but which has now become 'government land'. Anyone has the right to take up a piece of land to grow cassava in the designated area. In the last few years, the amount of land under cassava has thus increased greatly, and the extra production of this crop has rendered the village much more self-sufficient in food. However, cassava is considered a man's crop, since the main tasks associated with it are clearing bush and building a fence, and although women sometimes help their husbands by weeding the plot no woman cultivates cassava alone.

Another kind of land in some northern villages is meadow land (dawe). This is wetter and more fertile than bush land, and it lies within the residential and coconut area. Most tracts of this land are associated with descent groups, just as is the residential and coconut land, but some people claim rights to it by virtue of their ownership of coconut trees which border it. (Since most people own trees in wards associated with their descent groups, this rarely creates a contradiction.) Meadow land can be worked for a number of years at a stretch, particularly if cattle are tethered on it between crops to fertilise it.

Women can and often do work this kind of land themselves. They will also make considerable efforts to gain or retain rights in it. For example, a woman married into a village which has no meadow land can return to her natal village and 'beg' her mother for some of her meadow land. Some women will be prepared to walk several miles each week during the agricultural season back to their natal village in order to produce a meadow-land crop, as well as cultivating a bush field with their husbands. Women try to ensure that when coconut trees are inherited, they receive some near to meadow land. Thus this kind of land tends to be cultivated more by women than men, and especially by divorced and widowed women, who rarely cultivate bush land.

In terms of ownership, meadow land is more problematic than bush land, and falls somewhat uneasily between the categories of communally and privately-held property. It is not surprising therefore to find that most land disputes concerned meadow land, particularly after the new land laws brought in after independence had made the situation even more ambiguous (see below).

It is important to note that land is usually gained by virtue of a person's status as a member of a descent group, and that women and men are relatively equal in this regard. Furthermore a woman can cultivate on her own to feed herself and her children. She can either get a bush field by requesting a brother or other male relative to clear one for her, or she may herself have rights to meadow land, or can use those of a female relative.

Private Property: Coconut Trees

Coconut trees (and the considerably fewer cashewnut trees) are a very different category of property. Historically, their development has been much more recent. Copra production appears to have intensified with the rise of the Zanzibar Sultanate, and, as previously stated, large plantations were developed in some areas, such as southern Mafia. In the marginal areas such as northern Mafia, more coconuts were planted at the end of the nineteenth century (sometimes using a little slave labour) but the push in this region came during the brief period of German rule at the beginning of the twentieth century, when it was mandatory for every male to plant at least one hundred trees.

Coconut trees begin bearing when they are between five and seven years old, and continue for at least another 40 years, after which their productivity begins to decline, although they may still produce nuts for another few decades. A single tree, when bearing fully, produces around 40 nuts a year, and at the time of field-work between 1965 and 1967, this raised a net cash income of around 6 shillings per tree, just over 1 per cent of a male's cash income needs, and about 2 per cent of that of a female [4] (cf. Caplan, 1975, p.11 et seq.).

Ownership of trees is registered in the local government office on an individual basis. They can also be bought and sold for cash, although there are informal restrictions at the village level on selling trees to 'outsiders', a category which is defined as all non-villagers, and very often meaning people who do not have membership of the descent group associated with the residential land on which the trees are growing.

27

Trees are inherited according to Islamic law, which means that a woman gets only half of a man's share, and she can never be a sole heir (if for example she is an only child). This disadvantages women but nonetheless, in northern Mafia, women do inherit the trees to which they are entitled, and there is no attempt made (as in other Islamic societies) to prevent women from getting their rightful shares.

Other methods of acquiring trees are by planting, which women never do alone, only together with their husbands. If a divorce later takes place, the trees are evenly divided if the couple worked together on their cultivation, but if the husband planted them on his own, a wife might get only one third. If a man plants trees before his marriage, his wife is not entitled to claim a share later.

Trees which are bought for cash are the sole property of the person who purchased them. However, since women have less access to cash than do men, they rarely acquire trees in this way.

The only other way in which women are likely to obtain coconut trees is through their marriage payment (mahari) - the amount of goods which a husband promises to give his wife at the time of their marriage (see details below). Mahari is often paid in the form of coconut trees rather than cash.

The net result of all this is that men own more than three times as many trees per capita as do women, and thus have a much higher cash income from the sale of copra.

Table 1.

Minazini Village, 1965: Ownership

of Coconut Trees

Trees numbers	Men per	Women cent
0	27	62
1-50	22	27.7
50-100	22.7	5.5
100-200	18	4
200-500	8	0.7
500 plus	1.1	0

On average, adult males own 125 trees per head, while adult females own only 36. To some extent this is compensated for by the generally accepted Islamic rule that men are responsible for maintaining their wives and children in terms of goods bought for cash (i.e. some food and all clothes) whereas women are free to spend their cash as they please. Since however maintenance is very rarely paid after divorce and women usually take the children, most divorced women are relatively poor.

Other Forms of Property

The other major forms of property on the coast are animals, such as cattle and donkeys, and boats. Cattle are kept for milk and meat; they are slaughtered for most important rituals. More men than women own cattle, which are usually acquired for cash. Both male and female owners usually give their animals to a herdsman who receives some milk and a proportion of the calves born as payment. Donkeys are very rarely owned by women, partly because they are much more expensive than cattle, and also because their owners use them for carrying goods for other people from the northern villages to the south of the island, an occupation in which women never engage.

Boats are also never owned by women, both because of lack of cash with which to pay the specialists who make them, and also because women in this area neither fish nor handle boats. A significant number of men do practise fishing, although only a small minority own even a canoe, much less a larger boat capable of off-shore fishing and/or travelling to the mainland to sell the resultant catch. None of the fishermen or traders however is a full-time specialist.

As the above discussion shows, men have many more ways of making cash and investing in capital than do women. They can trade or fish, and in addition a few of the younger men migrate to look for work on the mainland, usually in Dar es Salaam. Women on the other hand have few opportunities for acquiring cash. The produce from coconut trees apart, virtually their sole means of earning money is by making the plaited grass mats for which the island is famous, and selling them to male traders from their villages. Although all women, from very young girls to great-grandmothers plait their grass strips and sew them into mats on every conceivable occasion, they only make a fairly minimal income from all this activity. Nonetheless, it is usually this income which enables divorced and widowed women to manage on their own and supply their cash needs, albeit meagrely.

Thus far I have considered individuals and their rights over private and communal property. I now turn to examine the notion which is fundamental to many studies of peasant societies - that they are characterised by the existence of households (i.e. economic units of production, consumption and reproduction), usually made up of people who are members of a 'family' who form a corporate body in terms of property-holding.

Housing and Households

The household is not a very useful concept to use in northern Mafia (see Caplan, n.d.). If it must be used at all, it is as an 'odd-job' word (cf. Yanagisako, 1979) rather than a theoretical concept. In this area, the household is chiefly definable as a residential and commensal unit; and it is not a basic building block of society partly because it is not a corporate unit which owns property, and partly because it is not the major production and consumption unit. There is no word in Swahili for household, although the term nyumba can sometimes mean a residential group as well as a dwelling place. Houses in this area, unlike coconut trees, are not commodities, or at least, they have not been until very recently. Houses on the coast are of three types. Small huts (banda) are built of a framework of mangrove poles, covered in plaited coconut palm fronds; these can be erected quickly but usually only last for a couple of years. The more usual type of house (nyumba) has a larger mangrove-pole framework, filled in with mud and thatched with coconut palm fronds. Such a house, if kept in reasonable repair, can last for many years. Thirdly, larger houses with cement floors, whitewashed walls, and perhaps a corrugated iron roof are more usually found in urban or plantation areas; it is only this latter category, which utilises specialist labour and imported materials, which can be classed as a capital asset.

Houses of the first two categories can be built by almost anyone, although sometimes specialist labour is used if a fancy wooden door or window is required. Someone wishing to build a house usually calls a work-party - the men cut the mangrove poles and erect the frame, and the women collect the mud and fill in the walls. Both women and men know how to prepare palm-leaf thatching (makuti) but the task usually falls to the latter, as does that of putting the thatching on the roof.

Houses normally consist of two or three rooms, a verandah at the front, and a courtyard at the back, together with separate kitchen and bathroom huts. Huts on the other hand are only a single room. Such structures are generally occupied by specific social categories. First of all, young adolescent boys move out of their parents' house at the age of about thirteen, and build a hut alongside. They continue however to eat with their parents and siblings. Around this time, they also begin to make a serious contribution to horticulture, and may soon cultivate their own small fields.

The second category of hut dwellers are elderly people who feel the need to live near to a son or daughter when their spouse has died. If a woman, such a person will continue to cook for herself unless totally incapable, when she will be fed from the main kitchen; a man cooks for himself, and he too will be fed by his son or daughter.

The third category of hut dwellers are divorced or widowed women, who generally move near to their own kin, and may build a hut in the vicinity of their house. Such huts do not form part of the commensal unit, for these women will have their own kitchen, but they do form part of a larger unit which I have termed a cluster (Caplan, 1975).

The building of houses or huts does not therefore require large investments of time, labour or money, and they are not considered as private property. They do not form part of a deceased person's estate, and are not fought over by a divorcing couple. The relative ease with which a simple house can be erected means that there is great flexibility in meeting people's housing needs, which inevitably change over time.

The above discussion demonstrates that a house is not necessarily co-terminous with a household. A household (commensal unit) may consist of several houses, as for instance when a young boy builds his first hut alongside his parents. A house however never contains more than one household, for in this area no two adults other than a married couple ever share a house, and thus a marriage or a divorce always involves the setting up of a new residential/commensal unit. Even co-wives of the small minority of men who are polygynously married live in separate houses, and usually in separate clusters, or even different villages. The widowed and the divorced always have their own houses, even when quite elderly. Old people continue to cook for themselves and also to cultivate their own fields (albeit with some help) for as long as possible.

Half the houses (including huts) in Minazini village are grouped into clusters usually composed of near relatives. Frequently, they are situated near a grave site of which the cluster residents are 'owners', in the sense that they have the right to be buried there, and they usually organise the annual rituals at the graves which are attended by other non-resident 'owners'. Cluster members are somewhat more likely to exchange services with one another than with outsiders, and they often work co-operatively in their fields. Some clusters constitute a small segment of a descent group - for instance a senior man and his wife, their adult sons, divorced daughters and their children, and perhaps an elderly parent. Such a cluster is likely to build up only if the man who is its focus is relatively wealthy and has high socio-economic status. Other clusters do not have such a focus - they are simply groups of houses in close proximity whose inhabitants usually have particularly close ties, e.g. a group of siblings who have inherited coconut trees (and hence residential rights) in the same locality.

Thus even a minimal definition of a household as a co-residential unit has to be seen in context; clusters are also co-residential units and may also form ritual units.

Domestic Units and Relations Between Spouses

Following Radcliffe-Brown (1952), anthropologists have distinguished between the rights which a husband has in his wife in terms of jus in rem (rights in her as an object) and jus in personam (rights in her services). Bohannan (1949) has further elaborated this distinction, suggesting that a distinction must be made between jus in uxorem and jus in genetricem (rights in a woman as a wife, and rights in a woman's reproductive power). In all of these discussions, the rights which a wife has in her husband are much less often mentioned, let alone categorised in this way.

In order to understand the reciprocal rights which husbands and wives have in each other, it is necessary to examine the nature of marriage. The most important point to note is that in this area (as in most Islamic societies) marriage is a contract between two individuals, not a religious sacrament. A marriage ceremony includes very little religious ritual, apart from a few prayers. The kadhi (officiant) asks the couple if they are willing to marry, declares the amount of marriage payment (mahari) which the groom promises the bride, and then tells them 'Live together with goodness, and if you divorce, do this also with goodness.' Right at the time of the inception of the contract, then, the possibility of its being broken is foreseen.

Islamic law lays down very clearly the circumstances in which this may happen, but divorce is very much easier for a man than for a woman. A man can divorce his wife by repeating the formula; after three times it becomes irrevocable. A woman, on the other hand, must either persuade her husband to divorce her, or else seek a divorce through the courts.

Islamic law also clearly defines the terms of the conjugal contract for the duration of the marriage. A husband must support his wife by providing her with a house, food and clothes. In return a woman should give her husband domestic and sexual services. Women should prepare food (although technically, according to Islam, they are not obliged to cultivate), a long and arduous process where grain has to be pounded in a wooden pestle and mortar, and firewood and water fetched from far away.

Islam is very clear that it is a husband's support of his wife that gives him authority: 'Men have authority over women because Allah has made the one superior to the other and because they (men) spend their wealth to maintain them.' (Koran, verse 'Women'). However, if a husband fails to maintain his wife adequately by local standards, she can sue for a divorce in the courts; given the relative poverty of most villagers in northern Mafia it is not too difficult for women to obtain divorces. Husbands also owe their wives a fair share of sexual attention; a woman can divorce a husband for impotence, and if her husband has more than one wife, he must cohabit equally with each in turn. One woman sued successfully for a divorce on the grounds that her husband was away working in Dar es Salaam, and therefore had failed both to maintain her or satisfy her sexually.

Nonetheless, although women do have rights in their husbands, these are usually limited. For example, a man can take more than one wife, even without the consent of the first. And while adultery is a sin for both sexes in Islam, an aggrieved husband can divorce his wife, while a wife would have to take her husband to court and seek a divorce on grounds other than adultery.

A woman should technically seek her husband's permission before leaving the house, while a man is under no such obligation to his wife. In Islam too, a woman does not have the right to leave her husband without his agreement. If he wishes to divorce her, he 'takes' her back to her parents' house. A woman who leaves of her own accord, can, if the husband is determined enough, and his wife cannot show just cause for leaving him (i.e. lack of maintenance or impotence) be ordered to return to him by the <u>kadhi's</u> court. But the strictures of Islamic law are mitigated by the concepts embedded in the customary <u>mila</u> complex. This recognises a much greater freedom in sexual matters for both women and men. Women's sexuality is celebrated (as in the girls' puberty ritual and the boys' circumcision ritual) both as important in itself, and because it leads to the bearing of children. Many aspects of these two rituals make it plain that they are preparing young people for sexual activity both inside and outside marriage (cf. Caplan, 1976).

There might appear to be irresolvable contradictions here in matters like attitudes to adultery, but in fact these rarely surface. The point is that because marriage is a contract, and is clearly recognised as such by Islamic law (unlike other major religions such as Hinduism or Christianity where it is a religious sacrament) husband and wife each remain separate individuals. One example of this is the fact that women do not take their husbands' names on marriage. Rights and duties within marriage are to a large extent reciprocal, and the failure of one partner to fulfill obligations leads to recriminations, and possibly a withdrawal of services by the other partner. Thus many women told me that if husbands failed to provide adequately according to their means, they would refuse to sleep with them. A song frequently sung by women at rituals is 'What are you waking me up for if you haven't brought me earrings or a nose-pin?'

In many senses, a household is a group of property-owning individuals; there is very little property that is owned by the household as a unit. A woman, like a man, retains her private property e.g. coconut trees, on marriage and this is one of the most important rights which Islam confers upon women. Indeed, if a woman has wealth, and a man does not, then a man can only 'borrow' from his wife and he must repay her. Furthermore, a woman's property is hers to do with as she pleases. Given the relative poverty of most villagers, women often do contribute, if they are able, to the cash needs of the household, for example by purchasing food which cannot be grown (e.g. tea, coffee, sugar) but they are under no obligation to do so. They can use their individual income for other purposes if they see fit, and many choose to contribute to their own kin, rather than to their marital household.

This is equally true of the produce from the fields. If a woman cultivates a field alone, then the harvest is hers to do with as she sees fit. Many women, if they know that a close relative is having a big ritual to which they want to make a generous contribution, will endeavour in the preceding months to cultivate an extra field in order to be able to help. For crops which are cultivated by the joint labour of husband and wife, the situation is a bit more complex. Generally, such food is eaten by the household, but in theory, a woman has a right to a portion of it to use in other ways if she wants to. When disputes over crops came before the village council, women were sometimes awarded half of the crop, sometimes the Islamic formula of two-thirds and one third in favour of men was used. It is not infrequent for couples to divide the crop at harvest and store it separately. This then is a situation in which men do not control women's productive labour.

People are very clear about who owns what within a household, and this was brought home to me forcibly when at the end of filming in one village in northern Mafia, the film crew sold off various items of household equipment. Husbands and wives invariably came separately to purchase goods, and when on one occasion I ventured to remark to one woman that her husband had already purchased a similar item, she looked at me in amazement and asked what his purchases had to do with hers?

Personal items such as clothes, jewellery, radios, watches and bicycles are invariably individually owned. They are however very unlikely, except in the case of the first two, to be owned by women, who would not have the cash to purchase such items. They are the sort of goods which only wealthier men, or young men who have spent periods working in Dar es Salaam, possess.

Because such emphasis is placed upon the individual ownership of personal possessions, women are not responsible for their husband's possessions. They do not wash their clothes, for example; men wash their own, and women wash their own, and a father or mother may wash the clothes of a child too young to do its own laundry. Similarly, women do not mend their husband's clothes; indeed, they do not sew at all in this area. Clothes are made by specialist tailors, except that many men embroider the intricate little caps that they wear.

In any important sense then, the household is a collection of individuals engaged in productive activities, but retaining the fruits of their own labour to a large extent. Relations within the household are characterised by exchange rather than pooling, (cf. Sahlins, 1974) since ownership is vested in individuals, and not in the household as a unit.

Reproduction and the 'Ownership' of Children

Production and consumption are two chief functions often attributed to the household and/or 'family'. Even more basic is thought to be reproduction, particularly in the sense of raising the next generation. To this extent, as Harris (1981) has pointed out, the household and family appear to be 'natural' units arising out of biological needs. Yet parenting, as much recent work (cf. e.g. E. Goody, 1981) reminds us, is a culturally and not a biologically defined activity. We have noted already the now classic distinction of the rights which a husband has in his wife as jus in uxorem, and jus in genetricem. The payment of bridewealth is frequently explained, at least in part, as primarily in order to obtain rights in children - 'childwealth' rather than 'bridewealth'.

On the coast of East Africa, bridewealth, in the classic African sense, is not paid. There are a number of payments associated with marriage, primarily paid by the groom and his kin to the bride and her kin. These are divided into two categories, customary and Islamic. 'Customary' payments include the cash paid to the bride's father, which is known as kilemba (turban) and to the bride's mother, which is called mkaja (a belt worn by women after childbirth). A groom must pay a smaller sum to the girl's sexual instructress (somo or mkunga, usually her grandmother or aunt) when he goes to consummate the marriage, and this is known as kipa mkono (the gift of the hand); it is a recompense for this woman's teaching of the bride. In addition, the groom provides the bride with a trousseau in the form of a complete set of clothes (sanduku, literally 'box').

The bride's parents provide her with a set of household equipment and furniture – bed, mattress, cooking pots, crockery and other goods, and in this they are usually assisted by the girl's sexual instructress. The equipment given to the girl by her parents constitutes her personal property, and is retained by her in the event of a divorce. It does not form part of an early inheritance, and no account of the amount spent is made after the death of a parent when his or her estate is divided up. The other major expenses incurred by the bride's parents are the costs of the wedding ceremony and the feasts which precede and follow it. Thus the expenses of the bride's family tend to be somewhat greater than those of the groom's side, although in both cases, help in meeting expenses is forthcoming from the extended family and its network (cf. Caplan, 1975, p.32ff).

Lavish expenditure is only incurred on the occasion of a girl's first marriage, which is seen as part of her rite of passage into adulthood. Subsequent marriages are much quieter affairs, with few if any of the customary payments being made, and no large feasts, only a small wedding breakfast. Such marriages are much more the affair of the couple concerned, rather than being arranged by parents and grandparents, as is the case for the first marriages of both women and men.

In all marriages, however, the payment demanded by Islamic law, the mahari, has to be paid or promised. Islamic law conceives of this as a sum given to or held in trust for the bride in case her marriage should fail. Often it is not handed over at the time of marriage, but a wife is entitled to claim it at any time. If a man dies before paying the mahari, then a woman has first claim for it on the estate. If a couple divorces, the husband must pay any outstanding mahari, although what frequently happens is that a husband who is reluctant to divorce his wife is persuaded to do so if she agrees to 'forgive' him his payment of her mahari.

The payment of mahari, or the promise to do so, then is a sine qua non of the legitimacy of a marriage, and hence of the legitimacy of children, according to Islamic law. It also establishes a husband's sexual rights in his wife, and hers in him. Customary law also recognises this. During the girl's puberty ritual, she is told by the 'expert' officiating 'Your husband has not paid for your hand, nor for your face, he has paid for your vagina, so do not refuse him'. Nonetheless, while Islamic law gives a husband <u>sole</u> access to his wife's sexuality, customary law is more liberal. The ritual expert also tells the newly-pubescent girl 'Always wash your vagina well before going on a journey. You never know who you might meet on the path and want to go with.'

There is a similar difference in the way in which the rights over children are regarded; under Islamic law, the father has more rights than the mother, and should take any children after divorce if they are over seven years old. His consent must always be sought before their marriage, circumcision (for boys) or ear-piercing (for girls). Customary law, on the other hand, gives women far greater rights than Islamic law. A child is born as a result of 'the work of father and mother' - a phrase used frequently in the boys' circumcision ritual. A child inherits its group membership, as I have already stated, from both parents, and in this respect, under customary law, illegitimacy is relatively unimportant. 'After all, a child can't really be illegitimate on its mother's side, only on its father's' I was told. Islamic law, on the other hand, does stigmatise illegitimacy, and of course, given the inheritance patterns of private property, it means that children born outside of marriage, who will inherit only from their mothers, are likely to be poorer than their counterparts who inherit from two parents.

Legitimate parents, then, are those from whom the child will inherit. They are however not necessarily the ones who rear it, for the institution of fostering is widespread on the coast of East Africa (as indeed it is in most of Sub-Saharan Africa). In one village in northern Mafia, I found a quarter of the children were being raised by people other than their parents, while an earlier study of the mainland Pangani region by Tanner (1962) yields a figure as high as 37 per cent. Children are sent to be fostered by other kin, because these people have certain claims on them. Grandparents, for instance are often said to have more authority than parents over children, and a request from a grandparent to foster a child is difficult to refuse. One woman had only two children, and both of them had been taken by grandparents. I asked her how she felt about this, and she said 'I could not refuse - they wanted them, and they are their grandparents'. Very few old people live without a young child in the house, partly, it is said, so that they have 'a pair of legs' to do the errands for them.

Parents' siblings who are themselves childless may request a child from a more fertile brother or sister, and this too is unlikely to be refused. In this way, children from large sibling groups are re-distributed over the extended family network.

The second reason why children are fostered concerns the high divorce rate. As I have already explained, divorce is relatively easily obtained in this society, and although it was difficult to obtain very precise figures, I found that men and women of between 55 and 60 years old or more had had an average of 2.5 and 2.0 partners respectively. Some marriages do endure for long periods; others end quickly and certain people are notorious for their constant changing of partners. Upon divorce, women almost always take the children with them, but it is often quite difficult for a woman to manage over an extended period if she has several children, unless she is unusually wealthy. This however is less of a problem than if the woman wants to remarry. Few men will agree to maintain the children of another man, and what usually happens is that the children go to be fostered by grandparents, chiefly the mother's mother. Older women are usually in a better position than younger ones to rear children from a financial viewpoint because they are likely to own more coconut trees, having either inherited property or received their mahari by the time they reach middle life.

Nonetheless, children are not regarded as so many pawns to be moved around as a result of marital games. They are very much encouraged to make their own decisions. One woman whom I knew well had sent her young daughter to be fostered by her sister. The girl walked back alone from a village several miles away from her parents' house, and her mother asked her whether she preferred to stay there or return to her aunt.

Children in fact achieve some independence early. They are encouraged to participate in chores as soon as possible, particularly looking after younger siblings. This task falls more heavily upon girls than boys, who have far more time for play than do girls. But by early adolescence, both sexes are helping parents in cultivation, and this is recognised as valuable. One man described to me how he and his wife had grown sim-sim (a cash crop) and divided the money raised not just between themselves, but also with those of their children who had helped, each in proportion to the amount of labour they had been able to contribute.

By around 15 years of age, both boys and girls may have their own separate fields, as well as helping on the school's communal farm [6]. This is also the time at which a boy moves into his own house, and is in many respects defined as an adult. A girl however remains under parental control until she has been married in her middle-teens (or as soon as she has finished primary school nowadays). The period between pubescence and marriage is one in which women are more restricted than at any other time during their lives since virginity on marriage is given importance. During this time however, girls begin selling their own mats, and usually have a little cash to spend; in general, they use it to buy themselves clothes, particularly school uniform.

It is thus very difficult to assign the 'ownership' of children to one particular person. Islamic law gives a father greater rights and more authority over children than it does a mother. But customary law again gives more or less equal rights, and in many situations, people respect the rights of both parents over their children; both should give permission for a marriage or other rite of passage to take place for instance. But in many significant ways, children are much less the property of their parents, and particularly of their fathers in this society than elsewhere. The children's own wishes are consulted upon matters from an early age. In addition, rights of

relatives other than the parents can considerably mitigate the powers
of the parents - grandparents and parents' siblings have clearly
recognised rights, as is shown at rituals when they (or their
representatives) must all be present.

To return, then to the distinction between jus in rem and jus in
personam, and between jus in genetricem and jus in uxorem. Are
these of any use in helping us to answer the question of whether
women themselves, and their children, are perceived as forms of
property? In order to do this we must ask the question both ways
round - we must define the rights which men and women acquire in
each other through marriage. Only by comparing them can we arrive
at a meaningful answer to this question. As I have shown, the
marital contract is a reciprocal contract in many respects - a
husband provides maintenance, and a wife provides domestic labour,
which is seen to include sexual services. But in providing first a
mahari, or the promise of it, at the time of marriage, and then in
supporting his wife, a husband acquires rights in his wife which are
not just in personam, but also in rem because he theoretically
(under Islamic law) holds these rights 'against the world'. In other
words, his rights to her services, especially sexual are exclusive.
She too acquires rights in his sexual services (hence divorce for
impotence or neglect) but they are not exclusive, since a husband
can take another wife, and since too, adultery is regarded as
somewhat less serious for men than for women.

In the context of the East Coast, a definitive answer to these
questions is difficult to arrive at, for one is operating on two levels
- that of Islamic law (itself subject to differing interpretations, cf.
note 3) and that of customary law. Women do have a considerable
amount of leverage within their marriages, and ultimately, they can
(and do) leave; because of their descent group membership, and the
support of their own kin, it is not usually difficult for them to free
themselves from their husbands and marriages. Given too the division
of labour, which allocates to women the main burden of rearing
children, they do not lose them at divorce. In any case, the children
of a couple, in a society based upon cognatic descent, belong equally
to both sides. Thus it is through membership of strong kin-based
groups that women are able to act as autonomous individuals.

The East Coast as a Whole

From a perusal of the literature available on the East Coast (cf.
Caplan, 1982) it seems likely that the situation in northern Mafia is
not an isolated example. First of all, on most parts of the East Coast
where subsistence cultivation is still paramount, cognatic descent is
the normal pattern, although descent groups are not found in all
areas.

Secondly, most anthropologists who have worked on the East
Coast comment upon the relative lack of importance of the domestic
unit or household. Tanner, writing about the Pangani District
comments that 'The married family is very impermanent and does not

form an agricultural unit ... most of them (women) prefer to cultivate separately' (1969, p.16). Widjeyewardene, who worked in villages on both the Kenyan and Tanzanian coasts, states that 'The domestic unit, the household, is in some measure a production and consumption unit ... but important qualifications must be made. In the first place, the only legal bond within the household is between husband and wife ... As a general principle one may say that the economic product of any individual is his or her own' (1961, pp.273-4).

All commentators remark upon the high divorce rates, and stress that marriage is seen primarily as a contract which may be broken. Several of them state that households are matrifocal. Bujra, writing of 'Atu' in northern Kenya, finds that many households are composed of co-residential female kin, especially mothers and daughters (1977, p.71) and that at the time of her field work in 1965, no fewer than 40 per cent of the village women were either divorcees or widows. Similarly Landberg also found that in her northern Tanzanian coastal village there was a large proportion of matrifocal households and women living with other female kin (1977, chapter 5). She states that even where women are married and reside with their husbands, they may cultivate with their female kin, rather than with those husbands (ibid). Widjeyewardene remarks upon a similar phenomenon: 'The chief point of importance that emerges from this is the role of women in the formation of domestic groups ... in no case is there a household without an adult woman' (1961, p.262).

Divorced women thus can and do live alone with their children, or with other female kin, independently of a man. Several authors note that such women may bear children who suffer little stigma; Landberg found that 'Children born outside of marriage are not isolated or ostracised. As members of their mothers' descent groups, they have legitimate positions within the community' (ibid. pp.219-20; cf. also p.143).

Recent Changes in Property Law:
Can Socialism be Bad for Women?

Since independence, and particularly since the Arusha Declaration (cf. Nyerere, 1968) Tanzania has embarked on a policy which it defines as African socialism (ujamaa). The government is committed to a policy of development for all the citizens of the country and is opposed to a form of development which benefits only a minority. Many of the efforts of the last few years have borne fruit - most children (girls as well as boys) now attend primary school, and few villages are out of reach of medical care. Nonetheless, the policies themselves, and particularly the method of their implementation, are not beyond criticism. Some policies have been carried out with scant regard for establishing first exactly what needed to be changed. In other words, there has been an assumption that peasants need to be 'modernised' without first finding out either what peasants thought, or whether the 'traditional' system had valid ecological or other reasons for its existence. Secondly, some of the assumptions underlying the formulation of policies, particularly regarding women, their property and other rights, and their work loads have remained, with certain notable exceptions [7], largely unspoken and unexamined. Some recent policy changes which may affect women in an important way relate to land tenure, encouragement of cash-cropping, the 'villagisation' policy and that of 'better housing'.

Soon after independence, the government abolished the concept of freehold land introduced during the colonial period, and declared that all unoccupied land is government land, and may be cultivated by anyone. The intention was to prevent accumulation of land by speculators. Nonetheless, it strikes at the very basis of the system of land tenure practised in areas like northern Mafia where most of the land has of necessity to lie fallow for long periods, and where ownership is vested in descent groups. It is significant that in southern Mafia, most of which is now planted up with coconut trees, there are no descent groups, and there seems little doubt that if the land tenure system changes from a communal to an individual system, then the descent groups will be weakened. And so, it would seem, will the rights and status which women hold as descent group members. A second policy which thus far has had relatively little effect on this area is the encouragement of cash-cropping. Early attempts in the immediate post-independence era to persuade the villagers of nothern Mafia to grow cash crops (other than coconuts) were largely a failure (e.g. a scheme to cultivate cotton communally). Since that time in the mid 1960s, pressure to grow cash crops seems to have been relatively slight (apart from urging villagers to improve their coconut plantations); rather, the administration and Agricultural Office have concentrated on persuading the villagers to plant more subsistence crops, particularly cassava. In this they have been successful with the result that, as previously stated, the village is now more or less self-sufficient in food.

The villages of northern Mafia were also relatively unaffected by the ujamaa (creation of communal villages) policies of the early 1970s. However, since the implementation of the 'villagisation' policy, discussed below, villagers have once again been urged to grow more cash crops. As it is, the existing cash crop, coconuts, produces far more benefits for men than for women, and there seems little doubt that if cash-cropping is adopted on a large scale, the position of women vis-à-vis men would deteriorate further, as has happened in so many other parts of Africa (cf. Rogers, 1980).

The third policy - villagisation - has affected northern Mafia profoundly, although at the time of field work in 1976, it was too early to monitor changes precisely. After years in which the problems of rural people in Tanzania living in isolated homesteads were discussed by both colonial and independent governments, the Tanzanian government decided in the mid-1970s to act with some speed and implement a policy of immediate villagisation. 'Operation Sogeza' (moving) took place in most areas between 1974 and 1975, and villagers were moved into concentrated settlements whether they agreed or not. In northern Mafia there was considerable anger since the coastal belt, unlike the rest of the country, has always had nucleated settlements. Even people living in the centre of the village were asked to move, so each new house site could have an acre for a kitchen garden. Thus most villagers had to build new houses, as well as being urged to cultivate more land. Residential land was allocated regardless of descent group membership and its relation to the village wards or ownership of trees. It is not improbable that this will further weaken the cognatic descent groups, as land rights pass increasingly out of their control.

Soon after villagisation had been implemented, a 'better housing' (<u>nyumba</u> <u>bora</u>) campaign was begun. Villagers were urged to construct houses with cement floors and walls and a corrugated iron roof. Such a house would of course require imported materials and perhaps specialist labour, both of which would have to be paid for by cash. This obviously changes the nature of housing. Houses are likely to become private property, commodities which can be bought and sold for cash. Given the relative lack of access to the cash sector, it is unlikely that women will be able to acquire houses of their own [8].

The better housing campaign insists that <u>all</u> houses must be of superior quality, and the villagers have been told 'no more little huts'. This has implications for divorced and widowed women, who are likely to be living in huts, as well as for young boys and old people. Although better houses sound like an improvement in the standard of living, they imply less flexibility in housing, and a consequent loss of privacy.

What is particularly worrying, however, is not the campaigns in themselves, but rather many of the premisses behind their formulation which are also implicit in the way in which they are implemented. Much of the planning is based upon what I can only term the 'construction' of the household as a unit, to which are attributed functions which it certainly never possessed before. A village, under the 'Villages and <u>Ujamaa</u> Villages Act' (1975), is registered as a corporate body with a minimum (250) and a maximum (600) number of households. Households are units which hold land (e.g. a one acre kitchen garden), and also reside in a permanent structure - a house.

A new word has been drafted into the Swahili language - <u>familia</u> - from the English word 'family', and it is not surprising perhaps that a frequent context in which it is used is 'a man and <u>his</u> family', i.e. his 'dependents'. 'Families' which do not fit into such a pattern, i.e. families in which there are no adult males, are likely to be seen as 'problematic'. For example, in his study of 'Operation Sogeza' in one area of Tanzania, Mwapachu, then a senior government official, comments that it was difficult to move households which contained only women and children and that they needed help with building new houses (Mwapachu, 1979).

It would be paradoxical indeed if as a result of efforts to establish a genuinely socialist society and to bring about development to benefit all, women should thereby lose the very real autonomy which, in some areas such as northern Mafia, they previously possessed.

Conclusion - Engels Vindicated?

It is perhaps useful to look at the foregoing material in the light of Engels' analysis, and subsequent re-interpretations of it, particularly that of Sacks (1979). Here we have an area in which the state developed after the rise of the Zanzibar Sultanate, although its influence was uneven, and had less impact on areas like northern Mafia where subsistence cultivation, rather than a plantation economy, remained dominant. Even so, such areas were subject to the laws of the state, imposed through the kadhis' courts, and to the payment of taxes. With the development of the colonial state under the Germans and British this process continued, although recognition was given to customary as well as Islamic law (cf. Gray, 1956).

Given, however, the relative availability of land and lack of state interference, villages in areas like northern Mafia were able to continue their method of cultivation, utilising long-established customary land-tenure practices (to which the British also accorded partial recognition), as well as cultivating cash crops. But cash-cropping favoured males, because of the Islamic laws of inheritance, and so did other methods of making cash, most of which required skills (like fishing) or mobility (like trading) which women do not have.

The major factor in ensuring the coexistence for so long of these two sectors - communal and private property, subsistence and cash economy, Islamic and customary law - were twofold. Firstly, that Islam, crucially, gives women the right to hold property, and secondly, Islam's view of marriage as a contract. This has helped ensure that the household/family has not emerged, as it has elsewhere, into a corporate property-owning group under the control of a male head. Instead, it is a loose co-residential and commensal group in which individuals hold private property while also holding rights to communal property via their membership of descent groups.

This situation does not appear likely to continue. The state is now impinging upon this area more than at any other time in its history. In its construction of an entity which it terms 'the family', and in its assignation to such a unit of co-residential, productive, and reproductive functions, and above all, in its assignment of property-holding functions to this unit, the state seems likely to erode even further the autonomy which women previously enjoyed.

Notes

1. Field-work was financed in 1965-7 by the University of London and the Worshipful Company of Goldsmiths. A revisit in 1976 was made possible by the BBC.

I am grateful to the following people who heard or read drafts of this article and made helpful suggestions: Janet Bujra, Lionel Caplan, Olivia Harris, Renée Hirschon, and members of the Oxford Women's Studies Seminar.

2. These refer to themselves by such terms as Washirazii (based on their supposed descent from Persian immigrants), Wambwera (in Mafia), Wahadimu, Watumbatu and Wapemba (in Zanzibar and Pemba), the 'Twelve Tribes' (around Mombasa), and Bajuni (around Lamu).

3. Although the royal family of Zanzibar belonged to the Ibadhi sect, the Kadhis' courts administered Sunnite Shafe'i law. However, a further complication arose during the colonial period when for a time the British applied Indian Islamic law (which was of the Hanafi school) through the kadhis' courts. Today the kadhis' courts refer in matters of family law (except where these contradict more recent state legislation), to the classic Shafe'i texts (cf. El-Busaidy, 1962; Farsy, 1966).

4. I estimated that in 1967, a married man needed approximately 500 shillings cash income per annum. A married woman theoretically needed less because her husband was supposed to provide her with (bought) food and clothes, but a divorced or widowed woman, who receives no such support, would need more than her married sister.

5. In 1965-7, I had no children, but by my return in 1976, had one natural and one adopted child. The second child was very difficult for the villagers to accept; when they passed round photographs of the children, they would comment 'That is the one she bore herself, and that's the one she's just fostering'. Only when I explained that both my children would inherit my property equally did they concede that the adopted child was really 'mine'.

6. All schools in Tanzania lay emphasis upon practical as well as academic work, and most have a farm on which they grow crops.

7. Mbilinyi tackles some of these issues in her writing, notably in her 1975 article. Nyerere himself is also not unaware of some of the problems women face, as is evidenced in the following:

> The truth is that in the villages, the women work very hard. At times they work for twelve or fourteen hours per day. They even work on Sundays and public holidays. Women who live in the villages work harder than anyone else in Tanzania. But the men who live in the villages ... are on leave for half their lives. (Nyerere, 1968, p.245).

8. It is of course just possible that a situation similar to that described by Bujra on the north Kenya coast may emerge, where men inherit land, and women inherit houses. However, in that area, women do not cultivate at all (cf. Bujra, 1976).

3 THE EXCHANGE OF WOMEN AND PROPERTY: MARRIAGE IN POST-REVOLUTIONARY CHINA

Elisabeth Croll

Introduction

In examining women's relation to property two aspects can be considered: women's access to property, and women as a form of property. Post-revolutionary China makes an interesting study for there the State has explicitly set out (a) to restructure relations of authority within kinship groups which had previously exchanged women in marriage and had denied them access to property; and (b) to reconstitute the notion of property itself by reducing areas of private ownership. The interaction of these two areas of reform has determined women's relation to property in the past thirty years.

Before the twentieth century, China was a society in which women had virtually no property rights and where women's labour, fertility and person constituted a form of property, itself exchangeable in a number of transactions and chiefly in marriage. Thirty years ago in 1950, the government of China outlawed the subordination of women to men, the exchange of women in marriage, gave legal recognition to women's property rights and substantially reduced areas of private ownership and property. The negotiations and the transactions of gifts which accompany the ceremonies constituting marriage in contemporary China thus provide a rich source of data for determining how far reforms to deny men's rights in women and the acquisition of rights by women themselves have succeeded. This paper focuses on marriage for it is one of the major means by which the State has attempted to change the relations between women and property.

In the mid-1950s the Chinese government was confident that their projected reforms established most of the theoretical preconditions for redefining the relation of women to property, since they incorporated both economic policies to reduce private property and the popularisation of a new ideology changing the relation of women to property. They were mindful of Engels' premises that 'full freedom in marriage' can only become operative 'when the abolition of capitalist production, and of property relations created by it, has removed all these secondary economic considerations which exert so powerful an influence in the choice of partner, (Renmin Ribao, 13

44

Dec. 1963). No longer would the corporate socio-economic and political interests of households require the manipulation of its women members. However an examination of the negotiations and transactions which constitute marriage in contemporary China suggest that in peasant households, women have not yet achieved full rights to contract their own marriages and that the transfer of rights over women still constitutes an important goal of marriage, one which may well have increasingly deprived women of their own claims to familial property. This paper attempts to elucidate the factors which have prevented a radical redefinition of women's rights to property in China.

The Marriage Law of 1950

The Marriage Law of 1950 [1] was a radical break with the past; its intention was to abolish arranged marriage, that is the rights of kin groups or persons other than the bride and groom to negotiate the passage of women between virilocal households, and to abolish the elaborate negotiations and transactions which reflected the dependence of women on male kin. The Marriage Law also prohibited betrothal gifts which validated the transfer of rights in a woman from one kin group to another. In return for handing over rights in their daughter, the bride's kin, or the wife-givers, had traditionally received what was seen as compensation from the groom's family as part of the marriage negotiations. The form and amount of the betrothal gift, negotiated by the heads of households through a go-between, had normally involved the transfer of jewelry, clothing, household goods, food and cash. Of course, the constituents of the betrothal gifts had varied according to the socio-economic resources of the groom's family. Among those on the margins of subsistence for instance, it was entirely a cash payment or compensation received by the bride's family which formed the fund out of which brides were procured for their own sons. In richer households it was used by the bride's family to purchase goods for the dowry. The Marriage Law also abolished the elaborate series of rituals which had symbolised the separation of the bride and her removal from the custody of her father's line. Upon the bride's departure, the door of her natal home had always been firmly shut in her face to symbolise her separation and loss to her natal family. She was transported by sedan chair to the groom's house where followed certain rites of integration into the groom's family which symbolised their new authority over the daughter-in-law, her subordinate position and her rights and duties towards her husband's kin group.

The new Marriage Law abolished arranged marriage and advocated 'free-choice' marriage in which full rights to handle matrimonial affairs was devolved to the younger generation 'without obstruction from relatives, friends, family and the public, and without regard for social status, occupation and property' (Guangming Ribao, 27 Feb. 1957). The redistribution of power involved in the substitution of free-choice for arranged marriage had consequences for the traditional authority exercised by elders and kin groups and their rights over the circulation of female kin. The placing of the negotiations of marriage within the control of the individual parties, the basing of free-choice marriage on the congenial bonding of the partners, and the strengthening of the marital bond as opposed to all other familial and kin bonds invested marriage with a new significance for the younger generation and especially for women. Brides were to enter into freely chosen contracts as equal partners to their grooms who, it was assumed, would have none of the traditional rights over women: their labour, their fertility, their chief ritual attachments and persons. As there was to be no legal transfer of rights over the bride, no compensation was allowed for the bride's family. The new ideology of marriage prescribed a period of courtship which was to represent the changed status of individuals as equal partners in the marriage negotiations. The marriage was to be legitimated not by an elaborate series of prestations and ceremonial emphasising membership in larger kin groups, but by a simple registration ceremony at which the marriage contract between two freely chosen individual and equal partners was signed and thus obtained the legal recognition of the State. It was to be followed by a simple informal tea party for friends and relatives [2].

A number of educational campaigns followed the promulgation of the Marriage Law to introduce the new institutions of marriage and women's position within it. These campaigns of the early 1950s provided a forum for intensive and continual discussion 'to enable everyone to demarcate clearly the differences between the old and new marriage systems and to eliminate the influence of the social customs on the consciousness of the people' (Renmin Ribao, 20 March 1953). The movement to introduce new marriage customs has been generally described in ideological terms as a 'battle in which new ideas were pitted against the old' or 'a struggle to get people to change their ways of thought' (People's China, 16 Nov. 1957; Renmin Ribao, 13 Dec. 1963). Thus the government has concentrated on consciousness-raising, assuming that once people understand the meanings behind marriage rituals and the passage of gifts, they will voluntarily reject traditional forms. For instance, in the marriage campaigns the government has specifically linked the abolition of betrothal gifts to reforms to reduce the dependent status of women. In educational materials designed to popularise the new forms of marriage, the government has argued that in the past 'betrothal gifts' were nothing but a 'pretext for the buying and procuring of women with money and other goods' which symbolised the exchange of women between groups of men (Zhongguo Qingnian, 19 Nov. 1964). It had harmed countless numbers of women by reducing their independence of movement and likening them to 'a form of merchandise or private property to be exchanged at will' (ibid). The government argued that it was an outmoded practice in a society which was explicitly committed to redefining the roles and raising the status of women. Thus the campaigns to redefine marriage were explicitly linked with the rejection of male kinship rights in women's

46

labour, fertility and person, and the exchange of women between kin groups.

Traditional Practices

In traditional China the main form of property had been land. Rights to property, either those inherited through membership of a common descent group or acquired within a lifetime, had been solely invested in the males of the household and kin groups. As an anthropologist who made a study of inheritance in traditional China has noted 'every male born or fully adopted into a family, was from the moment of his birth as a son, a coparcener' (Freedman, 1966, pp.49-50). Women did not inherit except in rare cases where not a single male member of the lineage survived. Dowry provided for daughters at the time of marriage is sometimes interpreted as a form of pre-mortem inheritance to the bride (cf. Goody, 1976), but students of traditional China have often argued that it was the symbolic attributes of dowry rather than female claims on property which guided the possession of dowry. Most social anthropologists distinguish between the definite legal rights to inheritance enjoyed by the males as 'basic shareholders' in contrast with the privilege of receiving a dowry by women as 'optional shareholders'. At the discretion of the 'basic shareholders', women might or might not have received dowry consisting of movable as opposed to patrilineal property or land in marriage (McCreery, 1976). Thus daughters of the richer households had frequently been sent off with a substantial dowry in the form of jewelry, clothes, household furnishings and cash:

> not because the girl has any specific claims on them (she is not a member of the property-owning unit), but because their own status is at stake; a bride-giving family must, in order to assert itself against the family to which it has lost a woman, send her off in the greatest manner they can afford. And it is no accident, therefore that the dowry and trousseau are put on open display; they are not private benefactions to the girl, but a public demonstration of the means and standing of her natal family (Freedman, 1966, p.55).

In some cases, therefore, dowry made considerable economic claims on the resources of the bride's household. The wealthier the family, the more likely that a daughter would be provided with a substantial dowry, and in the poorer peasant and artisan households the dowry was more likely to be of a token nature. But even a very poor bride's family attempted to provide a small dowry in order to avoid talk of 'marriage by purchase' (M. Yang, 1945, p.103). Optional as it was however, dowry was part of a woman's property complex in that her personal possessions in the form of jewelry and clothes did not necessarily form part of the larger jia estate, or the property subject to family division, but remained part of the conjugal or of the woman's personal fund.

47

After 1950, a number of economic policies were introduced in support of the Marriage Law. These were intended to reduce the property base of the individual household and to decrease the differentials between men and women's access to property, but there was no mention of dowry. In the rural areas, the introduction of co-operatives and rural communes substituted collectivised production units for individual peasant producers; they owned the land and provided employment for young men and women away from the controls of the household head. The family was thus to be without landed property and the jia estate generally reduced to a few movable items such as furnishings, tools, consumer goods and, in some cases, housing to which in theory all family members, including the women, were to have equal access.

Marriage Transactions Today

The competition between the new ideology of free-choice marriage and the traditional custom of arranged marriage has given rise to a variety of patterns of marriage in rural areas which combine elements characteristic of both pre-existing marriage customs and concessions to the new ideology. Marriage negotiations are still initiated and controlled by the older generation, although they no longer monopolise these negotiations. There is now included a procedure providing for the consent of the younger generation who presently may operate the right of veto. This pattern became a common procedure and so widely-accepted that it has been given official recognition as an acceptable form of free-choice marriage. In 1955, the Central Committee for the Movement for the Thorough Implementation of the Marriage Law stated that marriage contracts in which the principals were first introduced to each other by third parties and then expressed their own agreement to the match were to be recognised as a form of 'free will'. 'It is incorrect', the statement concluded, 'to consider that the introduction by a third party means an arranged marriage' (New China News Analysis, 5 March 1955).

This semi-arranged form of marriage was often referred to in the villages as 'free-choice' marriage to be distinguished from marriage negotiations initiated and controlled by the younger generation which was termed 'free-choice marriage in the modern way'. As one resident of an Henan province village observed in the 1970s, the former was considered to be the accepted norm in this and other villages of its inhabitants' acquaintance, although they were also aware that elsewhere in China there might be alternative 'more modern' ways of negotiating marriage. However, these practices were not appropriate 'to their way of doing things' (J. Chen, 1973, p.72). More recently, a survey of marriage negotiations in two counties in Anhui province showed that 75 per cent of the marriages registered in 1979 had taken the semi-arranged form (China Reconstructs, March 1981).

Today a wide range of transactions continues to characterise marriage negotiations in rural villages. Despite the legal prohibition on money transactions, betrothal and its associated gifts continues to function as an important social institution in rural China. Although there were a number of reports in the mid-1950s referring to the practice of camouflaging the passage of betrothal gifts by various means, the transfer of a moderate number of gifts to the bride's family has remained an openly tolerated procedure in rural areas even to the present day. Betrothal gifts are frequently included in official reports listing traditional customs currently practised in rural China.

Today the normal value of the betrothal gifts probably averages about Y300 with a range between Y100 and Y500, although at times its value is estimated to have reached more than Y1000. In parts of south China in 1965, it was reported that betrothal payments were not less than Y300 and Y400 and about as much as Y600 to Y700, plus gifts of food (Nanfang Ribao, 18 Jan. 1965). In the 1960s, the likely constituents included a cash payment of about Y300, household items such as furniture, sets of bedding, a sewing machine, items of personal clothing and perishable goods including chickens, fish and meat. In poorer Henan province, the betrothal gifts in the 1970s included movable property such as a bicycle, sewing machine and a clock and household items valued at a total of Y60 to Y80 together with small amounts of cash (J. Chen, 1973, pp.80-5). In the process of computation there is apparently room for some bargaining and hence for some competition between the families of bride and groom, and between the families of prospective grooms, for a very desirable young woman. There have also been a few references in the media to the more extreme cases: families who have profited by negotiating betrothal agreements many times over. In the 1980s, the persistence of betrothal gifts and the high cost of marriage for the groom's family continues to receive some publicity. Recently in a village in Hebei province, it was reported that betrothal gifts and a wedding banquet cost about Y1000. Since this amount accounted for only a third of the marriage costs for the grooms' households, marriage transactions had evidently become much more expensive for young men in recent years (China Reconstructs, March 1981).

Ideology and Conservatism

A study of the initial negotiations and transactions which surround marriage in rural China suggest that marriage is still conceived as a contract negotiated between members of the older generation, and financial transactions continue to validate the transfer of rights over women. In China the government has tended to attribute the persistence of these old forms of marriage in rural areas to the 'conservatism' or 'backwardness' of the peasants and of women in adopting new forms of social behaviour. Since the 1950s, it has identified village customs as the chief obstacle to implementing the new Marriage Law; they correlated change in marriage customs with the degree of exposure to the new ideology of marriage. Thus, in the role models and reference groups described in the media for emulation, the point at which change takes place coincides with initial awareness of the symbolism of old customs. Understanding is apparently followed by the immediate acceptance of new forms. Up to 1975 for example, the women of one production brigade were described as having taken for granted the acceptance of the betrothal gift as 'a warm pleasantry' or 'harmless custom'. During the anti-Confucian and Lin Biao campaign, however, they were made to realise the degree to which the custom likened them to a commodity. As a direct result and to demonstrate their new consciousness of the meaning of the custom, twelve girls of this brigade set a precedent in the village: they went in person to return the betrothal gifts to the families of their betrothed but without cancelling their engagements (Xuexi yu Pipan, 10 Jan. 1975).

However, this explanation for the persistence of traditional forms of marriage is valid only if it can be demonstrated that there are significant differentials in the degree to which various sub-groups have been exposed to the new ideology, and this must be directly correlated with the retention of old forms of marriage. For contemporary China, however, this explanation does not hold since it can be argued that the government has made a sustained effort to familiarise every section of the population with the new ideology. In nearly every case recorded in the media, the correspondents whether urban- or rural-based, showed an awareness of the new ideology of marriage and that the initiatives in the negotiation of marriage should have passed to the younger generation as well as an understanding of the reasons why betrothal should be discarded. Although some of the correspondents did not necessarily agree with the new ideology and even argued vehemently against it, they were certainly aware of the changes which it advocated. Generally it can be said that no government has been so assiduous in educating its young people for marriage.

But as we have seen this widespread education in the new ideology does not of course mean that traditional norms have been displaced. Indeed there is plenty of evidence to suggest that they persist. For instance, among the older generation many continue to interpret any initiative in marriage by the younger generation as disobedience or rebellion against parental authority that threatens their hegemony within the household and results in their loss of 'face' in the local community. They have invoked the traditional sanctions of filial piety and the wrath of the ancestors in their support. For the younger generation, duty and gratitude as well as lack of alternative opportunities to meet potential spouses makes them reluctant to defy the traditional authority of their parents. Letters to the press reveal that the obligation of filial piety continues to invoke feelings of anxiety: a number of girl correspondents felt they should conform with tradition and follow the wishes of their parents who had taken the trouble and expense to bring them up and were now losing them to another family. Sons did not have the same economic reasons for a daughter's gratitude for they were expected to support their parents in their old age, but for them the Confucian ideal of filial piety had been especially instilled from an early age. However evidence of such traditional sentiments on the part of older and younger generations should not be interpreted as mere survivals, representations of the cultural backwardness or ignorance of peasants in rural China. Instead, explanations must be sought in the wider economic context of contemporary society because very real economic reasons explain why the old forms of marriage persist and are defined in terms of the exchange of women. Primarily these relate to the structure and function of the peasant household in contemporary China and the demands which the rural economy currently makes on the individual household.

The Peasant Household in the Rural Economy

The rural economy is made up of three sectors: the collective waged labour-force, private sideline activities, and the domestic labour or daily servicing of the household. Each of these sectors adds to the income, either in cash or in kind, and supplies staple and non-staple foods for consumption or reduces the cost of maintaining the household as an economic unit. Within the communes the peasant household is still a unit of production although greatly reduced in scope, and because community services are very unevenly distributed in rural areas, it is also the primary unit of consumption. Chiefly it must continue to mobilise its material and human resources in order to find solutions to two organisational problems - production, and the transformation of materials for consumption. Moreover, the performance of these functions by the domestic group no longer relies on the exploitation of the jia lands or estate, but on the paid and unpaid labour of its members. The continued existence of the household as a unit of production and consumption requires that a household maximise its labour resources and organise and distribute them between these three sectors of the rural economy. Furthermore it is women's labour alone which is expected to combine the three sectors.

Young married women normally work in the collective labour-force alongside their husbands, but in addition they also undertake the major private sideline activities and service the household. The portion of a woman's time allocated to each sector may vary according to stages in her life cycle. In more complex stem- or joint-households, for example, it is common for an older woman to semi-retire or retire from the collective sector to manage the sideline and domestic sectors. This happens on the occasion of her son's marriage with the recruitment of a young daughter-in-law who immediately enters the collective waged labour-force.

In addition the accumulated demands made by the rural economy on the labour resources of the peasant household, together with the absence of State pension-schemes in rural areas, results in greater economic interdependence of the generations. The elders continue to be dependent on the wage-labour of the young, while the young are dependent on the older generation for their labour in the private sector of the economy and domestic servicing. In a peasant household, the family budget is reckoned collectively and agricultural wages are frequently distributed in one wage-packet to the head of the household. Each household thus has one fund and one savings account out of which expenses are met, and movable property or consumer durables purchased. The size of the fund mainly depends on the wages of the young. At the same time, however, because of traditional patterns of familial control, the young are unlikely to have accumulated a fund of their own and are almost entirely dependent on the accumulated household savings for economic support. In brief, the socio-economic functions assigned to the peasant household by the rural economy and the consequent form that the domestic group takes has maintained the conceptualisation of marriage as instrumental in exchanging women between households.

In China, official definitions of the domestic group concentrate on the inter-personal relations which are bounded by it. The domestic group is generally defined as 'mainly a unit of life in which the husband and wife share their married life together, rear and educate their children and care for their elder near relatives together' (Peking Review, 13 March 1964). This definition has two limitations: it leaves the projected forms which the residential group or family form should take vague and it omits any reference to its property base or socio-economic functions.

Virilocal marriage, or the recruitment of wives to the domestic group in which the groom resided prior to marriage, was widely practised in traditional China, and nowhere are new rules of post-marital residence explicitly stated. Rather the domestic group or household is said to 'stem from the marital bond for either it functions to establish a new household completely or it perpetuates an old household for a further generation' (Lu Yang, 1964, p.7). Thus the government's periodic attempts since the early 1970s to promote uxorilocal marriage (the recruitment of grooms into brides' households) as a normal form of post-marital residence have produced no significant results. This was done as part of a campaign to upgrade the value of daughters as permanent members of their parents' household into which the sons-in-law would be recruited on marriage, but today it is still brides who largely continue to be circulated between peasant households. This transfer of women from their natal household to that of the groom's family on marriage means that daughters are thought of as 'lost' to another family. There is thus still a marked preference for sons in rural areas who are permanent members of the household and will provide for their elders in old age. It is particularly noticeable that families with a number of sons show a confidence and invest in the future of the domestic group which is not present in families with no sons or even only one son. The former households, the wife-takers, were looking forward to and planning and saving for their future expansion when all the sons would recruit wives and later perhaps divide into separate but neighbouring households. Families with daughters and no sons, wife-givers, did not have a future to invest in as their daughters would go to another family (Croll, 1977). Virilocal post-marital residence and the consequent demand for sons has not only retarded marriage reforms, but it has also hampered the implementation of family-planning policies. Even some production units have been hesitant to train and invest in the training of girls who will probably be lost to another production unit on marriage (Croll, 1978). Although daughters may still be secondary to sons, however, the economic demands on the peasant household mean that a high value is placed on a daughter-in-law's labour.

The new definition of the domestic group in China omits any reference to characteristics which usually underlie anthropological definitions of the domestic group as the unit of production, consumption and reproduction. This omission in part reflects the goals of the communes in rural areas which were designed to make the collective the effective owners of the means of production, the basic unit of accounting, planning and distribution of incomes and provider of consumer services. In terms of these ideals, the establishment of this collective unit would remove the property base of the peasant household. It would also mean that much production and consumption would take place outside of the individual household. The payment of wages to individual members of the household would further weaken the corporate interests of the peasant household and the interdependence of its members. Despite the new ideology of the collective and the policies designed to reduce the domestic group's economic basis, certain socio-economic factors specific to the peasant household continue to underlie its economy; these tend to encourage the peasant household to maximise its resources in defence of its own economic interests. The intervention of the older generation in the marriage of their sons and daughters in rural areas and their rationales for doing so, suggest that the older generation continue to view marriage as an important instrument of control over familial affairs and female kin which can be exercised to the advantage of the corporate interests of the peasant household.

Labour Needs and Marriage Strategies

One of the most common explanations given by the older generation in taking the initiative in marriage negotiations was the desirability of recruiting another labourer into the household. Parents often expressed their support for early marriage in terms of their desire to 'drink a cup of tea provided by a daughter-in-law'. If the household required labour the most obvious remedy was to arrange for the marriage of a son and import a new daughter-in-law. For example, an observer in one village study reports how a mother initiated marriage negotiations on behalf of her young son before it was appropriate on the grounds that it was time she had some extra help in the house (J. Chen, 1973, p.80). This strategy is particularly explicit where a parent has died and there are several younger family members to be cared for. In these circumstances an elder son might be urged to marry so that a daughter-in-law could contribute additional income and help service the household. This is illustrated in the case of a medical student who wrote to a youth magazine, describing how his mother had recently died leaving his father, himself and two younger children. On his return home during the vacation, his father had stressed that a housewife was needed in the family as 'cooking and cleaning gave them a great headache' and had asked him to take a wife as a solution to their problem. In the ensuing disagreement between father and son, friends and neighbours supported the father's action and accused the son of being 'unfilial', a criticism which greatly disturbed the young man (Zhongguo Qingnian, 12 Feb. 1963).

Not only was the acquisition of another wage-earner or service-worker a motivating factor in the continuing intervention of the older generation, but the reverse also occurred; that is, some households with a low ratio of wage-earners to dependents married their young daughters out, thus immediately reducing the number of wage-dependents. In two cases quoted in the national women's magazine in the mid-1960s, parents initiated marriage negotiations with wealthy families who would be able to meet the cost of their daughters' education and living expenses in order to lighten their current 'family burden' (Zhongguo Funu, 1 May 1964; 1 Feb. 1966).

As important as the acquisition of the labour of a daughter-in-law was the reproduction of the family's labour force. The older generation frequently expressed their preference for early marriage negotiated on their own initiative in terms of a desire for the early advent of grandchildren. Parents and kin often encouraged young people to marry early in the hope of living to see their grandchildren or more particularly grandsons. Young sons were habitually pressurised into early marriages by elderly parents who became increasingly worried about their marriage arrangements and the birth of the next generation. Many reported that they had married young at the behest of their parents who had openly wanted a male child early in line with the custom of 'finding a wife for one's son early so that one can soon enjoy a comfortable life' (Gongren Ribao, 27 Sept. 1962; 9 Oct. 1962). It was the ardent wish of one young boy's mother in another village to have a grandson which had caused her to openly defy both the law and the commune leaders in order to bring a wife into the household for her son, despite the fact that he had not yet reached twenty years of age, the legal age of marriage (J. Chen, 1973, p.78).

Although the intervention of the older generation is usually couched in terms of the personal satisfaction to be derived from the birth of a grandson or the services of a daughter-in-law, it is clear that practical considerations underlie these sentiments. These were made explicit in the following cases. One correspondent to a national newspaper suggested that, although he was only 23 years old, there were advantages in his getting married now. Not only could he and his wife work, but his parents, still in their early fifties, could also continue in agricultural employment, and, by the time his parents retired, his own children would be nearing the age of entry into the labour force. He thought that the common folk-saying: 'Plant seedlings early and you will harvest a rice crop early; have a daughter-in-law early and you will enjoy happiness (grandchildren) early' still had a certain validity in China today (<u>Gongren Ribao</u>, 11 Sept. 1962). The advantages, if not the necessity, of reproducing labour at an early age was most explicitly stated in a discussion which took place between peasants and a young educated youth residing in their village. In line with the official recommendations, the young man had suggested that people should get married at a later date, but in response the peasants had immediately retorted that he just did not understand their problem: if people waited to marry until they were 30 years old, then when they were 50 years old their first son would scarcely have had time to become an able-bodied labourer, and if they had become sick or ill in the meantime, or if for some reason there was no adult to support the household, then would not its members just sink into poverty? (Parish, 1975, p.618). In contrast to urban households where free-choice marriage at a later age is the preferred form, the older members in peasant households felt they had to intervene in the marriage negotiations of the members of their household at, or as near, the legal age as possible.

Likewise, the persistence of the betrothal gift in rural areas may be attributed to economic pressures. The most frequent explanation given by the older generation for the acceptability of the betrothal gift is that it is a form of compensation paid by the wife-takers to the wife-givers, recompensing the bride's parents for the expenses of the girl's upbringing. Some parents state that after many years of raising a daughter they ought to get a handsome sum in return; indeed it is not unknown for negotiations to be broken off because the gift was not sufficient compensation for the loss of a daughter. In one such case in the 1960s, a mother who rejected a betrothal gift because of its low value exclaimed to her daughter: 'I have raised and brought you up and do you think that this little sum of betrothal is enough? In the days of the past, at least twice this amount would have been asked for!' (<u>Zhongguo Qingnian</u>, 19 Nov. 1964). When conflict arises over the value of the gift, the requests of the girls' parents are quite likely to receive the support of most of the village, despite the law prohibiting monetary transactions in marriage. One girl's parents were greatly dissatisfied with the proffered gifts, saying that they 'had taken great pains for many years with the upbringing of their daughter, and were they now to be given so small a present in return, that it was not even enough for the exchange of a pig?'. Many of their fellow-villagers thought that the parents were being quite reasonable to ask for a moderate betrothal present. The villagers concluded that it was a matter of convention that when a daughter was to be given away in marriage, the groom's parents should give a betrothal gift to show their gratitude to the bride's parents for having raised their future daughter-in-law (<u>Nanfang Ribao</u>, 25 Dec. 1964). Village opinion has been slow to change. One young girl reported in the 1970s that when she had objected to the passage of a betrothal gift, she had been praised in the media as a good example to other girls, but many fellow-villagers thought she was foolish not to take the opportunity to ask for a few sets of clothing as a gift from her husband's family (Renmin Ribao, 24 Jan. 1972).

The fact that it is the parents of daughters rather than those of sons who most often insist on compensation in the form of bethrothal gifts again suggests that the older generation felt that investments in daughters should be recouped at marriage. Although for some parents of sons, especially those resident in the poorer and isolated infertile regions of China, the advantages of providing a larger betrothal gift to ensure brides for their sons outweighed the advantage of adopting the new ways, many grooms' families were only too pleased to adopt the recommended form and thus be relieved of their traditional obligations. One mother said she was very pleased when her son married in the new way for it meant that she didn't have to pay a penny for her daughter-in-law! (People's China, 1 June 1951).

Some parents operated a dual standard. Families who insisted on gifts in return for their daughters often encouraged their sons to marry in the new way. In another instance, a father who had paid dearly for his own wife and who certainly intended to get some of it back when his daughter married was heard to exclaim, 'Look at the cost of a daughter!'. The same father however had allowed all his sons to marry in the new way for this had meant that he did not need to pay anything for his daughters-in-law (Myrdal, 1967, pp.289-90). A similar rationalisation for the persistence of the custom was frequently offered by the future brides themselves. Many appeared to have believed that even if they had initiated the negotiations themselves, they should follow the wishes of their parents, and accept betrothal presents to show gratitude to the older generation who had invested in their upbringing and were now losing them to another family (Zhongguo Qingnian, 24 April 1962).

A common theme in the defence of continuing parental intervention and the exaction of gifts is the interest in the recruitment and reproduction of labour which directly reflects the demands made by the rural economy on the peasant household. It is thus the demands of the rural economy on the household as a unit of production and consumption that have encouraged its expansion in numbers at least for certain periods of its developmental cycles. The expanded or joint phase of the development cycle following the marriage of a son or sons may serve as a unique opportunity for the household to make use of its extended labour resources to specialise and diversify the economy of the domestic group and to accumulate wealth prior to eventual division. Indeed it may be argued that economic along with certain demographic factors have meant that the developmental cycle of peasant households may be more elaborate now than at any time during the recent past. If labour now forms the major part of the total means of production, and control over labour the major source of wealth and social differentiation, then the recruitment and reproduction of labour itself is in constant demand. Since the individual and private hiring of labour is prohibited by law in China, marriage becomes the major if not the only means of reproduction and direct recruitment of labour. Thus it is the immediate corporate interests of the peasant household which both encouraged and enabled the older generation to maintain their authority over marriage. The terms of these negotiations suggest that it is labour rather than property which now forms the most important of its resources. Indeed labour itself has become a form of property. But, as other studies suggest, those whose labour is exchanged need not necessarily be defined as objects (cf. Strathern, this volume) or be denied access to property themselves. In China, however, despite changes in marriage transactions and inheritance, there are indications that women themselves may well be deprived of property rights at present.

Dowry and Inheritance

The gifts which nowadays accompany the bride to the groom's household are not necessarily referred to as dowry, but simply as presents contributed by the family of the bride to the establishment of a new conjugal fund within that household. These gifts may take the form of personal effects, tools for production, or room furnishings (such as a bed, bedclothes, a wardrobe, chest, a desk or chair, a clock) or they may be other substantial items such as a bicycle, a sewing machine or an electric fan and, more recently, a television. Their provision by the kin of the bride is explained on the grounds that their absence would draw adverse attention to the bride's household and that they provide the material basis for the couple's room and their future household in the event of a family division into separate households. They are thus representative of and a contribution to the status of the bride's family vis a vis the groom's family and kin and neighbours. As the bride's family frequently responded, 'if we don't spend some money and provide you with some form of dowry, will not other people laugh at us?' (Zhongguo Qingnian, 16 Jan. 1966). Compared to other marriage customs though, the transfer of gifts which have all the connotations of the traditional dowry seemed to have given much less cause for concern by the authorities. In the new ideology there is no explicit prohibition of the dowry, and in the educational materials the marriage of role models is either marked by its absence or it is presented as an outmoded custom which is offered by the parents of the bride but rejected by the bride herself. Interestingly however, praise has also been bestowed on families who retain the form of the dowry, but invest it with a new political or revolutionary significance. In one case the bride's family provided their daughter with 'revolutionary ideas and farm tools' and in another 'four volumes of the Selected Works of Mao Zedong, two bamboo baskets, a spade and a pick' (Zhongguo Qingnian, 16 Jan. 1966; Renmin Ribao, 24 Jan. 1972). The dowry has always been invested with less economic or symbolic significance than the betrothal gift, and in 1980 it was reported in the Chinese media that very few brides bring any dowry to their marriages (China Reconstructs, March 1981). The reasons why this would seem to be so again have to do with post-marital residence patterns and the substitution of labour for property as the chief source of wealth accumulated by a peasant household.

Economic reforms, especially the collectivisation of land and the means of production, have reduced inheritable property in rural China, but the question of inheritance is by no means irrelevant. The Sixty Articles governing communes show that the State always intended that householders should own their own tools and house, have the right to buy, sell or rent their house, and according to the laws of inheritance pass it on to their children. The jia estate thus still includes residences, household effects (furniture, bedding, utensils, bicycles, watches, books and curios, clothing), farm tools and small numbers of domestic livestock. Legally, daughters share equal inheritance rights with sons, but because of post-marital residence patterns they are less likely to do so in rural areas. Where the dowry persists it does continue to give women a share in the property of her natal family, but, as we have seen, it seems to be a declining institution. Where the marriages of sons and daughters are spaced sufficiently apart to allow for the accumulation of familial funds to meet the expenses of both marriages, then daughters may well be provided with gifts or some form of movable property. However for the kin of the bride there is bound to be some conflict between the funds lost to them and the desire not to lose status, and where there was some competition between sons' and daughters' marriages, the daughter was seen to have less claim on familial funds (Croll, 1977). At this stage of the developmental cycle of the family, the claims of sons and the recruitment of daughters-in-law must take precedence in the allocation of familial funds over the claims of daughters who are lost to the household on marriage.

Nor is she likely to benefit at any other stage of the developmental cycle as virilocal residence also affects the inheritance of a married daughter in the event of the death of her parents. Her inheritance is ultimately dependent on whether there are any brothers, and if there are not, then the degree of support she has provided for her parents in their old age. If there is an only daughter who, although married and living elsewhere, has sent money to support her parents then she will inherit the house and household effects. Sometimes in fact the commune will contract with a married daughter that she supports her parent/s in return for the house upon their death. On the other hand if the collective has supported her parents as dependents under the Five Guarantee System [3] then the daughter's right to inherit goes by default, and the collective then reserves the right to take over the property on the parent's death.

Although the property base of the peasant family has declined, the effects of patriliny and post-marital residence on intra-familial inheritance patterns continues. Ironically it is the increased value attributed to women's labour which is largely responsible for the decline in the dowry.

The Value of Women's Labour

The large-scale entry of women into wage-labour in agriculture and industry in rural China in the last twenty-five years has placed a new value on daughters. This has given a greater impetus to the compensation of the bride's household through the transfer of the betrothal gift. As the amount of the betrothal gift and the cost to the groom's household has increased, so it has become more difficult for it to accumulate sufficient funds for the marriage of their sons. A recurrent theme in articles on marriage in the media in China in the last two years has been the rise in costs of brides and the consequent difficulties which young men have in obtaining brides. It seems likely though that the rise in the value of the betrothal gift has not only created difficulties for the groom's family, but has also had repercussions for the claims of daughters on family funds and property. Whereas, in the past the bride's family frequently returned the betrothal gift to the groom's household in the form of a dowry which also traditionally constituted a potential source of independence, now it seems much more probable that the bride's family will retain it and feed it into the familial fund out of which daughters-in-law are to be procured. Apparently some parents marry off their daughters first so they can accumulate enough cash for their son's wedding (Beijing Review, 9 March 1979). In the past few years therefore, daughters are less likely to be given a dowry even though they have now almost without exception contributed their wages to the familial fund for some years before marriage. The decline in the fund set aside for the dowry then does not take account of or recognise a daughter's earnings and her past contribution to family funds which in view of the rising age of marriage may be substantial.

The increase in value of the betrothal gift also has potential repercussions for the daughter-in-law. It is likely that after marriage her earnings are viewed by the groom's household as recompense for the expense entailed in procuring her. Like other members of the household her wages too are frequently incorporated directly into the single familial fund rather than offering a source of individual independence. At present then a woman may not only now be deprived of a dowry that once had formed a potential basis of any independence [4] but furthermore her earnings may not be recognised as hers by right after her marriage. Although by law, marriage gives women equal access to family property and equal inheritance [5], the acid test of such a rule must be the nature of division in the event of divorce or the death of husband and subsequent remarriage. In the rural virilocal household, the wife, daughter-in-law or mother usually remains in the household of her husband's kin upon his death and, unless she remarries, her husband's family will in all probability continue to support her and the joint property base may well remain intact. In these circumstances, her rights are only likely to be contested in the more unusual event of her divorce or remarriage as a young widow. Unfortunately there is so little evidence to go on that it is difficult to predict the likely form that division of property would take in these circumstances.

Although land has been extracted from the household estate and labour has replaced property as the primary economic base, it is housing, tools of production, movable property and savings which in rural China continue to represent the accumulated capital of the peasant household and the valorisation of the labour of its members. It is also increasingly apparent that although women contribute to this capital and have legal claim to this property, in practice, the immediate corporate interests of the peasant household circumscribe the rights and claims of women on family property.

Women, Marriage and Family Form

In contemporary rural China, marriage is one of the more important strategies employed by the domestic group to expand its labour resources. As this paper suggests, there is a direct correlation between the multifarious socio-economic functions demanded of the peasant household, its expanded size or complex structure, the persistence of parental intervention in marriage negotiations and the passage of the betrothal gift to the bride's household. This rural pattern of associations is in direct contrast to urban marriage patterns. In the cities there is a minimal, if non-existent private sector of the economy and there are institutionalised State and community provisions for retirement and for servicing and sharing in the maintainance of the household. This reduces the socio-economic functions of the city household and it is less a unit of production and consumption than its rural counterpart. Consequently the demands on the labour resources of the urban household are greatly reduced. In urban localities, housing is publicly owned and allocated, the household budget and expenses of the household are calculated on an individual basis and the costs divided among the wage-earning members. The remainder of an individual's income is at his or her disposal, and for young people, daughters as well as sons, one of the main expenses to be saved for out of their own savings is their marriage. Young people initiate their own marriage negotiations with the result that parental controls and interests in marriage are much reduced. The betrothal gift has all but disappeared in the cities. Thus urban women are much more likely to be equal partners in marriage and to have made a free-choice marriage in which they retain a certain portion of their own income and have their own savings and individual property.

In the rural areas where (a) post-marital residence is more likely to be virilocal, (b) the peasant household is still a unit of production, consumption and a single monetary unit demanding the recruitment and reproduction of labour, and (c) where all kinds of community services are less developed, then the corporate interests of the peasant household in the negotiation of the marriages of its sons and daughters are greater. The structure and socio-economic functions of the peasant household have tended to encourage the continuing interest of the older generation in marriage procedures in defiance of the new ideology of free-choice marriage. At the same time the increasing value placed on labour rather than on landed property has invested the circulation of female labour and fertility with a new significance. For the peasant household, women remain objects of exchange in marriage; paradoxically it is the rise in the value of women's labour which may well have penalised women themselves in terms of their access to dowry and other property.

Notes

1. For the text of the 1950 Marriage Law see Croll (1973), and for amendments in the Revised Marriage Law of 1980 see Women of China, December 1980.

2. For full description of marriage reforms see Croll (1981).

3. Under the Five Guarantees all persons in China are provided with basic food and fuel, clothing, shelter, primary education and burial.

4. In almost every case the women of the early twentieth century who had left home to attend school or marry a man of their own choice had converted the jewelry of their dowry into cash support. See Croll (1978).

5. A daughter's right to inherit property was again recently tested and affirmed in the law courts. See Women of China, March 1980.

6. For a further and full elaboration of this argument see Croll (1981).

4

DOWRY IN NORTH INDIA:
        ITS CONSEQUENCES FOR WOMEN

        Ursula Sharma

Dowry Divides Women

Traditionally, dowry in India was regarded as a burden for the
bride's parents but an honour for the bride. Feminists in India now
argue that this institution brings no honour to women, indeed the
pressure put upon young brides to persuade their parents to give
more dowry may lead to their humiliation, ill treatment or even
death. If this is the case, how has the dowry system survived for so
long and why are attempts to challenge it not more successful? In
order to answer such questions, it is necessary to look at dowry not
only as part of the symbolic order of Hindu society (as 'saying
something' about marriage and the relations between affines) but as a
concrete form of property in which the members of the household,
both men and women, have different kinds of interest and over which
they have different kinds of control. In North India dowry consists of
movable property made over to the husband's family, or to the newly
married pair at or soon after the wedding.
        According to the conventional ideology in North Indian society,
property accrues to the household as a corporate group rather than
to individual persons. Of course, land and houses will be officially
registered in the name of a single individual (usually the senior
male) but the property is administered by the senior members of the
household on behalf of all its members. Modern legislation assumes a
more individualistic notion of property. Where land is concerned the
corporate responsibility of the wider kin group (where it existed)
was eroded long ago during the British period. Recent legislation,
especially that concerning the inheritance rights of women, shows an
increased tendency to accentuate legal individualism. There is often a
tension between the legal and economic individualism demanded by
modern capitalism and the traditional more corporate attitude to
property which still operates informally within the domestic unit. To
give an example, a young woman who earns an individual wage -
whether as a stenographer or a farm hand - may be expected to
hand over her wages to her parents-in-law who will pool them with
those of other members of the family and make decisions about how
this income should be spent or saved. Obviously the prior rights of

individuals over goods of certain kinds will be recognised in practice (over items of clothing, for instance) and the particular circumstances of the household as well as the personalities of its members will affect the precise way in which day to day decisions are made.

But two main principles underlie the structure of authority in most households, those of seniority and of gender. Juniors of either sex are expected to defer to elders and women are expected to defer to men. Where these relations of authority correspond to relations of dependence this deference is easily exacted, but discrepancies do arise, as we should expect in a period of rapid economic change, and each household has its internal complexities. Broadly speaking, what all this means in relation to dowry and the position of women, is that as brides women have little control over the way in which dowry is given and received. As they become older they participate in the dowry system more actively as givers of dowry (mothers of brides) or as receivers and redistributors of dowry (mothers of sons). We cannot understand the consequences of dowry for women unless we look at the processes of decision-making and also at the relations of dependence within the household, especially since it is changes in this latter area which have, in my view, intensified the importance of dowry as an element in the marriage system.

I now turn to a description of marriage payments in North India, drawing on data collected during fieldwork conducted in Punjab and Himachal Pradesh in 1977-8 [1]. The following account will probably be valid for most Hindu communities in North India, although I realise that some of the differences in practice as between, for instance, different classes and between rural and urban areas may seem to have been glossed over as a result of my attempts to generalise.

The Organisation of Dowry in North India

The gifts subsumed by the term dowry (daj, dahej) are given at the time of the wedding or very soon after. They usually include household goods (furniture, utensils, bedding, perhaps electrical appliances) and clothes (most of which are destined to be redistributed among the groom's kin). There may also be certain goods designated more or less as personal gifts for the groom – clothes, a wristwatch, and in wealthy families even a motor scooter. Some cash may be given but in North India, land, agricultural equipment or cattle are never included to my knowledge, in spite of their central importance to the rural economy. Immovable property in the form of house sites may be given in the case of very wealthy urban families, but this seems to be a modern development, and on the whole dowry consists of movable property.

Whatever the dowry consists of, these gifts are given as part of a series of prestations made by the family of the bride to that of the groom. It commences with the sweets and cash conventionally made over at the engagement ceremony, and continues throughout the lifetime of the bride and into that of her children, for her brothers must make substantial contributions to her children's marriage expenses. When they arrange the marriage of a son, parents do not just look forward to the dowry they will receive at the wedding. They look to the bride's family's general capacity to give.

When the two families begin negotiations for the marriage, dowry is seldom given direct mention in the opening round of discussions. That would be in poor taste and bad manners. But negotiations are conducted on the assumption that the groom's family's expectations and the bride's family's capacity to give will be roughly matched. A certain amount of status can be 'bought' by a girl of undistinguished family who marries into a better family by means of a large dowry, but there is no point in marrying your daughter into a family whose expectations are likely to be too high, nor in creating such high expectations with over-generous opening gifts if this initial level of giving cannot be sustained. The ideology to which high caste groups try to conform, and which is respected by low caste groups as well, is the kanya dan marriage. Kanya dan means the gift of a virgin. The bride's parents make a 'gift' of their daughter, along with as big a dowry as can be provided, to the groom and his family [2]. This being the ideal, any element of explicit bargaining must be discreet and covert, so that the dominant ideology (the bride and her dowry as gifts freely given by the father from the happiness of his heart and to obtain religious merit, for which he desires nothing in return) is not violated. According to this ideology the groom's family cannot, of course, explicitly demand anything, but the reality is quite different as everyone knows. Every village can provide its horror stories of negotiations which foundered when it became clear that the groom's family expected more than the bride's family could give, however implicitly these demands were made known (Jeffery, 1979, p.81; Sharma, 1980, p.148).

Dowry Distribution and Control

Parents begin to collect items for a daughter's dowry well in advance of her wedding, even years in advance, depending on how many daughters they have to provide for and on their circumstances at the time. It is usual for the girl herself to prepare some of the items, e.g. embroidered bed-covers, cushions, etc., and nowadays wage-earning daughters may buy some items from their wages, although strictly speaking the ideology of kanya dan marriage does not countenance this. However most parents, whatever their financial status, will reckon on receiving some help from other relatives.

The bride herself will have very little say in what happens to her dowry once it leaves her parents' home. As a new bride she is in any case expected to behave in a modest and self-effacing manner and if she wishes to win her new family's favour she will not risk her future happiness by asserting her wishes until she has established a firm footing in her new household. If, as is common, the newly-married couple are to spend some time living together under the husband's parents' roof then the household dowry items will be merged with the common stock of household goods for the time being, on the understanding that most of them will be made available to the young couple if and when they eventually move out and set up house on their own. However, this separation of goods is not always easy once other members of the household have become used to enjoying use of the refrigerator, television or whatever the new bride brought with her. S.L. Hooja, in a perceptive discussion of the way in which dowry goods are redistributed, notes that there may well be conflict between the couple and the husband's parents on this issue. Such conflict arises from the contradiction between the traditional idea that since children are effectively the property of their parents, then the property of the children may be controlled by the parents, and the more modern notion that if a young man has the means to set up his own household independently of that of his parents he is entitled to complete autonomy so far as the organisation of this new household is concerned. It is not just the bride therefore who has only limited control over the dowry goods; even her husband may find it difficult to assert his rights in them (especially if he is very young) owing to the close relationship between seniority and authority in the family (see Hooja, 1969, pp.9-11).

Where household goods and items of clothing are concerned, it is likely to be the bride's mother-in-law who has the greatest say in how these items are distributed. This is partly by virtue of her position of seniority, but also relates to her position as senior woman. It is largely women, and especially senior women, who control the flow and pace of gift-giving both within the household and with other households. This is not the place for an extensive discussion of systems of ritual gift-exchange among women in South Asia (see Vatuk, 1972, and Eglar, 1960 for accounts) but suffice it to say that the proper regulation of gift-making at all important ritual occasions (life-cycle rites, seasonal festivals, etc.) is an important function of the women of the household, and where these gifts consist of goods (sweets, clothing, household items) as opposed to cash, it is the senior woman of the household who has the prime responsibility for seeing that obligations are met and proper relationships maintained. So one can see the control which the mother-in-law has over the goods which nominally are the property of the newly-wed couple partly in terms of the general authority which senior members of the household have over juniors, but also in terms of the senior women's responsibility to maintain correct relations of reciprocity within and outside the household. So when the mother-in-law appropriates items of clothing from the dowry and distributes them among her own married daughters or to other daughters-in-law, she may not just be exercising her prerogative over valuables entering the household, but will see herself as meeting obligations to make regular gifts to her daughters in their married homes, and to provide good things for the other junior women who are part of her household by virtue of having married into it.

What say do men have in this redistribution? The mother-in-law may well consult her husband when she hands out the clothing and other personal items as described above. But if any sums of cash are involved (and in middle class urban families this is more and more the case) they are likely to be under the immediate control of the father-in-law. It is up to him whether some portion of these funds are earmarked for the future use of the young couple or whether they are merged with the general funds of the household, although if the bridegroom is already living separately from his parents, as may be the case with urban employed men, it is more likely that he will have a measure of control over such important resources. The pattern of control in the process of redistribution therefore is in keeping with the informal principle that women (especially senior women) have immediate control over things in the household, and men (especially senior men) have immediate control over any large reserves of cash.

The ideology of the jointness of interest of the members of one household makes it very difficult to identify the kind of control over resources and property which individual members may exercise in empirical cases. Even when they do make unilateral decisions about the disposal of property they do not always recognise themselves as doing so. They will see themselves as members of the group on behalf of other members and will find it difficult to explicitly countenance any division of interest among the members. This problem besets the study of household decision-making generally in this kind of society. But even a scrutiny of the norms regarding relationships within the household (the ideology of seniority, of male competence, of the distinction between daughters and daughters-in-law) ought to suggest that the dowry property will not be under the control of the woman in whose name it is given, although that does not mean that it will not be controlled by other women. The Hindu bride's dowry may bring her self-respect and prestige in the household (and indeed in the community) if her parents have been particularly generous, but it will not of itself bring her economic power [3].

Forms of Marriage in North India:
Anthropological Theories and the North Indian Case

Kanya dan is the form of marriage to which the dominant ideology gives the most positive value, but it has never been the only form of marriage in North India. The literature is full of references to bridewealth marriages in all parts of South Asia. This form of marriage seems to be on the decline but was formerly very widespread and is still common in some communities, mainly low castes (see egs. Aziz, 1979, p.62; Mayer, 1960, pp.233-4). Unfortunately there are no detailed descriptions of such marriages, probably because families are often secretive about such marriages and ashamed to acknowledge them as they do not have the prestige of kanya dan marriages, but also because anthropologists have until recently tended to concentrate upon high caste groups among whom such marriages are rare nowadays. But it would seem that in all areas of North India there has been a tendency for dowry marriages to spread down the hierarchy, increasing at the expense of bridewealth marriages although not equally rapidly in all regions. (See Sharma, 1980, p.138ff for a discussion of this shift in Himachal Pradesh and Punjab).

The co-existence of two quite different forms of marriage payment in the same society, not accompanied by radical differences in kinship structure, cultural evaluation of women etc. presents a nice challenge to the possibilities of sociological generalisation.

Here, the 'cost-benefit ratio' type of analysis (see Comaroff 1980, p.6) seems to prove useful at first sight. In these terms marriage payments are seen as a form of compensation. Dowry compensates the groom's family for the addition of a dependent non-productive member, whilst bridewealth compensates the bride's family for the loss of an active productive member. This kind of theory has been very influential; many writers on South Asia have not bothered to confirm its validity, simply offering it as a common-sense assumption (see Nair, 1976, p.80; Mandelbaum, 1972, p.105). In India it is true that bridewealth occurs mainly amongst the low castes and tribal communities where the female members of the household are very likely to work outside the home for a wage (albeit a pitifully low one) and/or make a substantial contribution to the pool of family labour available to work owned or rented land. The highest dowries are usually paid in groups where women have traditionally been least likely to make substantial contributions to family income. So it would seem that the low caste groom is paying for the future services of an economically useful bride whilst a high caste groom is being paid to take on an economically dependent bride.

This could certainly explain the original distribution of marriage payment practices, but it does not explain the pattern of change. Nowadays, dowry is increasingly adopted by low castes and impoverished groups who formerly paid bridewealth, but the shift to dowry does not always seem to be related to any withdrawal of women from productive labour. Similarly, among high status groups who pay dowry, some educated women have begun to earn wages in professional and skilled occupations and make substantial contributions to the household in which they live, whether as daughters or wives. But this change is not accompanied by any substantial attrition of the institution of dowry, let alone a shift to bridewealth. In some areas, it is true, a bride with recognised earning capacity may be able to marry well with a slightly lower dowry than a woman without such qualifications (Van der Veen, 1972, p.40) but in other areas the girl's qualifications make no difference at all (Murickan, 1975, p.83).

However there is one sense in which the cost-benefit type of theory may have some validity. This is possible if we consider not the absolute amounts of wealth generated for the household by women's work, but changes in the proportion of their contribution in relation to that of men. It might be possible to show that the expansion of dowry has been accompanied by a decline in women's capacity to contribute to household income compared with that of men, even though there has been no absolute diminution of women's economic activity. New opportunities to earn cash wages in factories, in government employment and white collar occupations have expanded far more rapidly for men than for women, both in India and in many other ex-colonies, as the literature on women and development demonstrates (Boserup, 1970). While women in rural households may be doing about the same amount of productive work as they did before the Second World War – on their own farms or on the land of others – it is the men of the household who will earn the primary cash requirements of the household, whether as migrant labourers or home-based workers combining wage labour with part-time farming. Regardless of how much work they do, women in such households remain dependent upon men, for they cannot by themselves generate the cash needed by the household. Even if they can generate cash income the cash may not pass through their hands (for instance they may help to grow agricultural produce for sale, which is then marketed by men) or they may have little control over it. The cost-benefit ratio theory may have some limited value, therefore, if we do not interpret it too literally but concentrate on relations of dependence rather than absolute amounts of work performed or cash earned.

There is also a demographic version of the cost-benefit theory, according to which marriage payments refer to the scarcity value of women rather than to their economic value as workers. Thus, Loizos explains changes in the Greek Cypriot system of marriage payments in terms of the decrease in marriageable males due to out-migration and the consequent competition among women for eligible grooms (Loizos, 1975, p.512). This may have some limited applicability in India but if so, it applies at the local rather than at the national level. In the majority of Indian states there is an overall shortage of women. For instance in certain areas of North West India the ratio is as low as 960 women per 1000 men. Neither polygyny nor polyandry is practised widely enough to make the kind of difference to the marriage market that polygyny is supposed to make in some African societies. This means that few women who wish to get married fail to do so in the end, unless they are actually deformed or mentally defective. On the other hand, some men in families at the lower end of the social scale do fail to attract brides. This being so, the intense anxiety which parents express over the prospect of marrying off a number of daughters seems surprising at first. It is true that failure to marry is a greater disgrace for a woman than for a man, and that women are expected to marry at an earlier age than men, but the demographic situation is so much in their favour in this respect that it ought to be men who need to worry about inducing women to marry them rather than the reverse.

However, rather than marriage payments being the result of demographic imbalance it is at least as likely that they are a cause of such imbalance, albeit an indirect one. Miller has marshalled evidence which suggests that the imbalance of male-female ratios is due to differential care of girls and boys. This, she claims, is at least partly related to their differential economic rating in the household as either assets or liabilities, an evaluation in which dowry obviously plays an important part (Miller, 1981, p.133ff). It is fairly well known that female infanticide was practised among some social groups in the nineteenth century – not, as one might suppose, the poorest social groups but mainly among high status landowning groups, the substantial peasantry and the minor rural aristocracy (Panigrahi, 1972, p.11). It was among these groups that dowries were high and grooms hard to find, since the families concerned stood at the top of a particular local hypergamous hierarchy. In India hypergamy is common in some caste groups and a number of hypergamous marriages may take place between members of different castes. Where this is the case, the women of the families or sub-castes with the highest status will be in competition for husbands with women of lower status who can pay substantial dowries. The inevitable consquence of this is a general inflation of dowry rates at the top end of the local hierarchy. So although there is no overall excess of women (indeed there will be a shortage in all likelihood) there may be demographic imbalance within a particular section of the marriage market.

It is clear that dowry has the effect of controlling competition among women for the most desirable husbands in a hypergamous marriage market, whilst expanding the pool of desirable wives in the case of men. The amount of dowry your parents can give determines to a very large extent the league in which you play. To give a large dowry will also increase the prestige of the family, not just by attracting a wealthy or influential son-in-law but by determining the family's capacity to give freely without expectation of immediate return. Women are therefore important instruments in the competition for prestige.

Dowry and Inheritance

Hindus themselves say that the bride is given movable property for her dowry as her share of her parents' estate. It is regarded as a form of pre mortem inheritance which women receive when they leave the parental home at marriage. Sons remain members of the natal family and they receive the immovable property after the death of their father, divided equally between them either then or at some subsequent point. Daughters traditionally did not inherit land unless they had no brothers and although the law now allows them to do so, very few exercise this new right. In the course of my fieldwork I found that many women considered that a sister who claimed her share of land would seem greedy and might risk forfeiting her brothers' goodwill. Had she not already received her share of the family property at marriage?

Some anthropologists, such as Goody and Tambiah (1973) have also represented dowry as a form of inheritance. Goody treats dowry in India as one instance of a form of inheritance common in Eurasian societies. In 'diverging devolution' children of both sexes inherit, but women often receive their portion at marriage in the form of dowry property. Dowry also helps to ensure that women secure partners of at least equal and at best superior position, in short it contributes to class formation and maintenance, whereas in Africa bridewealth contributes to the maintenance of a fundamentally egalitarian distribution of goods and wealth among groups (Goody, 1976, p.9ff).

But if Hindus themselves represent dowry as a form of inheritance, are we obliged to view it in this way too? In some societies this is clearly a legitimate way of looking at dowry. Friedl notes that Greek brides are allocated land and/or house sites at marriage strictly equivalent to the share which their brothers receive later when their father dies, and that daughters thus endowed retain control over this property (Friedl, 1962, p.49). Goody would be correct in treating the dowry system here as part of a total system of inheritance which disperses property among sons and daughters. But in my opinion it would be stretching the term inheritance well beyond its conventional limits if we were to apply it to Hindu dowry, for reasons which I have demonstrated already.

Firstly the dowry does not represent a fixed share of a particular divisible estate; the amount is fixed with reference to the state of the marriage market (what prospective bridegrooms will accept) and the bride's family's circumstances (what they can afford) at the time of marriage. Secondly, as I have reiterated, the dowry is not paid to the bride herself but to her husband's family. If it is a form of inheritance, is it not really a form of inheritance by the son-in-law since he will have more control over it than the daughter herself? Better still, ought it not to be seen as the lateral transference of property between households but within the same generation since, as I have shown, it may well be the parents-in-law of the bride who have the greatest say initially as to how the dowry property should be used or distributed? If any proportion of the goods is designated as the bride's personal property this part of the dowry is usually small in relation to the whole (Van der Veen, 1972, p.44). Contrary to the dominant ideology and the terminology of traditional Hindu law, dowry property is not women's wealth, but wealth that goes <u>with</u> women. Women are the vehicles by which it is transmitted rather than its owners.

The Inflation of Marriage Expenses: Dowry as a Social Problem

The inflation of dowries which has taken place in most sections of Indian society is out of proportion to the general inflation (in prices in the Indian economy). So providing a dowry for a daughter nowadays constitutes a relatively greater strain on family resources than it might have, say, fifty years ago. In Punjab, and probably most areas of North India, the composition of the dowry used to be more or less conventionally determined and many of the items could be made in whole or in part by members of the bride's family themselves (e.g. rugs, clothing, bedding). As there was little change in the style of consumer goods or household furnishings, many items could be accumulated well in advance of the marriage, slowly and as household circumstances permitted; there was no pressure to provide the very latest style of bed or the most up-to-date type of cooking pans. I would argue that the quantitative increase in the amount of dowry given has led to a qualitative change in its significance for women. More than it ever used to be, the dowry is one of the major determinants of whom a woman may expect to marry and of how she will be treated by her in-laws after marriage. What a bride is worth is measured more and more by the amount of material goods and cash her family can provide rather than by the reputation and prestige with which they can endow her, the skills they have ensured she has acquired. In consequence, the provision of a dowry involves a great strain on the household and this encourages daughters to see themselves as burdens rather than blessings.

I do not think that this can be dismissed as an ethnocentric assessment of the situation because dowry has during the present century come to be regarded as a social evil by Hindus themselves, but somehow as an evil which no-one knows how to stop. Parents who bewail the need to accumulate dowry for a batch of daughters are unlikely to bring themselves to refuse it when the time comes for their son to marry. To a large extent the goods which enter a household when a son marries are actually substitutes for the goods which must leave it on the marriage of a daughter.

British administrators during the first decades of this century cast a disapproving eye on the practice of dowry as evidence of the extravagant customs which encouraged the honest hardworking peasant to waste his substance and prolong his dependence upon the money lender (although disapproval on these grounds had a lot to do with the fact that the honest hardworking peasant was regarded as a more useful and reliable prop to the Raj than were the commercial classes). However, Indian social reformers took a broadly similar view and, after Independence, laws were passed officially restricting marriage expenditure. But like so much other well-intentioned legislation, these laws have not been enforced. Indeed many rural Hindus are not aware that they exist (Murickan, 1975, p.85). Reports in the press, especially the Indian feminist journal Manushi, suggest that those who suffer most from the inflation of dowries must help themselves rather than look to the law. In recent years there have been numerous cases of 'dowry deaths' in which young wives in urban families have either been driven to suicide by their in-laws' excessive demands, or in which brides have actually been murdered by families disappointed in the first dowry and hoping to reap a second from the re-marriage of their son, trading on the qualifications of a young man with a secure job or good prospects. Manini Das describes one case which attracted a good deal of publicity, the case of a Delhi woman, Tarvinder Kaur. This young woman was, it seems, burnt to death by her mother-in-law when her parents failed to meet the constant demands for more gifts. Her relatives were able to mobilise a large number of people to demonstrate outside the in-laws' house, petition Parliament and give the case maximum publicity.

This case was followed by several similar ones, in which feminists and reformers joined with the families of women who had suffered in this way. Apart from public meetings, the main techniques of protest used were attempts to shame grasping in-laws through public exposure. Manini Das notes, however, that there is really very little hope of the police and judicial machinery providing a solution (Manushi, No.1, p.16). Police are unwilling to register or investigate cases of murder of women within the family [4]. In addition to this, if the in-laws are influential and wealthy people they will be able to see to it that the police will either change the case from one of murder to one of suicide, or that they drop the investigation altogether. Remember that, given the tendency in India for women to be married to status equals or superiors, few brides are likely to have parents who are more powerful and influential than their parents-in-law. Manini Das concludes that it will be difficult to do anything unless women cease to be divided amongst themselves. So long as they identify themselves in some situations as mothers (dowry-givers) but in others as mothers-in-law (dowry-takers) their interests appear forever divided and they cannot realise common cause as women.

The interpretation of dowry inflation in terms of the cash economy is supported by the evidence provided by elderly informants in the course of my fieldwork which suggests that in the early part of this century dowries in Himachal Pradesh (a much more backward area than Gujerat) were limited to a conventional number of sets of clothing, household items and jewelry, with very little variation. Only with the large scale injection of cash into isolated hill areas after the First World War did dowry rates begin to rise. But another possible factor is the relaxation of ritual and social barriers to marriage; in those areas where hypergamous marriage is usual, dowry property already provided a qualification for women to marry upwards into high status families. The erosion of some caste restrictions which we find in certain urban classes has really had the effect of introducing hypergamous competition among women in groups where it did not exist before, only this is a hypergamy based more on socio-economic factors than ritual aristocracy. Where caste is less of a barrier, any girl with some education from a moderately respectable family can compete in the scramble to get a husband who is an Indian Administrative Service officer, an Air India pilot, son of a large scale entrepreneur, etc. With this loosening up of conventional restrictions on marriage, dowry becomes more and more (not less and less) the criterion by which one respectable girl with an MA in History or Home Science is deemed more desirable than another.

These factors help to explain, I think, why dowry deaths a) have become more common in the past ten or twenty years, and b) why they appear to be confined to the urban middle classes and are not found among rural groups or the urban poor, groups who still observe more strictly the traditional barriers to marriage based on caste, language and religion.

Dowry favours and is favoured by a cultural ethos in which brides can be viewed as objects to be passed from one social group to another, both as a means for the procreation of children and as vehicles for aspirations to social prestige. Although there is no space here to deal with the extensive literature on bridewealth it is likely that exactly the same can be said of bridewealth, at least as it exists under modern conditions. In 'developing countries' the effects of capitalist relations of production are penetrating the household and transforming the relations between men and women in the household. Usually these effects are most immediately experienced in terms of the consequences of wage-labour, migration and a market economy in which cash is the medium of exchange. Usually this transformation involves a devaluation of the domestic sphere and the activities of women within it and an increased dependence of women upon men within the domestic group. There is considerable evidence from Africa, where bridewealth has always been more common than dowry, that these changes have brought about a similar inflation of marriage payments to that which we find in India. And this inflation has had rather similar consequences for women, in that their marital destinies are open to more (not less) manipulation by others as the types and amounts of property transferred at marriage become relatively more important considerations in marriage negotiations (see Obbo, 1980, p.36; Mair, 1969, p.146).

Looking at the matter from a feminist point of view, therefore, the opposition which anthropologists have traditionally drawn between dowry and bridewealth may not be so important as other distinctions made on the basis of the degree and kind of control which brides can exert over their own marital fortunes and over the property which is transferred at the time of marriage. It would seem that in India the rapid inflation of dowries in modern times has led to a situation in which brides are more controlled by than controllers of property. Feminists have grasped this very clearly and are active in their protest. However, if the institution of dowry diminishes the social power of brides and even endangers their lives, it strengthens the hand of the mother-in-law. Even the mother of the bride may derive a deep moral satisfaction from a public and honourable display of generosity. Feminists are hampered in their efforts by the fact that in this sphere, as in so many others, property divides women among themselves.

Notes

1. This fieldwork was funded by a grant from the SSRC, to whom I am grateful.
2. The very concept of the bride as a gift implies the idea that she herself can be represented as a kind of property to be made over by one family to another. The passivity of the bride in the wedding ritual supports this inference. She has to be picked up and carried by her father or her brother at various points in the ceremony, and at others is supported and guided by her mother

(since she is muffled under many wraps or veils and cannot easily see where she is going). See Van der Veen (1972), p.25ff for a full discussion of the kanya dan ideology.

3. In this respect it is interesting to compare the dowry system in North India with that obtaining in parts of rural Greece. In many respects they are similar, but in Greece land gifted as part of the dowry remains under the bride's control to the extent that it cannot be alienated without her formal consent. Potentially at least, the dowry property gives her a source of power in the household which the Hindu wife does not have (Friedl, 1962, p.59).

4. This invites comparison with the unwillingness of police in Britain to intervene in cases of domestic violence.

5

FEMALE POWER AND THE INEQUALITY OF WEALTH
      AND MOTHERHOOD IN NORTHWESTERN PORTUGAL

João de Pina-Cabral

This paper is based on fieldwork carried out between 1977 and 1981 in two adjoining rural parishes, Paço de S. Miguel and Couto de S. Fins in Alto Minho province, northwestern Portugal. The landless peasantry of these parishes approximates very closely the model of Laslett's 'bastardy prone sub-society':

> 'a series of bastard-producing women, living in the same locality, whose activities persisted over several generations, and who tended to be related by kinship or marriage. Many of the women were credited not with one illegitimate birth only, but with several' (1980, p.217).

Furthermore, it is interesting that the periods in which illegitimacy reached a peak over the past century (the 1890s and the 1930s) were, indeed bearing out Laslett's conclusion, 'times when proletarianisation was on the increase and when obstacles may have been placed in the way of proletarian marriage' (1980, p.226) [1]. But 'illegitimacy' or 'bastardy' does not have the same meaning everywhere. We have to understand the significance and meanings which a specific social group attaches to 'legitimate' motherhood before we can make sense of 'illegitimate' motherhood. The observable social and economic power of the married peasant women of the Alto Minho stands in sharp contrast with the ideological emphasis on female moral weakness, and also with the social position of unmarried women. For the minhoto peasant the most valued resource in both a material and an ideological sense is land. The material presented in this paper suggests that unequal access to inherited landed property is the key to the inequality of motherhood.

A predominantly agricultural region, the Alto Minho is administratively divided into boroughs which are headed by small market towns. These towns are the seats of the local representatives of the central administration, and of large commercial firms. Similarly, the locally elected body of greatest significance – the camara, municipality – is found here. The town is the centre for the rural élite – the provincial bourgeoisie. This élite is eager to distinguish itself from the rest of the population – the peasantry –

which it looks down upon as backward and uneducated.

Most peasants live in hamlets (lugares) scattered across the hillsides, which are composed of five to eighty households (casas) and which possess a definite social identity. Hamlets are associated with specific stretches of land whether or not all of this land is owned by hamlet residents. A number of hamlets, in turn, are centred around a church to form a parish (freguesia). The members of a parish or a hamlet are vizinhos (neighbours) to one another. This term can be used in two interconnected by nevertheless different meanings. When it is used to refer to individuals, it has much the same meaning as the English 'neighbour'; when it is used to refer to a household (and then it is often in the plural), it refers to those households which own land and reside permanently in a parish or a hamlet [2]. This practice not only stresses the association of the household with the land, but also denies implicitly the rights of residence of landless people. These do not form casas in the sense of permanent households, and both a parish and a hamlet are seen as composed of casas. The 'egalitarianism' of these minhoto peasants conceptually excludes landless labourers as a group, although it does not exclude them as individuals. The double meaning of the term vizinho reflects precisely this ambiguity.

A Patrôa - the Female Boss

The relative social power and independence manifested by the peasant women of Portuguese Minho and Spanish Galicia is one of the features which most noticeably distinguishes the northwest from the rest of the Iberian Peninsula (cf. Lisón, 1971). Oliveira Martins, a famous historian and politician, wrote of the women of Minho in 1881:

> In Minho, as in all other Celtic regions, the woman rules the home and the husband. She exceeds the man in courage, cunning and strength. She ploughs the fields and pushes the ox cart the whole day long. ...When she marries, the girl knows the value of her dowry (dote) and the marriage is a business deal which she personally bargains about and arranges. She is not a spouse, almost a serf, who is empowered to her husband, as is dictated by the semitic fashion which has penetrated the south of the country: she is rather a companion and associate whose business spirit dominates over the constitutional weakness of the men who are destitute of a lively intelligence. These women seem like men. (1925, vol.2, pp.186-7)

He was probably exaggerating, as his contemporary Camilo Castelo Branco remarked (1885, pp.66-71), but what he saw as an inversion of roles must not be completely discarded. To this day married women do have a strong position of power in the household and in parish life as a whole. Nevertheless, such a position is not only problematic to the members of the bourgeoisie, but also to the peasants themselves.

The peasant use of the expression patrôa and its male form patrão provides us with an example of the fact that, for them too, the power which women have at home presents problems. While the term patrão (male boss) tends to be employed mostly by outsiders to refer to the male head of the household, the female form is used mostly by members of the household, particularly the husband, to refer to his wife, when speaking to outsiders. In both cases the expression is ironical as there is a feeling that it is vaguely inappropriate for it implies excessive domination.

While, on the one hand, it is definitely stated that the male household head should have more power than the female (for males are thought to be more pure and rational), on the other, there is also a definite acknowledgement that the power of the woman at home is great, and often even greater than that of the husband. This inconsistency in the definition of roles is profoundly experienced by local residents. The use of the term patrôa by the husband for his wife expresses precisely this conflict; its ironical twist expresses implicitly both criticism and uneasiness. By overtly admitting that his wife is his boss, the husband is covertly denying it.

This is not the case with the use of the male form of the term. I never once heard a peasant woman call her husband patrão; this would either be too profound an implication of servitude (if it were said with a straight face) or (if said ironically) it would imply that she would presume to be more powerful than the man. Since women are considered naturally greedy and lacking in self-control, any implication on their part of equality with men would only further prove the extent of their greed and lack of control over their emotions and desires. Therefore, the male form of this expression, patrão, is only used by outsiders who do so ironically, half-implying that the man is not really 'the boss'.

This expression has not been adopted by the bourgeoisie. It would be considered course and improper to imply that a bourgeois husband is not fully dominant and therefore masculine, and hence his wife is not fully feminine in her servitude. Lisón argues that in Galicia the actual power of the male at home depends on the actual economic success and on the psychology of each particular man (1971, pp.258-9). He suggests that different standards are used by Galicians when talking to outsiders (who presume the existence of male domination) and when talking to insiders (who are aware of actual female domination). To me, however, this duality of standards between outsiders and insiders does not seem to account for the perceived inconsistency in the allocation of power between the spouses. For the peasants of Minho there is no doubt that women as a group are weak and impure. The fact that they wield so much power is just as dissonant within the peasant worldview as by comparison to that of the bourgeoisie.

Women and the Land

In rural Minho the relation of the social group and its geographic setting is so direct that one is incomprehensible without the other. There is no conception of the social group as independent from its land so that, when a peasant refers to his parish or to his household, he has both the people and the land in mind.

The household (casa) is the basic social unit. The very idea of a hamlet (as well as that of the parish, for that matter) is inconceivable without the concept of casa and it is to the household that the individual looks for his primary source of identification. Finally, the household is the unit of commensality, of residence, and of management of production.

The relationship between the social group and the land is not only one of use but also one of symbolic identification. The social unit is intrinsically rooted in a piece of land from which it gathers its strength and its identity. This symbolic identification is related but by no means totally reducible to the economic relation between the social group and the land as a means of production.

The Portuguese word terra, which I have translated so far as 'land', is a highly polysemic term. Taylor's Portuguese-English Dictionary gives us the following range of meanings: 'earth, world; soil, ground; land; loam, dirt; native land; country, region, province, nation'. But even this list does not exhaust all the possible meanings of the word. There are a further two uses which are particularly relevant to the present discussion. Firstly, arable land plays a dominant role in peasant life and consequently, when they use the term terra, rural minhotos are more likely to be referring to arable land than to all types of soil. Secondly, the peasant refers to 'this terra' by opposition to Heaven and Hell. Here the word assumes very much the same sense which is given to the word 'world' (mundo) in ecclesiastical circles. For example, the concept of 'wordly pleasures' is conveyed both by prazeres mundanos and prazeres terrenos. In this sense terra refers to the temporal life in opposition to spiritual life [3]. The deep concern of the minhoto peasant for the terra which has so often been noted, is not simply limited to the 'land' in the strict sense of productive soil, but it reflects a deeply-ingrained set of conceptions which articulate the peasant worldview.

Although they often comprise a nuclear family, peasant households are not necessarily limited to it and they may include parents, grandparents, siblings, aunts, uncles, nephews, and even friends of the head couple. As opposed to what happens among the minhoto bourgeoisie, these other members are in no way peripheral to the household.

A household may be headed by a single or a widowed person. Should it include a married couple, however, the latter will hold the headship. Peasants believe that the work of managing a household cannot be efficiently carried out by one person alone or by two people of the same sex. While women are mostly in charge of the tasks of housekeeping, men dedicate a greater portion of their time to external business such as earning money and all bureaucratic tasks. Each spouse is allocated a specific part of the household's management. Men look after the cattle, the fruit trees, the vines, the olive trees, the pinewoods; the women are more concerned with the pigs and the poultry, with maize, beans, potatoes, pumpkins, and the kitchen garden. Significantly too, there are activities which are absolutely prohibited for each sex: for men, it is forbidden to wash, sew, sweep the floor, etc.; for women, it is forbidden to climb trees and prune the vines.

In this sexual division of labour, males are more closely concerned with what the minhotos themselves call produtos do ar (literally, products of the air), that is, things which grow well above ground level. (It must be remembered that vines in this area are grown either on pergolas or on trees.) On the other hand, females are more consistently in charge of the produtos da terra, things which grow in or near the soil. Associated with this is the specific prohibition which applies to women: they must not climb trees, that is, they must not leave the ground (terra). But they are not only more rooted to the ground, in the sense that they ought not to leave it; women are also less mobile, they are attached to a particular stretch of land, their terra. While men are mobile and free to leave the land and migrate, women are held to be bound to it. Thus the tasks of keeping the household are left to women, and jobs which involve leaving the home for long periods of time are allocated to men [4].

This is often explained by the local residents with the adage 'Men look up, women look down.' This adage has three distinct meanings: it refers to the differences between male and female genitalia; it refers to the sexual division of labour; and, finally, it refers to a much wider utilisation of the dimensional opposition Above/Below as analogically related to oppositions such as Heaven/Hell, Life/Death, Mind and Spirit/Body, Human/Animal, Purity/Corruption, Social/Anti-Social.

The impurity of women is thought to manifest itself in particular during menstruation and pregnancy. During these periods women contain within themselves highly impure substances. The word used to explain their nature to me was podre (rotten). Thus the minhotos imply decomposition, corruption, and impurity.

One of the most common ways of referring to menstruation is a tristeza das mulheres (literally, the sadness of women), for it reminds the women of their condition as impure beings. The actual menstrual blood has to be very carefully dealt with for it is a very powerful substance; for example, it can kill olive trees if it falls on them, and it causes a skin disease in cattle. Similarly, women are not allowed to jump or step over goods which are displayed on the ground at a fair, because the vendors fear that the women may be menstruating. Should any drop of menstrual blood fall on the goods, they would not be sold because of a belief in its awesome magical powers.

The irritability and physical discomfort which most women experience at this time is interpreted as resulting from this impurity.

Moreover, during pregnancy, women are thought to have uncontrollable food cravings which are interpreted as a lack of control of their desires: a form of unreasonable, animal-like gluttony. These cravings are nevertheless satisfied at all costs, for fear that the pregnant woman would pass the evil eye to her yet unborn child and thus damage property and people.

A woman's need for the protection afforded by the household and by marriage derives not from the external dangers which besiege her, but from her own internal vulnerability to evil: to use Du Boulay's phrase, she needs to be 'protected from her own nature' (1974, p.124). A particularly interesting feature of peasant life in the northwest of the Iberian Peninsula is precisely this combination of women's moral inferiority in the face of their relative power and independence.

Inheritance and Property

Two aspects of the way rural minhotos relate to property should be highlighted here. Firstly, we are considering a peasant society for which land is the major source of livelihood and therefore of security and of status. Secondly, land being of such importance for the rural minhotos, people and households share some of their identity with the land which they own (much like Mauss's giver and the gift, cf. Strathern, this volume). This is demonstrated by the fact that a common way of referring to a person is to add to the person's name that of the plot where the house he or she lives in was built.

As such, attitudes to property are not uniform; not all property is alike. A plot of land may be equated with an amount of cash, for example, (as indeed it is for the purposes of dividing the household's property for inheritance) but the ownership of a plot of land per se has a value which is greater than the ownership of other goods which, in theory, are equally valued. This means that there is of necessity a permanent shortage of land and that, when one refers to peasant attitudes to property, one is invariably forced to stress landed property.

In general terms, in Paço de S. Miguel and Couto de S. Fins, residence after marriage can be said to be 'ambilocal', that is, in Goody's words, 'a married couple may choose to reside with either the kin of the bride, or of the groom, depending upon their relative position' (1969, p.63). Furthermore, inheritance is theoretically egalitarian, for the local residents state that all children have the same rights to parental property.

Within this broad framework, however, many alternatives are open to individuals or groups. In their reaction to the problems which confront them, individuals utilise specific strategies. These strategies are not often invented anew, for they present themselves within an historically-determined context (cf. Bourdieu, 1972, pp.1105-6). In the following passage I shall attempt to elicit the dominant strategies to which the residents of these parishes take recourse in matters of residence, marriage, and inheritance.

Weddings are practically always at the expense of the bride's parents, and take place in their home, or at least in the bride's parish of residence. The onus is therefore on the girl's father to provide most of the money required for the wedding. In order to marry off a daughter 'decently', a couple has to use up a considerable amount of their savings, for weddings are events at which social differentiation is openly declared, and a household's strength is measured by the success of the weddings of the daughters of the head couple.

After marriage, most couples take up residence at the house of the bride's parents. There are primarily three reasons for this. Firstly, women are more attached to the household and the land, while men are more mobile. Couples feel that their daughters have a greater allegiance to their households than sons. Secondly, women are seen as far less protected than men. They are thought to be more subject to risks. For this reason parents prefer to have their daughters at their side. Thirdly, the locals are very strongly aware of the demographic imbalance between the sexes in favour of women [5]. It is more difficult to marry off a daughter than a son. By taking in the young couple the parents are reducing the economic pressure on the couple during the first years of marriage and therefore they are facilitating their daughters' marriages.

At present, most weddings are accompanied by very small transfers of wealth. During the years preceding the wedding, the bride and her mother collect a trousseau (enxoval) which consists of prestigious household goods. The family of the groom, in turn, is supposed to buy new clothing for the groom and, if they are orgulhosos (literally, proud; in fact this expression generally means that they are wealthy), they give the couple a piece of furniture, usually a double bed.

A person's dote is a very important consideration when choosing a marriage partner. This term as used at present in these riverside parishes [6] has come to refer to an expectation for eventual inheritance. Thus, a spouse's dote is the amount of property which he or she will eventually contribute towards the common fund of the household. It must be understood that, while the word dote is correctly translated into English as 'dowry', and while there have been areas in Portugal where the practice of giving dowry to a daughter at marriage has been common, in these parishes, at present, the term dote has come to be equivalent to inherited property. When a woman from Paço or Couto says that a certain young person has a 'good dote', she means that when the young person's parents divide their household's property for the purposes of inheritance, the young man or woman will receive a large amount of property by local standards. As a household's property is usually divided when one of the spouses dies or when they both reach a ripe old age, most couples only come into the full fruition of their dote quite a few years after their marriage. In order to raise their child's marriageability, however, wealthy parents who can afford to do so promise to give part of the dote to their son or daughter at marriage. This often consists of a plot which produces maize and wine, but it may also be money or a house. Although it is entrusted to the young couple at marriage, this part of the dote given in advance is taken into account for the purposes of inheritance when the parental household's property comes to be divided. Therefore, and since it may also be given to a son, I suggest that the dote in this context is more constructively approached as a form of 'diverging devolution', as Goody would have it (e.g., 1973, p.1ff), rather than as a form of 'dowry' in particular.

When the part of the dote given in advance is a field, it is managed together with the land of the parental household where the young couple take up residence (usually the wife's). Some of its proceeds, however, are handed over to the young couple who, in this way, are allowed a modicum of economic independence. This part of the dote given in advance is seen as a compensation for the child's work for the parental household, and is only given if all of the child's work or earnings previous to the marriage have been handed over to his or her parents. As few male children still do this today, the practice is disappearing in the case of men. In the case of daughters, dotes given in advance are sometimes still offered by particularly wealthy parents.

Two married siblings are thought to be incapable of living in the same household. The situation would create too much friction. When the younger daughters reach marrying age, therefore, the elder daughter usually finds a house in the vicinity of the parental home. The youngest married daughter is generally the one who remains at home looking after the parents during their old age.

Thus, there is a strong tendency for the creation of matrifocal stem-families, that is, for two or three generations related by women to live together in the same household. These households of sisters help each other informally and two decades ago it was still common for first cousins to marry, in order to reunite their grandparents' land. Male siblings, who usually set up residence away from their natal hamlets, slowly lose contact with their sisters. These households of sisters form the core of hamlet-centred and predominantly matrilateral informal kin groups. These are reflected in the kindred nicknames which, in local society, are the most important means of marking a person's social identity.

Inheritance is partible but the child who marries at home is often benefited with either a third or a sixth of the property before the division among all the siblings is effected. Also, the youngest child has a privilege of choice of the lot which he or she wants. As the child who remains at home is generally the youngest daughter, this in fact means that this daughter inherits considerably more both in quantity and quality than the other siblings. Furthermore, in spite of what the informants often claimed, the study of actual cases of division of property made it clear that, as a whole, daughters are privileged over sons. It is felt that a woman is generally in greater need than a man, for he can always go out and earn a living for himself while she is bound to stay with what she receives. Therefore, if there is not enough to go round, the daughters are usually benefited at the expense of the sons.

82

As a rule, women receive a larger part of their share in arable land rather than movable property or forest land. This in fact is a privilege, for arable land is preferred. Men go abroad to earn money, or engage in paid employment and their salaries are then invested in houses or in land. This means that while men are the creators of wealth, the producers, women are its maintainers, the reproducers.

We are now capable of assessing the position of a married woman in her home. As the guardians of the household, the activities of women are not restricted to the household itself; rather women are in charge of the greater part of the agricultural activities of the household. As a rule they live in their native hamlet, surrounded by their sisters and the friends of their youth. They do not give up their surname at marriage, nor do they adopt their husbands'. On the contrary, in the daily life of the hamlets, husbands are usually called by their wives' names or kindred nicknames. The couple's property has been largely inherited by the wife and she is always very conscious of her rights as owner and does not yield all executive powers to her husband. There is no sense in which the property is passed from the wife's father to her husband. As everyone in these parishes insists on marrying in 'community of property', the husband cannot alienate any significant part of the common property without the wife's consent. Among the bourgeoisie this may be merely a legalistic formula which does not correspond to any real balance of power; among the peasantry, however, wives are conscious of their rights and privileges as owners and they utilise them if necessary. It is furthermore interesting to note that, even though the couples are married in 'community of property', a vague separation in rights over property remains throughout the married life. When one spouse dies at an early age leaving offspring and there is a possibility of the other remarrying, the property of the couple is usually divided in such a way that the children receive that which the deceased partner brought into the marriage, and the surviving partner keeps what he or she had brought.

Peasant society does not distinguish as does the urban, bourgeois society of Minho between the realm of production - the economy, the world-out-there - and the realm of consumption - the family, the home. For the peasants both coincide in the household. The central economic significance of women, therefore, is directly related and not opposed to their roles as keepers of the home.

The situation of the women at home, therefore, is one of privilege and power. Although women systematically claim to obey their husbands (so as to protect themselves against being accused of letting their anti-social nature come to the fore), in fact the husband has no more power at home than the wife.

This situation is not considerably altered during widowhood. Upon the death of her husband an old woman usually divides most of her property among her children. But she always keeps control over a part of it. By threatening to give it to another person, she ensures that the child she lives with treats her in the fashion which she desires.

This position of power and prestige for women is, however, strictly dependent on marriage. Through marriage a woman assumes control of property and power over its management, on the one hand, and, on the other, the expression of her sexuality is socially sanctioned.

But marriage is not equally accessible to all women. Until the 1950s and to a lesser extent the 1960s, a woman who belonged to a landless family would not be able to find a husband. To this day, the chances of such poor women marrying locally are still slim, even though the local availability of paid employment since the 1960s has meant that people who do not own land can marry and live off their salaries. The residents of Paço and Couto still often recite the old saying that 'whoever has no <u>dote</u>, house, or money for (the wedding) expenses, cannot marry,' even though it is no longer strictly true. By paying for the wedding, by taking in the young couple to live with them, and by assuring their daughters a decent inheritance in arable land, the bride's parents are creating the conditions without which their daughters would find no husband.

The 'Bastardy Prone Sub-Society'

<u>Caseiros</u>, share-croppers who work the land of absentee landlords, bequeath the right to work this land and to inhabit the house which is attached to it to the married child who remains at home, generally a daughter. As they owned little land of their own, before the 1950s the other daughters had to remain unmarried. The same happened with owner-farmers who had very little land. Their daughters either went to the cities to work as housemaids or remained at home unmarried. It was therefore very commonplace for people to remain single. Nowadays, female emigration and the emergence of alternative sources of income explain why most people do get married (cf. Bourdieu, 1962).

Women who were completely landless were in a still less enviable position than the daughters of <u>caseiros</u>, not only would they fail to find a husband, but also they did not have the security of an agricultural household since their mothers themselves had often been unmarried. They did not own houses and were forced to live in temporary make-shift lodgings such as barns, stables, and rented houses. Since they were paid for their work on a daily basis and their employment was therefore seasonal, they often found it necessary to have sexual relations with wealthy farmers as a means of acquiring food and other necessities during the winter months (cf. Furtado Coelho, 1861, p.2). Hence, the fathers of their children were often their employers, or other wealthy peasants in the vicinity. Sometimes such relationships could be profitable. Camilo Castelo Branco, a 19th century novelist, provides an illustration:

> 'Brazilians' - money lenders who returned from Brazil after having closed their shops in that far-off land - dishonour girls, and then give them dowries (<u>dotes</u>) the contents of

which are already pre-established by accepted usage; the
contenders to the hands of the girls who receive these dowries,
dispute by means of cudgel-fights for the legitimate enjoyment
of the girl who is now able to become a bride (Castelo Branco,
1885, pp.70-1).

What horrified Camilo and his contemporary Oliveira Martins (see
quote above) was that these girls had failed to find a husband not
because they were not virgins, but because they had no land. Once
endowed, many men would be willing to marry them. Camilo quotes
Oliveira Martins and agrees with him when he says that 'Many, many
girls who are not virgins get married, and this, though it is common
knowledge, is not considered scandalous' (ibid. and Oliveira Martins,
1925, p.189).

It is worth noting that the sexual morality of the minhoto
peasants is not very restrictive. Sexual intercourse between young
people is known to occur regularly, and this results in a high
number of pre-marital pregnancies. If a girl's parents are reasonably
wealthy, her lover is usually easily convinced to marry her. In cases
where the lover refuses to do so an abortion is usually procured. If
the affair had become public knowledge, however, the girl's
marriageability will have decreased and she may have to lower her
expectations. Her parents may be forced to give her a reasonably
good advance on her dote at the time of marriage. The residents of
Paço and Couto are adamant, however, about the fact that unmarried
couples should not form a household. Local residents do not object
to sexual intercourse between unmarried people; but the creation of a
household which is not based on the sacrament of marriage is
considered to be an offence to the whole hamlet [7].

Landless women who become pregnant find it difficult to marry
and furthermore they do not always receive help from their lovers in
bringing up the child. Landless women who did not succeed in
marrying would bring up their children in their mothers' homes.
Their sons were likely to emigrate and seldom returned to the
parish; their daughters would follow their mothers' lifestyle and one
finds cases of women today whose grandmothers too were unmarried
mothers.

Illegitimacy was very common until the 1950s, but it is now
disappearing. Nevertheless, today, 8.33 per cent of all households
in Couto, and 3.73 per cent in Paço, are headed by unmarried
mothers. From 1860 to 1940 (at which time illegitimacy rates started
to decrease) the percentages of illegitimate baptisms per decade
oscillated between 14.3 per cent and 22.5 per cent in Couto and
between 5.8 per cent and 12.5 per cent in Paço (see Fig.1) [8].

The noticeable difference in illegitimacy rates between the two
parishes is in itself significant. In Couto, where illegitimacy rates
are higher, most of the land was in the hands of absentee landlords.
In Paço, where illegitimacy rates are lower, the land was and is still
today mostly in the hands of local owner-farmers. Illegitimacy in the
Alto Minho shows a definite correlation with landlessness.

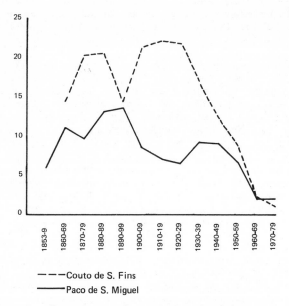

– – –Couto de S. Fins

Paco de S. Miguel

Fig. 1   Percentage of baptisms of illegitimate children per decade in the two parishes (Source: Parish Registers).

In the late 1960s as other European economies prospered, we find an unprecedented rise in emigration numbers. Between 1961 and 1970, 13.4 per cent of the population of the district of Viana as recorded by the census of 1960 had emigrated legally, and in the borough which includes the two parishes on which this study is based, legal emigrants made up for 15.3 per cent of the population in 1960. If we consider that during the same period the number of clandestine emigrants made up between 40 per cent and 60 per cent of the whole emigration, the real magnitude of the phenomenon becomes clear. Landless peasants, who previously had been incapable of funding their trips abroad, could now go to France, Germany, and even the United States in search of better pay for their labour. At the same time the cash returns of emigrants and the development of the capitalist sector of the Portuguese economy in the 1960s meant that local paid employment in non-agricultural tasks became available. This greatly raised the salaries for agricultural work.

Since the 1960s landless peasants could find alternative sources of income and could therefore marry. Concomitantly, returned emigrants started to buy up the land of the absentee landlords, and people who had previously been landless were no longer so. This had the effect of practically ending illegitimacy. The percentage of baptisms of illegitimate children in both parishes together in the 1970s was 1.56 per cent.

Motherhood and Marriage

When Camilo and Oliveira Martins complained that peasant society had no great concern with virginity, they were correct, and they would still be correct today. Women are not valued as a form of property, they are rather seen as vehicles and keepers of property (in that they inherit), and as sources of property (in that their labour is an essential aspect in the reproduction and possible growth of the household's property). Their behaviour previous to the marriage is therefore less important than their value as potential heirs.

But this is not to say that women are not feared for their sexuality. In a very basic way, women are thought to be incapable of controlling their sexual urges. Indeed the idea of blaming a man for his sexual behaviour is a recent import into the rural areas, one which is still not fully accepted. This is the moral behind many of the proverbs, jokes and sayings which punctuate the speech of local residents. For example, 'Do you know why the rooster has no hands? Because the chicken has no breasts'; or 'If a woman does not bend over, you cannot see her arse' (in Portuguese 'bend over' is translated as 'to lower oneself', which brings an added meaning to this sentence).

The minhoto peasant's attitude to sex is truly dualistic: sex is evil and if it were not controlled it would reduce society to moral chaos. The household and marriage are important precisely because they control this potential chaos. Marriage mediates between the need to have children, and the evilness of sex. It provides the context for reproduction and sexuality to take place without threatening the moral order. Through marriage, furthermore, women's sexuality is redeemed (cf. Hirschon, 1978, p.67ff). This explains why the idea of common law marriages is unthinkable, and why civil register marriages are called 'cow's weddings', for they do not redeem sexuality.

Unmarried mothers, whose sexuality has not been redeemed by marriage, are not feared or ostracised because of their 'illegitimate motherhood', rather they are despised and considered somewhat impure. It is often said of their offspring that 'they are brought up like little goats', thus pointing to the fact that in some sense they are animal-like.

Individually, unmarried mothers are considered inferior; but, as a group, landless peasants are all inferior, for they cannot be said to form casas (households). For there to be a household there has to be a stable relationship between a group of people, a building, and land. Landless peasants are seen as mobile and called deprecatingly cabaneiros. Literally, this word refers to a person who dwells in a hut, a temporary house; figuratively, however, the term is far richer in meaning. Having asked a wealthy peasant what it meant, I received the following answer: 'A cabaneiro is a puny person, who cannot deal with anything; a "dead" person who belongs to the Do-Not-Bother Company Ltd. Such a person is a cul-de-sac.' Landless people do not have a strong link to the land. They are, therefore, conceptually excluded from the peasant society proper [9].

Unmarried mothers, then, are more resented than pitied, for they are blamed for what is seen as loose sexual behaviour. But that is not all, as there is a feeling that whoever does not have land, does not deserve to have it.

Female Power and Emigration

A notable feature of the agriculture of Minho and Galicia is that most of the agricultural labour is carried out by women. In 1966, Cailler-Boisvert, writing about Soajo, argues that 'l'agriculture est confie éntièrement aux femmes' (1966, p.255). But already in 1861, Furtado Coelho tells us that 'there is in this district the very ancient habit of handing over to the women most of the work in the fields. Here, women plough the land, hoe and spread the manure, while the men are either abroad or, those who remain behind, occupy themselves with other tasks' (1861, p.10). This practice appears to be truly ancient. This is what Silius Italicus has to say in 344-353 B.C. about the soldiers from this region who joined Hannibal's army:

> Rich Gallicia sent her people, men who have knowledge concerning the entrails of beasts, the flight of birds, and the lightnings of heaven; they delight, at one time, to chant the rude songs of their native tongue, at another to stamp the ground in the dance and clash their noisy shields in time to the music. Such is the relaxation and sport of men, and such their solemn rejoicings. All other labour is done by the women: the men think it unmanly to throw seed in the furrow and turn the soil by pressure of the plough; but the wife of the Gallician is never still and performs every task but that of stern war (1934, vol. 1, p.139).

Similarly, Justin, the Roman historian, says: 'The women do exercise themselves in household affairs, and in manuring of the ground; the men do live by their swords and by their plunder' (1672, p.426).

But peasant women are not mere slaves, 'pack horses' for their husbands as Camilo would have us believe (1885). The fact that the women's role is mostly limited to the household and the market place should not be taken to mean what it does for the bourgeoisie, that women are deprived of economic power. On the contrary, not only is the labour which they provide central to the economy of the household, but they also hold significant economic power.

Emigration has been a feature of this area for many centuries (cf. Serrão, 1974). Whether this sexual division of labour is at the basis of the notorious tendency of <u>minhoto</u> males to emigrate or vice versa is a matter for dispute. The rise in emigration since the 1890s, however, and in particular in the late 1960s and early 1970s, has been such that it is likely to have had effects upon gender roles and the sexual division of labour.

The fact that the average age of marriage was higher for women than men up until the 1890s is a particularly interesting feature of this part of the Alto Minho which appears to be related to the practices of uxorilocality, and of yielding the headship of the household to a daughter rather than to a son. If, as the evidence seems to suggest, these practices were more rigidly followed in the second half of the nineteenth century than they are today, the decision to marry depended on the woman's chances of inheriting the headship of her parental household, which may explain why women get married later in life.

It has been argued that the increase in male emigration trends since the 1890s has had the effect of giving more power to women in local life. In a simplistic sense, this is indeed true: if the husband is not at home, the wife's leadership is more crucial. It is in this sense that Cailler-Boisvert calls Soajo 'une communaute féminine rurale'.

In effect, however, and in the long run, precisely the contrary is taking place. Economically speaking, the significance of women in minhoto peasant society is attached to the crucial role of agriculture and arable land. As the economic importance of emigration started to increase, and particularly after the 1950s, the role of agriculture was progressively reduced. Concomitantly, the penetration of the capitalist sector into the rural areas has had the same effect. The peasant population became progressively more dependent on cash income from wages. But it is men who emigrate and it is men who earn wages (particularly in these inland areas). It is also men who invest their earnings and develop small businesses (although in this case, male domination is less blatant).

An interesting side effect of this process is the decrease in the female age of marriage. Since the new couple is no longer dependent upon the inheritance of the headship of the household, but predominantly on the husband's capacity to earn an income, female age of marriage decreases. In the 1880s, in these two parishes together, the average age of marriage for men was 28.5 and for women it was 29.9. In the 1960s, it was 27.6 for men and 23.9 for women. It is only in the 1970s, due to a further increase in local opportunities for wage earning in the capitalist sector, that the male age of marriage decreased to 25.7 (female age 23.1).

At the same time as this was taking place the penetration of the bourgeois worldview into the rural areas via the media and the schooling system has had the effect of reducing the power and independence of peasant women. Ironically, those women who adopt urban mannerisms in order to increase their short-term prestige, are in fact abdicating from what I have tried to demonstrate to be their age-old position of relative power and independence (cf. Pina-Cabral, 1981).

Conclusion: An Inequality in Motherhood

In considering the position of women in local society we are confronted with what could be called an inequality in motherhood. On the one hand, we have the 'female bosses' (the patrôa) whose motherhood is redeemed by the sacrament of marriage and is likened to that of the Madonna. They have power over property and over people and they share in the prestige of the household for together with their husbands they are the heads of the households. On the other hand, we have unmarried mothers whose motherhood is likened to that of animals and whose sexuality is considered to be uncontrollable and therefore threatening to the group. They are at the bottom of the local scale of prestige and they have no power over property or people.

Access to land is the measure which determines the course of the life of each unmarried girl. In the past, without land there was no marriage. But even today landless girls are hard put to find a husband locally and many have started to emigrate in search of jobs and husbands. This is the reason why the residents of Paço and Couto favour their daughters when they divide their property. It is also the reason why they maintain that o casamento é para as mulheres: 'marriage is for the benefit of women'.

Notes

I wish to thank Dr. John Campbell, Dr. Renée Hirschon, and Dr. Manuel V. Cabral, in particular, for their useful criticisms of earlier versions of this paper. All translations of books cited in Portuguese, Spanish or French are by the author.

1. Cf. M.H. Pereira, 1971.
2. Vizinhos: 'Name given to the inhabitants of the concelho who enjoy municipal rights to the full. It must be stressed, however, that the mere accidental co-residence in the same village was not sufficient to allow an individual to be a member of the municipality, since, because the concelho was in reality a "moral person", it was necessary to undergo a kind of political incorporation' (Serrão, 1965, vol. 4, pp.340-1).
3. In pointing to the complex meaning of this term I am attempting to stress the fact that, by using the same word in so many different contexts and meanings, an analogical identification between various concepts is being made by the people themselves.
4. In other areas of Minho (particularly coastal areas) women have been working in factories which are found near their parishes of origin. In the Alto Minho, however, this is not the norm.
5. In 1911, in the borough where these two parishes are situated, women amounted to 54.69 per cent of the population; in 1930, 55.45 per cent; and in 1970, 56.8 per cent (Recenceamentos da População, Instituto Nacional de Estatística, Lisboa).
6. Regional variation is very high in the Alto Minho, even within borough boundaries. It should therefore be stressed that the strategies which are described here are not necessarily those followed by the eastern parishes of the borough, which are situated in mountainous terrain.

7. In the two parishes studied I only came across two such households, both located in a roadside hamlet of Couto which has been particularly affected by bourgeois values. It is interesting that, even though they were very poor, both couples in question did not pool their income or their savings.

8. The following are the percentages on the basis of which Figure 1 was obtained:

Baptisms of Illegitimate Children (per centage)

Decades	Paço	Couto
1850s	5.81	–
1860s	11.11	14.29
1870s	9.64	20.25
1880s	11.97	20.47
1890s	12.55	14.29
1900s	8.96	21.14
1910s	7.19	22.58
1920s	6.50	21.88
1930s	9.26	16.60
1940s	9.12	12.37
1950s	6.65	8.92
1960s	2.25	2.44
1970s	1.82	1.14

9. In a different context, Ariès makes a similar point when he argues that 'pendant longtemps on n'a pas distingué les notions, aujourd'hui bien separées, de paternité et de proprieté, de famille et de patrimoine. La Fontaine au XVIIe siècle faisait la même confusion que Saint Jérome au IVe. Celui-ci traduisait par pater familias le mot grec oikodespotes, litteralement maître de la maison. Le pater familias de la Vulgate n'est pas necessairement un père de famille, au sens d'aujourd'hui, mais un possesseur d'hommes et de biens: le maître de la vigne. Il faut en conclure qu'un pauvre ne pouvait être pater familias (1975, p.144).

6 THE LEGAL AND SOCIAL TRANSFORMATION OF RURAL WOMEN IN AEGEAN TURKEY

June Starr

Introduction

This paper links three independent ideas. First, it provides an alternative model to Engels' provocative theory, expounded in The Origin of the Family, Private Property and the State, (first published in 1884) [1]. Engels suggested that women lose out in the historical process at exactly the point in time that capitalist enterprise develops in each society. Not only do women get squeezed out of the right to claim property for themselves and their children, but as marriage systems change from plural spouses to monogamy, women themselves become a kind of property for men. Monogamous marriage, according to Engels, makes women dependent on men for economic support. Thus men become dominant and women become subordinate and submissive to protect themselves and their young [2].

Second, it asserts – contrary to much existing theory – that both written and unwritten law is never neutral on the issue of the relationship between the sexes. When law is silent, it supports the dominant power structure and cultural values of a society. The power structure is almost always controlled by adult males (sometimes with a few token women). When written laws specifically promote norms of equality, however, as in the case of Turkey, they provide a useful option for overturning the cultural bias which favours male dominance.

Third, it builds on the Ardeners' suggestive notion that women's models of the world may be quite different from men's, because the men have generated the norms for the arenas of reasoned public argument. Women thus may not be as good as men at articulating their unverbalised thoughts because they have not been socialised into modes of 'public discourse' which is characteristically male-dominated (S. Ardener, 1975: xi-xvii).

Although Engels foresaw that women would be excluded from owning land as the economic system evolved from transhumance to settled capital intensive agriculture, he foresaw neither how the legal system nor how specific cultural systems would interact with the changing productive and marketing systems. This essay argues that the penetration of capitalist agriculture into the Bodrum region produced a class system which made marriages within a village an advantageous way of consolidating landholdings. Such marriages aid women in two ways. First, it keeps females in close proximity to their mothers, mother's sisters, and own siblings who provide a daily work and supportive group. This prevents young, impressionable brides from being psychologically intimidated into submission by a husband and his kin. Second, a wife's legal right to her share of the patrimony provides a powerful sanction to make a husband treat her well, because the new laws also allow a comparatively easy divorce [3] for mistreatment. I argue that the gradual exposure of females to the law system in Bodrum allows them to learn the necessary forms of behaviour to use the law courts to their advantage. Finally, I suggest that laws providing female access to land, in combination with judicial willingness to enforce these laws, is a powerful mechanism for female emancipation in Aegean Turkey.

Bodrum: A Changing Region

Many feminist scholars consider the modernisation process [4] as always adversely affecting the position of women [5]. Islam, too, is commonly thought to provide a cultural system in which women for the most part are totally subordinate to men, have few legal rights and little or no autonomy [6]. Turkey thus provides a unique situation in which to study problems of development relating to women because ninety per cent of its population are Moslem, and European legal codes were introduced in the 1920s. Furthermore, it is geographically, culturally and historically diverse. This diversity allows female/male relations to be contrasted across temporal, spatial, and cultural dimensions.

The particular focus of this paper is in the southwestern part of Turkey where the region takes its name from the town of Bodrum. In this essay we examine how male and female relationships are mediated by rights to property. In western countries property is identified with valuable resources such as land, houses, jewels and other highly-valued material goods which can be converted into saleable items on the market. In the Turkish region where I lived, orchards, houses, and productive fields were considered valuable property, as were cows, donkeys, camels, bicycles, jeeps, trucks and boats. Because women did not ride bicycles and were not taught to drive other vehicles, jeeps, trucks, bicycles and boats were owned and used only by men and do not figure further in this discussion.

In addition to material property, in Middle Eastern and Mediterranean cultures there is another valued resource, albeit intangible. This is honour. This essay argues that honour or reputation is also a valued possession, that is worth protecting and that it is as valuable to women as to men [7]. Furthermore, how a woman behaves affects the honour of her husband if she is married, and always that of her father and her brothers. This gives males social control over females, lessening women's autonomy. Much of female behaviour in the village intensively studied and in nearby Bodrum town only becomes understandable by knowing that honour and shame play a significant part in daily affairs. Like property, honour or reputation can be accumulated and can be lost [8]. It is a scarce resource.

Questions raised in the paper are: how does access to property and other resources defined as scarce by the society, affect male/female relationships? Under what conditions do women begin to assert their legally granted but customarily withheld rights to land, houses and other inheritance? Does a woman's changing relationship to property facilitate her emergence as an independent person with a growing ability to assert control over certain aspects of her life?

Turkey today is a complex nation-state involved economically with the European Common Market, Nato, and with its eastern neighbours [9]. It has a small but growing industrial sector which was hard hit by the oil crisis of 1973-74. Close to 65 per cent of the country is still agricultural. Poverty and lack of opportunities in rural areas led hundreds of thousands of migrant workers between 1960 and 1974 to seek employment in European countries [10].

Turkey is divided into sixty-seven different administrative provinces (il, vilayet). There are strong class divisions, sharp cleavages between urban and rural dwellers (although migrant workers begin to blur these distinctions among the poor) and at least seven historic, cultural and geographic areas with rich distinctiveness [11]. Differences exist between the two religious groups: the dominant Sunni and the minority Alevi (or Shi'ites, some of them remarkably heterodox). Throughout the 1970s tremendous political instability occurred, caused by violence among rival political groups. In September 1980 a military junta took over in a bloodless coup, ostensibly to restore order and to return to the principles of Ataturk.

Answers to questions concerning gender relationships and property need to be regionally, culturally and historically specific. Within the context of a changing social order this essay examines data collected from a village, Mandalinci, (cf. mandalina, 'tangerines') (population 1,000) and a district town, Bodrum (population 5,200) from December 1966 through August 1968 [12].

Bodrum region (kaza) is 66,000 hectares [13] of which 22,614 hectares or just over one-third is farmed land. Bodrum town [14] is the administrative centre for the thirty surrounding villages which vary in size from 293 to 2,000 people. In 1966 tangerines were grown in walled irrigated fields in Bodrum and the villages to its west, while animals, tobacco, and wheat were cash crops grown in villages on the Mumcular plateau to Bodrum's east.

Geopolitics and Economics

This section of the essay argues that marriage patterns changed with the changing economic, legal and social order. For centuries the

Bodrum coastal region was inhabited by two ethnic groups: Christian Orthodox, Greek-speaking townspeople who inhabited harbour areas and Sunni Moslem, Turkish-speaking Yörük sheep herders who practised transhumance (cf. Ramsay, 1917, pp.31, 83). The Greeks farmed coastal valleys around harbours on the Ottoman mainland and were good sailors. The Turkish transhumants migrated between summer pastures near the sea and winter grazing areas further inland on the Bodrum peninsula.

A second Turkish-speaking ethnic group, remnants of the once powerful Turcoman confederacy [15], occupied an ecological niche on the higher, inland plain commencing about 25 miles east of Bodrum town. These pastoral nomads had migrated over several centuries down to the region from the Anatolian plateau. They gradually settled into eight villages on the Mumcular plain about 125 years ago [16]. For cultural and religious reasons none of these three groups inter-married.

Between 1900 and 1919 the Greek and Turkish populations were on friendly terms. The Greek population farmed figs, olives, and wheat, and were the craftsmen of the region. They were carpenters, lime-makers, and house builders [17]. The area now known as Mandalinci village was a summer camp ground (yayla) for Turkish-speaking Yörük transhumants. Their winter quarters (kışla) were more protected. The Greek population also was larger in summer than in winter as attested to by ruins of houses and cafes along Mandalinci's deep water harbour (Starr, 1978, pp.23-4) [18]. The population in the entire Bodrum region was in 1912, 8,817 Turkish people and 5,060 Greeks (Soteriadis, 1918, p.9) [19].

In this period Turkish women from nearby islands were considered the most beautiful and were desired as wives by Turkish-speaking men [20]. Thus marriage practices reveal special socio-economic concerns: far-flung networks, embedded in transhumance, provided pastoral households access to diverse pastures, lands, brides, and information. For women, outward stretching networks meant that after marriage at the age of twelve to fourteen a girl was separated from her natal household for much of the year, because the groom was obligated to give labour to his father who had provided the bridewealth for his marriage. This created a virilocal post-marital residence pattern. But, groups moved with flocks between traditional camp grounds, population pressure was not considerable, land was not scarce, and mostly the Greeks owned private farmlands.

The increasing animosity between the Ottoman homeland and Greece from 1919 onward changed the situation. As news of the fighting between Greek and Turkish peoples in the Izmir area spread southward, Greek-speaking families fled from their Mandalinci seaside farmlands and cafes, abandoning the entire area to Turkish transhumant households. During the population exchanges of 1923 between Greece and Turkey, the Turkish government took an interest in Greek landholdings in the village area. Several elite Turkish households were granted farmlands in Mandalinci for their role in the war of 1919-1922 (Starr, 1978, pp.23-27). Moslem Turkish-speaking people from Crete were moved into 'Rum' ward in Bodrum, now called Kumbahçe (in Turkish Rum means Greek) [21].

In the early 1930s tangerine agriculture was introduced from Rhodes into Betes, a seaside hamlet near Bodrum town [22]. The first orchard of tangerines in Mandalinci dates from 1940. To grow tangerines required a capital investment in three year old trees, as well as in a deep water well or overland cement waterways. It meant that soil had to be checked during dry months of summer (from mid-May until mid-October) to determine when the orchard should be flooded with irrigation water. Such water is raised from ground wells by mechanical lifts or motorised pumps.

Capital for intensive cultivation could be obtained through a bank loan, but to negotiate one, a person needed a legal title (tapu) and not merely usufruct rights to land. Elite families, of course, already had ties to banking personnel and they obtained much of the best farmland at valley level. Other villagers did obtain legal titles, while others still continued with traditional use rights to grazing lands or fields. These were recognised under village customary law-ways, but they had marginal status under state law until converted through the state legal system into a legally recognised form of ownership [23]. Households owning a tangerine orchard (the only crop raised on irrigated land) tended to invest profits into building a house at the edge of their orchard.

The transformation to single Turkish occupancy of the region and to cash-cropping agriculture led to settled village life. This made privately-owned orchards a prime resource. Marriage between children of orchard-owning families developed, creating both dense kin ties within each seaside village, and an incipient class structure.

The impact of capitalistic agriculture, settled village life and an emergent class structure had profound effects on female/male relations and on females' access to property. But to comprehend fully these changes, we need to consider the third variable, the cultural system.

The Cultural Framework

In this essay culture has an ideological, institutional and behavioural component. It is viewed as the product of specific historical processes. But, cultural codes of behaviour, developed to cope with particular stresses in a certain historic period, may live on into a new era. Thus they can be viewed as transcending one productive system to emerge side-by-side with more adaptive forms of behaviour exhibited by some members of the group.

The value systems of the Turkish ethnic groups were based on male control of females and a rather loose adherence to Islamic religion. Islamic attitudes toward women had co-mingled for centuries with Hellenistic attitudes in the Bodrum region [24]. Moreover, transhumant populations by and large are not known for their religious ardour [25]. A daughter was under her father's control until marriage. After that her husband had strict control and responsibility for her behaviour. Like most transhumant people in Western Turkey, veiling was not practised. Bridewealth was given by the fiance to the girl's father in the form of sheep, and some gold coins were given to the girl. Lineages were shallow and blood feuding did not develop. The ideology of honour and shame, however, tended to keep males watchful of female actions.

The transition from transhumance to settled village life did not undercut the ideology of honour and shame, despite the pragmatic views of an emerging entrepreneurial class. Thus the Islamic notions of male dominance/female submission became pitted against the secular notions of the Turkish state which had enacted legislation giving equal rights to women.

Three types of Marriage

The increase of capitalist agriculture and the involvement with the market prompted marriages to be arranged within the village between orchard-owning households. Marriages within the village consolidated property and focused, mobilised and united resources. The effect for women was to forge dense kin networks within a community. Keeping a young bride near (or in the same village as) the parental household gave her some protection from an aggressive or cruel husband and some leverage against a demanding domineering mother-in-law.

Villagers distinguish three marriage modes: marriage by engagement negotiations, marriage by connivance and marriage by abduction.

Marriages arranged by negotiation (nikah) are never handled directly by the boy or girl. A mother first makes casual enquiries of her relatives and friends as to the whereabouts of a suitable mate for her child. Then a series of negotiations is carried out first by the boy's father or father's brother on behalf of the youth, and at a later stage by the boy's father and mother with the father and mother of the bride-to-be.

During these negotiations what is discussed is the amount and kind of land and houses each spouse is due to inherit at the division of the patrimony. Types of land include a house and lot, irrigated orchards, fields and woodlands or grazing pastures. Discussions also include the amount and kinds of gifts the groom will give his bride in the bridewealth.

In Mandalinci the groom gives the gifts to the bride at the time the actual engagement (nisan) is celebrated. He cannot go with his parents when they carry his gifts to his fiance. The bridewealth for a middle class agricultural family customarily includes four or more gold bracelets, some gold coins for the girl to wear around her neck or forehead, a watch, head scarves, some cloth for dresses for the bride, her mother and her sisters. Shoes are given to the girl's father, and socks and handkerchieves to her brothers. The cost of such gifts in 1967 ran from seven hundred to three thousand Turkish lira ($700 to $3,000). In one instance, a 28 year old Mandalinci man and his father mortgaged the first good crop of their newly planted tangerine orchard to the man who lent them money to buy the engagement gifts so the youth could marry.

It is normal to wait at least three months between the giving of engagement gifts and the village wedding (düğün). But in Mandalinci the engagement often lasts much longer, because the groom may need to be away for military service, or the girl is not yet ready to leave home, or all the bridewealth has not yet been accumulated and given.

There are two modes of engagement and marriage in Mandalinci - early and later - reflecting economic differences, and especially the difficulties of poor households to accumulate the cash necessary for the bridewealth. The most approved form of marriage (and the only marriage mode available to the wealthy) is for the groom to marry when he is eighteen or nineteen a female of about fourteen or fifteen. The marriage is celebrated and consummated before the groom leaves the village for two years of compulsory military service. In this case the new bride is brought to live at the parental house of the groom where a room or even a house is provided for the couple (the word for bride, gelin, also means daughter-in-law and is from gel - 'to come').

Most households cannot amass sufficient capital for early male marriages. Youths from impoverished families earn their own bridewealth which means they marry much later, around 26 to 30 years of age. They work in the village as day labourers and tenant-farmers or outside the village as more job opportunities occurred with the expanding Turkish road system of the 1950s. The improved transportation also allowed more production of perishables and with it developed a prosperous fishing trade. Jobs were also available in sponge-diving and boat-building industries of Bodrum town.

The breakdown in obligations across the father/son generation in combination with tangerine agriculture has meant that virilocal residence patterns are giving way towards more neolocal households (compare Stirling, 1974). A newly-married couple still may begin with virilocal residence (depending on the marriage mode and who provided the bridewealth), but many develop their own home separate from the groom's family. Ritual and emotional ties to both sets of parents are maintained, however.

A girl who did not wish to accept a proposal or whose parents were arranging a marriage not to her liking needed to convince her parents why that union was unacceptable. She might threaten suicide if they persisted. More usually, however, she found a youth she liked better and persuaded him to elope with her. A boy had many more options for avoiding a marriage not to his liking, thus under-lining once again the gender asymmetry of rural Turkish society.

The second type of marriage is by connivance, or elopement, (kız kaçırma).

The advantages of elopement is that the groom does not have to give any bridewealth. It also allows both males and females to marry the person of their own choosing. The girl often is the one to suggest it. The usual pattern is for the couple to flee in the night, have sexual relations and then go to the house of a friendly relative who will plead their cause to the girl's parents.

When the girl's parents notice her absence, they immediately report it to the nearest police station. The police will search for the couple. Once apprehended, they bring them back and formal charges are brought against the youth. Or the couple will reappear on their own and plead with the girl's family that they be allowed to marry. Because everyone assumes they have had sexual relations (whether they have or not), the girl is no longer desirable as a local bride, since virginity is a prime requirement. Thus, unless the parents are vindictive they allow them to marry. The fate of a girl who has eloped and not married is a worse shame to a family than a less wealthy bridegroom.

Whether they are apprehended or reappear on their own, a criminal case would be opened against the boy by the Public Prosecutor in Bodrum. Charges would be dropped when they produced a marriage licence for the court to see. The girl's active role in marriage by connivance challenges western stereotypes about submissive Turkish women.

The third marriage type is by abduction (zorla kız kaçırma). Turkish villagers and Turkish criminal law distinguish between elopement by mutual consent (kız kaçırma) and forcible abduction (zorla kız kaçırma). The Bodrum court and written law recognise a number of different actions and degrees of guilt, each carrying more severe penalties. Thus, rape of a virgin who is a minor is more severe than rape of a virgin of legal age to marry. Kidnapping and rape of a married woman also carried severe penalties.

A girl who has been forcibly abducted, kept against her will, and forced to have sexual intercourse, after a time may agree to marry her abductor as the only solution to her future. It is the major way she can be reunited with her family and be re-admitted to local community life, albeit now as a married woman. Because of the norms regarding virginity in a bride (which are supported by the pervasive notions of honour and shame) the girl may realise that if she wishes to marry at all, she must agree to marry her abductor. Here is one victim's story:

> I was on my way to school when he came with two friends and put me into his car and carried me off. He was a driver of a jeep between Milas and Bodrum and had noticed me. I was just a small girl. I didn't know about men. I didn't think about marriage. I was only twelve. He forced me to have sex with him... My father didn't open a court case against him because by the time they found us I was pregnant... It was hard at first, but now I am more used to him [26].

By the summer of 1968, after five years of marriage, they had two small children and had moved to a neighbourhood of Bodrum, near the girl's parents.

In the three year period 1965 through 1967 the Bodrum Middle Criminal Court (Asliye Ceza) processed 29 cases ranging from voluntary elopement to forcible abduction and rape (see Figure 1). In 17 of these cases the couple married, so charges against the youth were dropped. We can assume that most of these were voluntary elopements on the girl's part. In three cases, each boy was sentenced to large fines and prison which suggests forcible abduction. (We can draw no conclusions from the five cases which had not finished by the time court records were copied, nor from the three cases where charges were dropped for insufficient evidence.) Thus 3 of 20 cases or 15 per cent were clear instances of violence against women.

Two of the five cases I witnessed were noteworthy. In one a girl changed her testimony. At the police station she had said she had gone willingly; in court she said it was under duress. Whether the police forced her to say she was willing to protect the lad, or whether her father forced her in court to say it was by force is unclear. In another case a girl said she loved the youth and they had eloped at her suggestion. When asked if they would marry, she looked downcast while her father stated, 'I have already married her to another' [27]. There was nothing the judge could do to save the ill-starred romance. Paternal control had overpowered female autonomy and independence, and this father had outwitted the legal norms promoting female rights.

Figure 1

Cases Ranging from Voluntary Elopement

to Forcible Abduction and Rape

(1965 - 1967 inclusive)

Married	17
Charges dropped	3
Innocent of Charges	1
Unfinished	5
Fine and Prison Sentence	3
Total	29

Post-Marital Residence and Social Class

Although Bodrum people still affirm the virilocal residence ideal, actual post-marital residence is linked to class, mode of production, resources and bridewealth. By the late 1960s an emerging pattern of class structure had developed, based on intermarriage of land-owning households in the village. The strata were:

(1) absentee landowning households, which controlled citrus orchards, which were farmed by tenant farmers (ortakçı);

(2) resident orchard-owning households, who did their own farming, hiring day labourers as needed, or had an ortakçı;

(3) resident field-owning households with no hired labourers;

(4) landless households, whose heads are tenant farmers or day labourers for others.

With capitalist agriculture came absentee landowners and tenant farming. Tenant farmers were provided a small rent-free cottage for their services, which for women from poorer strata meant their own home, separated from their mother-in-law. Wives of day labourers often worked in the fields or orchards for wages themselves in order to add to the household income. In this stratum newly-married couples lived in whatever accommodation could be provided for them by either family.

It was the wealthier households who could demand virilocal residence, because the father had the resources to build a room for the newly-wedded couple adjoining his house, and to provide the bridewealth which obligated the son to work his farmlands. Yet, some wealthier patriarchs chose to set up their older sons in small businesses in Izmir or Aydın. In two cases they married their younger daughters to village men with whom they established tenant farming arrangements. Such a son-in-law is called an iç güvey (literally the groom who marries in). This allowed a young girl to stay in close contact with her natal household and provided a father with an assistant who may be more docile than his own sons. It also assured the girl's parents that they could mediate to a great extent the ways their daughter's husband behaved toward her.

Female kin living in adjoining households co-operated in food preparation, fieldwork, childcare, and sometimes in gathering vegetables and cutting tangerines. Mutual cooperation among female kin occurred even when sisters and mothers lived in separate parts of the village. Socialisation of village girls and also Bodrum women de-emphasised female rivalry and emphasised warm, mutually supportive relationships. Most girls thought it was a great advantage to remain near their mothers and sisters after marriage. The most adventurous village girls, however, dreamed of being married to a youth in Izmir or at least in Bodrum.

Mothers were also glad not to be separated from their daughters. Even more important, it meant they would be taken care of in their old age.

The Legal Framework

Islamic Law of the Ottoman Empire

During the 19th century several reforms in Ottoman Law affected the legal and social status of women. The major Ottoman innovation, however, its civil code, affected women only tangentially. Known as the Mecelle, it was simply a modern-looking codification of pure Hanafi law. The committee prepared the code between 1869 and 1888, and published it sequentially between 1870 and 1877. The project was abandoned in 1888 when it proved politically unwise to produce a modern codification of Islamic family law (Onar, 1955, p.295). Thus it left untouched the Şeriat, the core of Islamic family law which governed all aspects of family life and personal status including marriage, renunciation of wives, inheritance, and adoption of children.

Other Ottoman reforms affected women directly. For example, the old Ottoman tax on brides (aruş resmi) – of 60 aspers for girls and 40 or 30 for widows and divorcees – was replaced by a fee for permission to marry, given to the local Islamic judge (kadı). The new fee charged 10 piastres for girls and 5 for widows. Under the old Ottoman tax the amount and destination of payment was determined by the status of a bride's father. For widows' remarriage, however, the tax was paid where she resided or married (B. Lewis, 1960, p.679). The significance of the new fee was its implicit recognition of a relationship between an unmarried female and the place she lived. Ataturk's secular laws continued the payment of a fee for marriage, which became a fee paid to a secular civil servant for a licence to marry.

Ottoman domestic legislation limited the bridewealth to a maximum of 1,000 piastres and specified that no gifts might be exchanged among the relatives of the bride and groom, nor brought by the wedding guests. The bridal dinner was limited to soup, wedding cake, and five other dishes. The bride was to buy her own cosmetics, but the groom was to pay for her use of the public baths (Young, 1905, vol. II, pp.209-10) [28].

Attempts to limit the amount of bridewealth and of gifts exchanged among relatives of the bride and groom again appear in the reformist Ottoman Family Laws of 1915 and 1917. But, the importance of the law of 1917, called the Ottoman Law of Family Rights, was its expanded application of the Şeriat. It allowed whatever school of Islamic law couples wished to use to be applied. This meant that the most flexible rule of any school, Hanafi, might be used. It also allowed a woman to have written into her marriage contract her right to annulment should her husband take a second wife. This was a major concession to those Europeanised reformers who were pushing for a monogamous marriage law in Turkey [29].

The Ottoman Family Law of 1917 gave women rights to divorce on grounds such as impotence, insanity or abandonment. If a woman wished to divorce her husband on grounds of extreme cruelty or incompatibility, the law provided that three male family members must first attempt reconciliation of the couple before divorce was possible. Age limits were set, for the first time in Ottoman history, below which females and males could not marry [30].

But, inheritance practices continued as they had under the Şeriat. When a man died his widow had the right to one-eighth of his estate, and the remainder was to be divided among all his children (one-quarter if there were no children); each female share was to be half that of a male's. In practice in rural Turkey women rarely obtained their land in Ottoman times, and in Anatolian and Southeastern Turkey even in the early 1950s and 1960s women were denied access to the patrimony (Stirling, 1965, pp.121-2; Aswad, 1978, p.475) [31].

In conclusion, despite the contractual nature of Moslem marriages, women suffered a number of disabilities under Islamic law. Girls moved from control by their father to the authority of their husbands. They had the status of a minor and could not act as independent persons. Women's share of the patrimony was half that of their brothers', and the widow's one-eighth share of the husband's estate was not much reward for a lifetime of service. Furthermore, according to the law, a husband could turn a wife out at will by renouncing her in front of three witnesses; he had rights to the children produced by their marriage, she did not. Culture and circumstances may make this right of males under Islam less absolute than the law provides, but strict application means children always belong to the agnatic line.

Secular Law Reforms of Atatürk

Under Atatürk's revolutionary vision of the early 1920s, women's rights in Turkey were brought closer to men's. The new Turkish Civil Code, adapted in 1926 from the Swiss Civil Code, abolished male's right to divorce by renunciation and his right to plural wives. Monogamous marriage was established as the only form recognised by the State. A civil certificate, obtainable from a town clerk was the necessary prerequisite for registering a marriage with the state. To obtain a divorce, each party had to apply to the new secular law courts. Polygamy and bigamy were both made punishable by law, and children of polygamous unions were only given legitimate status by a series of separate legislative Acts [32]. Women's rights to their paternal inheritance were now legally recognised as equal to their brothers'. A widow's share was increased to one-fourth the estate, and she got the first choice.

Age limits for marriages were again set; this time males were allowed to marry at eighteen, females at seventeen, and in exceptional cases both could marry at fifteen. The Turkish legislature in 1938 reduced the ages of marriage to seventeen for males and fifteen for females, and in exceptional circumstances with a judge's permission to fourteen for females and fifteen for males (Velidedeoğlu, 1957, p.63).

Atatürk's policies strongly opposed social and cultural symbols, such as the male fez and the female veil (çarşaf). Turkish friends remember their mothers' stories of walking in city streets in the early 1930s and seeing soldiers rip veils off women. In rural areas of western Turkey, however, agricultural and nomadic women rarely were veiled as it was a hindrance during work in the fields or with animals.

These new policies, codes and legislation promoting equality for women were put in place by a small western-oriented elite. They did not occur in response to demands of a large segment of society, mobilised for action if rights were not granted. In 1934 this small elite even obtained by legislative act the right of Turkish women to vote in all elections (G. Lewis, personal communication).

Sir Henry Maine once remarked that law is always out of step with society; there is always a gap between the legal rules and the existing social reality (Maine, 1861, p.69). Thus, it is an empirical matter to establish the extent to which cultural practices changed under the impact of the new legislation. The remainder of the paper uses data from fieldwork in 1966 through 1968 to assess the consequences of these new rights for women, especially the ways women's rights to property are changing their relationships to men in rural areas of the Bodrum region.

Women's Access to Valuables

Earlier we defined property as bridewealth, land, and houses. Reputation is also a valuable resource. It is hoarded in the required virginity of a bride, and in the care with which wives present a modest public demeanour. It is lost through careless and unchaste behaviour of women. A great compliment to a rural Turkish woman is to call her temiz, which means clean, virtuous.

Under the new codes a woman can defend her honour and reputation at court in lawsuits against men who attempt to seduce her, who solicit her favours, or who abduct and rape her. She can bring suit against other women and men for spreading rumours and slander about her, and for bearing false witness. She can oppose her husband's attempt to divorce her to marry a new wife and she can sue him if he takes a common-law wife. In other words, she has become a legal person with full adult status to act on her own behalf with legal rights that no Islamic law system ever gave her.

The extent to which she is using these rights is explored, in a preliminary way, below. But, first we discuss tangible property because it is an implicit premises of this paper that access to self-sufficiency through owning fields, the means of food production, is an important value.

Through Her Life Cycle

Women's access to valuable property in Mandalinci combines both traditional practices and the growing penetration of the market into everyday life. The significant markers in the female life cycle which mediate her access to property are:

(1) engagement when she is given the bridewealth;
(2) marriage at about fifteen years of age when the moveable trousseau which she prepared is transferred to her new home;
(3) the death of her father, when the patrimony is divided;

(4) widowhood, when the patrimony of her husband is divided, and;

(5) old age (which may occur with (4) above), when she becomes a dependent person in the home usually of a married daughter, but sometimes of a married son.

From the ages of eleven to fourteen a girl will begin to embroider pillow cases, bed sheets, curtains and hand towels in anticipation of her marriage. The sheeting is bought for her by her parents.

During the bridewealth negotiations prior to marriage, she will have learned how much land, houses and family heirlooms (e.g. old pots, kilims, carpets, and some painted pottery) she will inherit when her father dies and his estate is divided. At the celebration of the engagement (nikah) she will be given the bridewealth, her fiance's gifts to her. In middle strata households these include gold bracelets, gold coins, perhaps a watch and cloth for dresses.

At the celebration of the village wedding, a bride will be given a small amount of cash by her parents and close relatives at the moment she is ready to leave her parent's house and mount the horse to be carried to the groom's house (or enter the hired jeep to travel to a village further away). Her parents also give her a winter coat, guests bring cooking pots, cooking utensils, towels, plates, cups and other useful household items as gifts.

Bridewealth: Broken Engagements and Divorce [33]

When an engagement is broken, no matter who is at fault all the gold and all the other gifts are returned to the fiance. If the cloth has already been made into dresses then the dresses themselves are returned. The candies and Turkish delights are the only things not returned, because they would no longer be fresh or might already have been eaten.

At divorce, however, none of the gold or presents are returned no matter if the woman is at fault. The bridewealth is considered 'the price of her virginity'. Only if a man married a woman to discover on her wedding night that she is not a virgin can he obtain the return of his bridewealth. But, a provident mother has probably tucked into the bosom of her daughter's wedding dress a handkerchief dipped in chicken blood. Not only is the nuptial room a traumatic occasion for the couple, but they must produce a bloodied handkerchief for the ritual benefit of the groom's sisters waiting outside the door. At divorce all the 'things of the house', the blankets, quilts, bedding, kilim, rugs, cooking utensils, pottery, heirlooms and sewing machine if there is one, belong to the woman. The house itself belongs to the spouse whose family provided it.

Orchards and Houses

Generally, the first opportunity a village woman has to own land is when her father dies. However, I have documented one situation in which a married woman sued her brother for her share of the patrimony and won rights to a house and grounds while her father was still alive (Starr, 1978, pp.213-23). This was accomplished with her husband's help. He not only acted as her legal representative (vekil) in the lawsuit, but quietened her down during the court's visit to the disputed house and house lot in the village, when she began shouting at her brother (Starr, 1978, pp.216-7). As the angry woman and her husband already owned a house in which they lived, this represents a clear example of accumulation of property by asserting a woman's rights to her father's estate.

This contrasts sharply with Anatolia in the late 1940s where 'a simple division of land between sons seems to have been the normal customary procedure' (Stirling, 1965, p.122). It differs also from the Hatay region of southeastern Turkey in 1965, where 'women are also denied access to land through inheritance unless they are brotherless' (Aswad, 1971; 1978, p.475). In the Bodrum region by the mid-1960s husbands were realising they could markedly increase their household's prosperity by utilising the wife's legal rights to land. Furthermore, during a year's observation at the Bodrum courts I saw numerous cases of division of patrimony in which female siblings actually appeared in court. Inheritance cases (veraset) and land division cases (taksim) which represented 'routine' (as opposed to disputed) land cases made up the vast majority of the caseload in the High Court in Bodrum (Asliye Hukuk) [34].

Land at Divorce

In the three year period 1965 through 1967, 138 divorce cases were heard, and half were brought by wives. The usual grounds were incompatibility and hence most divorces were uncontested. The person who became complainant usually lived nearer the court or desired the divorce more avidly. No stigma was attached to being either defendant or complainant.

Division of land is comparatively easy at divorce, according to the judge interviewed, because each spouse keeps control of her/his orchard during the marriage. If a woman inherited an orchard from her father, the husband merely worked in it. If he bought a motorised pump for the orchard, he could take the pump out of the orchard at divorce. But, if the husband bought the fruit trees while the wife owned the land, the trees belong to the orchard, based on the legal principle 'the person who owns the land owns the trees' (toprak kimin, ağaç onun). If the husband built a house on her land, and there was no contract, the house belonged to the person who owned the land. If there was a contract, the person who owned the more expensive thing, would buy the other out. (For a more detailed discussion of divorce cases, cf. Starr, 1983.)

Land at Widowhood

An estate is divided at the death of the patriarch. The legal principle is that the widow gets first choice of one-fourth of the estate, and the remaining parts are divided among all his legitimate heirs equally, regardless of gender. If the wife took the house and remarried, she could live there with her new husband. If the house was given to a child and she remarried, the child could ask her to leave when he/she was of legal age. If a man and woman had no children when he died, the wife still got one-fourth his estate and the rest was divided equally between the dead man's mother and father. But, if there was even one child, the wife still got one-fourth and the child the remainder. His parents then got no part of his estate. Property only went to the deceased's brothers and sisters if he had no children and his parents were not living.

When women were widowed after thirty or forty years of age they may have chosen not to remarry but to live near a married child. They then helped with cooking and childcare, and when they were too old to work they would be looked after by their children till they died.

Women's Use of the Courts

Women's interaction with the Bodrum courts is in part a function of their position in the life cycle and in part a reflection of their growing sophistication in defending their position in society. A young female is slowly socialised into viewing the courts as an institution capable of helping her in a crisis. As a child she may have watched the judge and court recorder come to their village to hold a court hearing to award title to land or to view the place of a serious crime or of a land dispute. Perhaps she had to apply to a judge to have her age raised as her father registered her birth several years after the fact, and without proper age she is too young to marry. Or she may need to waive the required fifteen day period between obtaining a state licence to marry and celebration of the wedding. If she has eloped, she will have to appear in court to clear her husband of charges of abduction. If she was abducted, her testimony in court will determine his freedom or prison sentence. Later she may be called as a witness to a crime or to a neighbour's application for land title. She and her brothers may need judicial advice about how to divide their father's property. The largest number of civil cases in the Bodrum court concerns land division (taksim and veraset cases).

Thus in mid-life she is prepared to view the court as a major resource when her husband or brothers fail her [35]. For example, in August 1967, a woman entered the Bodrum judge's office and requested that the judge appoint her as guardian for her mother, who was 'insane'. 'She is giving land to all my brothers and sisters, but not to me' she said. The judge accepted the case and asked that the mother have a doctor's evaluation [36].

In a different case, Ayse, a fifty year old woman went to the Director of Bodrum (Kaymakam) to ask his intervention in a dispute with her neighbour, Hasan. The fifty year old man had built a wall for his orchard on Ayse's field. After viewing the disputed ground, the Director gave a verdict that Hasan must take the wall down from Ayse's land. When he didn't remove the wall, Ayse opened a criminal lawsuit against him in court. She paid for witnesses to appear and eventually she won her case [37].

In a third case, Zehra, a forty-five year old woman asked the kaymakam to prohibit Mehmet's farming of land she had bought. After reviewing the title and the site, the Kaymakam made judgment in her favour. But, Mehmet refused to leave. Zehra then opened a lawsuit claiming, 'I just bought this land a year ago, and I find him still farming it.'

Mehmet answered, 'We have been farming this land for thirty years now.'

The judge asked, 'Who has the title?' Zehra responded that she did. 'But', the defendant said, 'It is not her land. She went to the Kaymakam and he stopped my farming of it.'

Eventually, Zehra won [38]. Here we see a woman who not only knows about farm titles but actively opposes a man who had usufruct land rights only. This case demonstrates a situation where usufruct was predominant but is now being replaced by notions of private ownership and a woman is able to take advantage of these changing conceptions of property rights.

Women are using the courts not only to gain and keep their property, but also to protect that intangible valuable, reputation.

For example, Hafise, a widow of sixty-five years, had lived in her house for thirty-seven years, raising eight children there. A civil servant inherited (from his mother) the house next door to Hafise. Although Turkish law specifies that windows cannot be put into a side of a house overlooking someone else's walled courtyard, he had built a window in the back of his house, overlooking Hafise's backyard. In making the extension on his home, he had also cut down most of Hafise's almond tree. In the summer of 1968 I went to Hafise's neighbourhood to find out how that case had ended. The following is part of an extended interview I had with Hafise:

Hafise said:

> The cases are not finished and I have been in court for one year and three months now. I have hired a legal representative (vekil) so that I don't have to go every week to court. The case about cutting down the tree was decided in his favour, but we sent it to Appeal court in Ankara.

I asked if Hafise had opened a case to gain restitution for the destruction of the tree. Hafise answered:

> No. I sent the dossier to the Appeal Court. I want to wait and see what they will do first. Maybe they will send him to jail

... He wanted to buy my wall. Do you remember that 'viewing' the court had of my garden and wall? Well, that 'viewing' determined the wall was mine. I said I'd sell the wall to him for 26,000 Turkish lira, but he offered me only 24,000 T.L. We then opened a different court case to determine the value of the wall. In this 'viewing' the judge only looked at the wall. They established that the wall was worth 1,300 T.L., but they neglected to look at the land it stood on. We are waiting for a viewing of the ground ... I'll only sell if he pays my price ... But, I still don't want his window open. Look, I wash in that garden. My toilet is there. I bathe there. I am an old lady. Sometimes I go out in my <u>don</u> (baggy pants). Can he be always looking at me? I saw apartment buildings in Ankara; they are all open, but this isn't Ankara. Bodrum is a small, old town. We are not so modern here. He should have his window on a street or in his garden ... [39].

Thus Hafise used the court to protect her modesty and her property. She had never been to court before this dispute. Nevertheless she pursued the restitution for her almond tree and the issue of his window through three different cases against her male neighbour, and when too many court hearings and postponements taxed her energies, she hired a local legal expert (<u>vekil</u>) for legal advice and court appearances.

In a final example, a twenty-two year old married woman, named Sevcihan, from Saz village (to Bodrum's east, adjoining the government forest) brought criminal charges at court. She accused a forest ranger, Mehmet, of molesting her after drinking with her husband while spending the night in their house. In court she told how two other forest rangers had offered her 500 T.L. to drop charges against their friend. Nevertheless, she pursued her grievance through five separate hearings over a five month time period. For each hearing she needed to travel twenty-five miles over rough terrain to court. On at least two occasions she had to bring witnesses and pay their expenses. On three different occasions she had had to retell the events of that night:

The woman, Sevcihan, in court:
That night the forest ranger and my husband came. They had been drinking at the coffee-house. They brought another bottle of <u>rakı</u> to our house, and my husband told me to make some food ready. And then my husband became drunk and he fell asleep. I went to my husband's father, and I called him. He came to the house for a while and then he left. I went to bed next to my husband. I went to sleep. Someone is touching me and I woke up.
Judge:
How is he touching you? Where is he touching you?
Sevcihan:
He is stroking my neck, my breasts, my arms, my hands. I ran outside. He followed me. I came back again. I went to the

room where my husband was sleeping and I locked the door. He knocked at the window, saying, 'Come. I am waiting for you.' I went again to bed next to my husband.
Mehmet's version:
I went home with her husband. We had been drinking at the coffee-house, and we had a bottle of rakı with us. And then her husband got drunk. He went to sleep. Later his father came and I offered him some rakı, but he said, 'I do not drink.' When he left I went to the bed they gave me. When I woke up in the morning I went to wash my face. She came to me, and I asked where her husband was. She said, 'He went. He went to the coffee-house.' (He is the proprietor.) She gave me a cup of water. I drank it and then said, 'Say good-bye to your husband for me.'
Judge:
Do you go to their house often?
Mehmet:
This is the first time.
Lawyer for Mehmet:
That girl and her husband made a plan to get 500 T.L. from my client.
Judge:
Do you have proof? What kind is it?
Lawyer:
Witnesses. Next time I will give a list of witnesses.
Sevcihan:
That's not true. The next day two forest rangers came to me by Jeep. They said if you will give up this court case, we will give you 500 T.L.. But, I didn't want to give up this case.

The testimony of the witnesses can be summarised as follows:

One witness had said, 'I drive a jeep for hire. The day after that event I carried two forest rangers to her village, and they went to her house, but I didn't overhear the conversation there.' Another witness had testified that he saw two forest rangers going to her village, and had seen the defendant and her husband drinking in the village coffee-house the night of the alleged event. A third witness, a twenty-three year old woman, testifying for Sevcihan said:

About a month ago we were stringing tobacco leaves onto thread. This man comes up to Sevcihan and said, 'My dear, Sevcihan, why do you not come to me? Are you angry with me?' She didn't go to him ... No, I didn't see him touching her [40].

Eventually, the charges against the forester were dismissed for insufficient evidence, despite the female witness' testimony which implied that Mehmet was aggressively pursuing Sevcihan.
From a different perspective Sevcihan can be seen to have won her goal. Her ardent pursuit of justice through the court made

Mehmet's actions public - his co-workers, her villagers, and even her debauched husband must now recognise his lecherous inclinations toward her. After five months of fearing a large fine and jail sentence (which would have meant loss of his job), Mehmet's lusts were probably tempered by prudence. Sevcihan's use of a district level court thus provided her the opportunity to vindicate her honour and safeguard her reputation.

Broader Implications

In the Bodrum region factors which allowed women to develop more self-sufficient lives were: changing land-use patterns which constructed the daily work routines for both females and males; a change in post-marital residence in response to the emergence of a new class structure, which occurred as a result of the penetration of capitalist agriculture. And third, the law. Judges' willingness to enforce legislation promoting norms of equality in union with women's growing knowledge of how to activate the official law system were emancipating mechanisms in western Turkey. In central and eastern Anatolia women's independence is apparently less advanced [41]. I would argue this is due to differences in the agrarian hierarchy, land use patterns, culture, historic conditions, and type of integration into the world market.

An explanation of Bodrum's successful acceptance of the new Civil Code may lie in several directions. Bodrum has a unique geographic and political position as a frontier of Turkish-Greek contact, and it was early pacified by the new Republic of Turkey. With good reason officials in Ankara would have wanted to keep Aegean Turkey pacified, economically productive and indoctrinated into the values of nation-statehood. Bodrum is much too accessible to the Greek Islands to let it remain a backwater, illustrating the failure of the nation to maintain a western democratic outlook. Furthermore, it is an area of increasing productivity since the 1940s, and since 1968 Bodrum town has had a huge economic boom in summer months due to tourism. The winter population of the town has doubled between 1965 and 1980 [42].

Earlier I suggested that in Aegean Turkey, Hellenistic and Islamic attitudes toward women had long co-existed as Turkish-speaking nomads over a period of several hundred years migrated into and settled in the region now called Bodrum. The ecology of transhumance required far-flung networks for the Yörük sheep herders to gain access to diverse pastures in this multi-ethnic region. Marrying daughters to Turkish-speaking transhumants of different camps within the same ethnic group cemented pastoral relations. The Islamic ideology concerning male dominance and the required submission of females was supported by the institutions of bridewealth, post-marital virilocal residence, divorce by renunciation and the ideology of honour and shame.

Yet, despite the change from pastoral life to settled capitalist agriculture, cultural institutions such as bridewealth and virilocal post-marital residence remained as 'ideal forms'. Writing about European manners and cultural change in the emerging Renaissance Europe, Elias (1939) demonstrated that two or three hundred years may be necessary for ideas, etiquette, and new cultural practices to diffuse throughout a society. Yet, in the Bodrum region, work routines changed rapidly in response to new crops and a new productive system. Marriage patterns changed, too, as cash-cropping agriculture and the transformation of the class structure made marriages within the village a way to consolidate land holdings for middle and upper strata peasants. And third, the norms of sexual equality promoted by the secular legal system through both written law and judicial decisions, provided a way for females to gain control of resources, especially productive land, which for women (as for anyone), are a bridge to autonomous personage.

Thus, Engels', dynamic theory of the process of change from pre-capitalist social formations to capitalist relations neglected the positive role law and culture play. In the region of Bodrum law balanced the disruptive effect that capitalist agriculture and the emergence of private ownership had on women's lives. With increasing scarcity of land for intensive agriculture, the norms of equal division of patrimony had become salient to husbands as a way to increase household land holdings. Elsewhere I noted that tangerine cultivation promotes nuclear households because two adults and two teenage children can provide all the needed labour from within (see Starr, 1978, pp.38-42). Mastery of the economic processes behind tangerine marketing is information easily accessible to any female who keeps her ears open.

Thus, I can unequivocally state that less than fifty years after the introduction of European Civil and Criminal codes in Turkey, women in the Bodrum region were reaping the benefits of laws of equality. They were able to hold titles to land in their own names. Some women successfully opposed husbands' attempts to usurp their economic resources during marriage and at divorce, and many women went to court to protect their landed interests and their reputations.

Some might argue that under the older system women were protected by fathers, husbands, and brothers; that going to court clearly indicates the breakdown of the older protective system [43]. Didn't women lead better lives, they ask, in a material, social and qualitative sense in the past? I answer, that depends upon your goals for women. Data presented here clearly indicate, I think, that husbands, brothers and fathers do not always look out for a wife's, sister's or daughter's best interests. They may not even know them (even if they wished to) because some women may not be sure what their best interests are, while others may not be able to develop a plan which they can communicate by reasoned argument (cf. S. Ardener, 1975, pp.xi-xviii; E. Ardener, 1975). Given these facts it is better that women have ways to look out for their own interests, that they judge for themselves what these interests are, and that they develop habitual modes of thought and action which allow them to do so.

Therefore, the Bodrum example suggests that several factors

need to intersect for women's emergence as more autonomous adults. The implication for policy makers is that legal rights and economic opportunities for women and for men must go hand in hand. The Bodrum study also suggests that we need to take a longer time span than twenty-five years [44] in deciding whether the results of change have improved women's lives. Of course we need to study the processes along the way. But, fifty years after the introduction of new secular codes, and twenty or more years after the gradual emergence of settled village life, we can see ways that women's access to valuables – land, houses, and reputation – are changing their relations to men, allowing them to become fully responsible persons.

Notes

1. Engels, of course, was not the only nineteenth century anthropologist to discuss woman's position in society in an evolutionary framework. But, precisely because his writing is the culmination of an anthropological perspective beginning with Maine, and developed by Bachofen, McLennan, Lubbock and Morgan, I choose to confront Engels's theories. Two recent critiques of Engels (1884) are Leacock (1981) and Sacks (1974).

2. See Engels (1981, pp.120-21, 142-44).

3. Divorce is now easier for women and harder for men than it had been under the previous Islamic law system of the 20th century Ottoman Empire. Divorce was now accessible under the new Civil Code of 1926 by a spouse applying to the nearest secular district court on one of the six grounds: adultery, dishonourable life of the spouse, desertion, mental infirmity, or incompatibility (Ansay and Wallace, 1966, p.122). For a more detailed discussion Starr (1983).

4. Modernisation is here roughly defined as integration of the group into a nation-state. The linkages between the group and the state may, of course, be imperfectly achieved, e.g., the Kurds in Turkey.

5. See Boserup (1970), Bossen (1975), Papanek (1977), and Nelson (1981).

6. Even those sympathetic to the cultural system of Islam and who advocate reform within Islamic law rather than a complete break, acknowledge Islamic law provides few rights for women and many disabilities when women's rights are compared to men's. See, for example, Coulson and Hinchcliffe (1978) and White (1978, pp.52-3).

7. The organising force of codes of honour and shame in Mediterranean countries has been argued by Campbell (1964), Davis (1977), Peristiany (1965), Schneider (1971), Schneider and Schneider (1976, p.2) and others.

8. See Stirling (1965, pp.98, 168, 230-3); Starr (1978, p.56); Abel (1979).

9. Approximately half of Turkey's trade in 1982 has been with

Islamic countries (The Guardian, 12th May, 1982) and in the same year Turkey signed a major Trade Pact with Russia for 600 million lira (New York Times, 20th January, 1982, p.A7).

10. In 1960, 22,700 workers left Turkey (Abadan-Unat, 1981, p.2). The figure continued to rise each year until the oil crisis of 1973-4. In 1980 the combined figure of Turkish residents in France, Germany, the Netherlands, Sweden and Switzerland was 1,762.9 thousand (SOPEMI, 1981, p.3).

11. Fisher (1963, pp.293-338) divides Turkey into five geographic regions, the Anatolian plateau, the Black sea coast, eastern Turkey, the Mediterranean, and the Aegean coast, but I suggest six. European Turkey ought to be separated from Aegean and Mediterranean Turkey at the Meander River.

12. The field research between 1966-68 was financed by a United States National Institute of Mental Health Predoctoral Fellowship and Grant and I gratefully acknowledge this support.

13. A hectare is 100 ares or 2.471 acres.

14. For a very interesting study of Bodrum town, see Mansur (1972).

15. Fieldwork revealed cultural differences between villagers on the Bodrum peninsula to Bodrum's west, and those on the Mumcular plain to Bodrum's east which villagers themselves recognise. saying 'They are very different from us'. Identifying which villagers were Yurük and which Turcoman was harder and is the topic of current research. But see Field (1881, pp.62-3), De Planhol (1958, pp.526, 528, 531) and Ramsay (1897, pp.100-1; 1917, pp.31, 83).

16. The transition from pastoralism to settled village life and the identity of these villages was first suggested to me by Osman Nuri Bilgin, Director of the Primary School in Bodrum, and a historian of the Bodrum region.

17. Interview with the Director of Rural Agriculture, Bodrum.

18. In the later 19th century the Turkish population was losing control of the Aegean areas to Greek-speaking farmers and shepherds. (Ramsay, 1897, pp.130-31, 133), see also Starr (1978, pp.23-5).

19. The population from the 1965 Census lists Bodrum town as having 5,136 while the surrounding villages are placed at 20,675 (Genel Nüfus Sayımı 1965, p.483).

20. Most women fifty years or older also remember Greek, for they came from islands of Kos and Kalimnos as brides.

21. See note 17.

22. Marketing tangerines only became feasible with the completion of a dirt road linking Bodrum to Milas in 1927, because tangerines ripen between December and March, the period of sudden, violent storms on the Aegean. This makes sea transport particularly precarious at this season.

23. The procedure of converting usufruct rights to a state recognised legal title (tapu) involved going to court and applying under Art. 639 of the Turkish Civil Code. 'If the land is not previously registered in the Land Registry and if the person occupies

and uses the land as if he were the real owner for 20 years without interruption and dispute, he may request a court to order the registration of the land in his name.' (Letter from Prof. T. Ansay, Dean of Ankara University Law Faculty. 14 December 1980).

24. Cosar (1978, p.131) astutely observes that as one moves from east to west in Turkey the 'situation of women improves with the general socio-economic situation'.

25. The lack of religious behaviour among Turkish-speaking transhumants has been noted by Barth for the Basseri (1961, p.135) and by R. Tapper for the Shahsevan (1975, pp.2, 155, 158, 164). But, see Beck for women's religious and ritual practices among the Turkish-speaking Qashqa'i (1978, pp.363-5).

26. Interview with Ayhan A., concerning Bodrum Court Case, B.C. 62. Bodrum Court Cases File. Also see Case 11 on film, 'Adliye: An Ethnography of a Turkish Rural Court', 1968.

27. Fieldnotes, filed under Kız Kaçırma (Elopement) Cases, 1967.

28. This is interesting as an attempt to use legislation to regulate custom and tradition.

29. See Allen (1935, pp.137-9), Coulson (1964, p.184), Starr (1978, ftn.2, pp.1-2).

30. See B. Lewis (1961, pp.225-6).

31. Maher (1978, p.102) makes the same point for rural Moroccan women. The male lineage members justify this deprivation of inheritance by saying that if daughters were given their land, it would be transferred to another lineage when they married.

32. The Turkish National Assembly enacted laws legitimising children of irregular marriages in 1932, 1934, 1945, 1950, 1955, 1965 and 1974.

33. The following is a summary of two days of discussions I had in August 1967 with the senior court judge and the Public Prosecutor concerning female and male property rights and bridewealth, at critical times in the life cycle or when engagements were broken or marriages were dissolved.

34. See, Starr and Pool (1974, pp.552-54) for an analysis of women and men's use of the courts in Bodrum. Also Starr (1983) for women versus men in divorce suits.

35. Additional confirmation of this assertion is available. Female complainants against male defendants as a total of all cases processed in the Bodrum Middle Criminal Court rose from 14 per cent in 1950 to 28 per cent in 1967 (Starr and Pool, 1974, p.353).

36. Witnessed by me 7 August 1967. Filed under Conversations with Bodrum judges and Public Prosecutor, p.33, titled, 'Opening a Case, Sulh Hukuk (Lower Civil Court)'.

37. Bodrum Court Cases, File. Sulh Ceza (Lower Criminal Court), B.C. 23, 1967.

38. Bodrum Court Cases, File. Sulh Hukuk (Lower Civil Court), B.C. 78.

39. Bodrum Court Cases, File. Asliye Hukuk (Higher Civil Court) B.C. 72 and Asliye Ceza (Middle Criminal Court) B.C. 85.

40. Bodrum Court Cases, File. Sulh Ceza (Lower Criminal

Court) B.. 41B.

41. For overviews and comparative statements about women in Turkey, see Abadan-Unat (1963, 1978 and forthcoming), Cosar (1978), and Kandiyoti (1977, 1980). For ethnographic accounts of women's position, see Aswad (1967, 1974, 1978).

42. Winter population figures for 1980 were: Bodrum town - 10,000 people; Bodrum district (kaza) including the town and all the villages had 38,000 people. (Personal communication, Mrs. Emine Cam, Director of Tourism Bureau in Bodrum.

43. Nader (1964, 1965) hypothesised that women in Oaxaca, Mexico used the court only when they did not have a husband, father or brother to protect their interests. In Turkey, however, family structures, law and the market interact so that it is frequently a brother or husband who has usurped the women's resources (see Stirling, 1957, p.27); or a father may exploit his daughter for his own financial gain (see Stirling, 1957, p.31). Even in areas of strong kin group control, 'the "protection" of the lineage which had previously been to the economic advantage of the woman is turning increasingly into dominance and exploitation' (Aswad, 1978, p.475).

44. Twenty-five years was the time period of the evaluative conference in Istanbul, entitled the 'Reception of Foreign Law in Turkey', which essentially was pessimistic (see Stirling, 1957, and Velidedeoğlu, 1957).

Acknowledgements

I owe a debt of gratitude to Dr Geoffrey Lewis, Oriental Institute, Oxford for taking the time to read critically this manuscript, although I take responsibility for its remaining faults. I also acknowledge with pleasure conversations and careful readings of the essay by Helen Callaway, Shirley Ardener, and especially Renée Hirschon.

7   DIVORCE AND THE DISADVANTAGED: AFRICAN WOMEN IN URBAN SOUTH AFRICA

Sandra Burman

The Apartheid System

In South Africa today changes occurring in African families in many parts of Africa (Goode, 1963) are being both accentuated and distorted by the government policy of racial segregation or apartheid. The phenomenon of migratory African labour, mainly male, predates the advent of the Nationalist Government (which has been in power since 1948). In various less systematised forms it can be traced back to the nineteenth century. With the penetration of the African societies of southern Africa by capitalism, migration greatly accelerated from the early twentieth century. But although African workers are required in the urban areas, what is not permitted under apartheid is the urbanisation of African families. In its attempt to prevent further African urbanisation, the government has created a battery of regulations and controls to keep African families in the rural areas and to draw African labour to the cities on a short-term basis. These 'influx controls' aim to admit only those who are able-bodied, willing to work on short-term contracts, and, usually, who are male. Thus one of the chief features of contemporary South Africa is the legislated disruption of African family life. This results from the contradiction between the economic and social pull of the urban areas and the government's policy of creating rural 'homelands' for Africans.

Today the 'homelands' have a vastly disproportionate number of old men, women and children, while the men of working age are away most of the year in the cities. The cities have disproportionately few women, with large numbers of men accommodated in single quarters. These men return once a year to their families in the 'homelands', where they are obliged to go if they wish to renew their contracts and their permits to remain in the cities. The effect on the entire way of life within families, both rural and urban, has been enormous, including perforce not only a redistribution of family labour, but also of decision-making within the family, and the accumulation and control of family property. This is in turn affecting relationships within the household, both between men and women and between generations, though the changes are being mediated by long-established norms in African family life.

This paper focuses on one aspect of the effects of apartheid on urban African families: what is happening to the control of property within families in urban areas and the consequences of the changes taking place. Property is defined, first, broadly, as rights in material objects (including money) which a person or family in practice thereby control sufficiently to use as a resource for their needs. Then follows a discussion of what effect changes in the control of family property have had on the very definition of property in so far as African women and their children are concerned. In particular, the question is considered whether they might be regarded formerly, or even now, as so much the objects of a system of property transaction as to be property themselves, and with what consequences.

The effects of the system of 'influx control' are most acute and clearly discernible in Cape Town, which is the second largest city in South Africa. It is the only city to fall within the Coloured Labour Preference Area, an area of South Africa which the government wishes to keep as clear of African urbanisation as possible. In order to do this, job preference is given by law to the so-called 'Coloured' population of South Africa [1]. The data presented in this paper have been collected in Cape Town and the 'homelands' from which most of the Cape Town African population comes – mainly the Xhosa-speaking areas of the Ciskei and Transkei. Further, as many assumptions about property and relations within the family are first explicated only at family crisis points, divorce has been used as the main focus for studying these assumptions, the underlying relations, and their consequences [2].

The African Family in Cape Town

Changes in contemporary urban African marriages have been documented among the Xhosa in Cape Town and the Eastern Cape during the 1960s and early 1970s (Wilson and Mafeje, 1963; Mayer and Mayer, 1961, 2nd edn 1971; Pauw, 1963, 2nd edn 1973). In the 1980s change appears in equally, and possibly even more, complex variety in Cape Town, with the development of a new township occupied by many recent migrants. The result is that African marriages in Cape Town now span a variety of practices which vary quite widely between those of families resident in Cape Town for several generations, with no rural connections, and those of the recent migrants still oscillating between city and rural area, observing mainly rural practices in connection with their marriages.

Officially Cape Town is a city of 1,458,620 people, of whom in 1980 183,360 were classified as Black, 775,600 as Coloured, 17,420 as Asiatic (mainly descended from immigrants from the Indian sub-continent), and 482,240 as White (1980 Census). Practically all the Africans are members of the working class, though in this context 'race' classification overrides class to a great extent in determining life style and affiliations. Each 'population group' has been or is still being moved to separate suburbs. In the 1970s the Africans were confined to three townships on the city's outskirts: Langa, Nyanga and Guguletu, though more than 25,000 also lived in illegal squatter camps [3]. It is in fact generally accepted that the actual number of Africans in Cape Town for at least the last decade has been considerably above the official figure, with the usual census undernumeration aggravated by the illegality of up to 50 per cent of the Africans in Cape Town (Simkins, 1981; West, 1981). The waiting lists for housing in the Cape Town urban area townships are enormously long already and informants had sometimes waited 10 or 12 years for houses, while conditions of gross overcrowding are common in the townships as a result.

In 1978, after a number of illegal squatter camps had been bulldozed by the authorities, a national and international campaign to preserve one such large site of about 20,000 people, called Crossroads, was organised by its inhabitants, together with white sympathisers. With the spotlight of world attention focused on the situation, the government agreed in 1979 to legalise most Crossroads inhabitants. Cape Town had been declared part of the Coloured Labour Preference Area in 1954, and a combination of tough influx controls and virtually no house-building for over a decade had ensured that by 1980 the three established townships had a high proportion of inhabitants either born in the city or else long resident there. (All legal housing for Africans in Cape Town was either council housing or that provided by white employees.) In Crossroads, on the other hand, there were both illegal immigrant families and also heads of families who were themselves legally in Cape Town but unable to obtain a home because their families were illegally in the Cape Town area, driven there by the extreme poverty of the 'homelands' and a desire to maintain family life. Two surveys of Crossroads between 1975 and 1978 (Graaf and Robb, 1978), found that approximately half of all householders were legally in Cape Town (and this included families where both spouses were legally in Cape Town but unable to obtain a house). There were also many women whose husbands had acquired girlfriends or civil law wives in the city and ceased to send home any money, leaving their rural wives with the choice between starvation or coming to the city illegally in search of their husbands and/or work.

The residents of Crossroads tend to observe many rural customs and are often eyed askance by the inhabitants of the more settled townships, who resent the ex-squatters' competition for jobs and housing and find aspects of the rural way of life strange or undesirable. Crossroads women are more likely to observe the practice of regularly going with their children to stay with their husbands' families in the country as a dutiful daughter-in-law should, though this custom is still observed to a lesser extent even by other town women whose parents-in-law are in either rural or urban areas. Other marriage customs, such as marriage by 'abduction' (ukuthwala in Xhosa) are no longer common in the townships but frequently occur in Crossroads and the rural areas, particularly the Transkei, from which the majority of Crossroads residents originate. In

119

ukuthwala cases the girl is seized by the young man and his friends, with or without her advance knowledge, and much of the expense of the normal bridewealth negotiations and marriage ceremony are short-circuited in this way. The girl's family may, even where the girl is unwilling, either connive at the seizure or discourage her return, since the man must pay her family bridewealth for her, and the usual marriage cost to the girl's family in ceremonial expenses and probably 'trousseau' will be considerably less. Several informants told of seizure in this way. In very few cases had the girl connived with the man in advance. In some instances she was strongly discouraged by her family from returning home, even being sent back to the man after running away to her family. One informant, M.P., for example, told of how she had always been her father's favourite child. When her mother died, she was sent to her mother's sister to be brought up, and a deep affection developed between them. Her father became so jealous of the relationship that, despite her and her aunt's strong objections to a particular suitor, her father actually encouraged the young man to thwala her and then forbade the aunt to receive her back into the household.

A rather different example of lack of family support was provided by another informant, N.N., who was a schoolgirl in the Transkei aged 17, when seized by a much older man home on his annual leave. She was brought to Cape Town by him immediately and, at the first opportunity, ran away to her father's brother in Guguletu. However, the man had already instituted bridewealth negotiations with her family, and her uncle insisted on her returning to live with her captor while these continued. After a few weeks she ran away to her uncle again and begged him not to force her to return. As by this time the negotiations had run into difficulties, her uncle was much more sympathetic, and even talked of assisting her to return to school, where she had been doing well and wished to continue. His wife, however, was dubious about the prospect of yet another mouth to feed in the house, and insisted that N.N. be sent for a pregnancy test. She was found to be several weeks pregnant, and her fate was sealed. She was returned to her abductor forthwith. Since women are themselves part of the society being described and have usually internalised its values, it is perhaps not as surprising as non-Africans sometimes find it, that major pressure to accept the marriage tends to come also from the girl's contemporaries and non-related women, who refuse to accept her back into the group of unmarried girls. (If still a schoolgirl, she will also often not be accepted back at school and may lose any school scholarship she has.)

Jobs for Urban Women

The labour market is not a tempting, or often even a viable, alternative to women seeking to escape unwelcome marriages. Bozzoli (1981) has shown how, as a result of the position of women in the African family structure and of the way capitalism developed in South

Africa, African women were the last of all the groups in South Africa to join the urban proletariat. They finally left the rural areas in large numbers only in the mid-twentieth century, when the increasing impoverishment of the over-crowded reserves led to economic crisis, malnutrition and starvation. By then, white men and women and African men had become proletarianised, and the industrial sector had become the monopoly of African male and/or white workers. In Cape Town there was the additional competition of the long-established Coloured communities. African women in Cape Town therefore have few opportunities for good jobs, becoming predominantly domestic workers, liquor brewers and sellers, and prostitutes. As Bozzoli shows (1981), these occupations are often vulnerable to cyclical variation in the economy, stratification, and exploitation, while organised resistance is particularly difficult to achieve. In Cape Town, too, the Coloured Labour Preference Area policy further complicates the picture, since African women without residential rights [4] cannot obtain factory work. Coloured competition and a quota system for African workers in factories ensures that a lower proportion of African women are employed in factories than in the rest of the country. Moreover, as a result of the Coloured Labour Preference Area policy, no training as either teachers or nurses, the two most common forms of independent access into the middle class for African women in the rest of the country, is available in Cape Town, and for the same reason there are very few employment opportunities in these spheres. African women in Cape Town are therefore even more marginal to the mainstream of economic activity than are their counterparts in other South African cities, and an African woman who does not have family support is particularly vulnerable economically.

Women's Legal Position in Customary Law Unions

In 1910 four states of southern Africa came together in the union of South Africa and in 1927 the government of the Union passed the Native Affairs Administration Act (No. 38 of 1927). This sought to unify the diverse approaches of the states to the recognition and enforcement of local African customary law; in addition the act used the institution of chieftainship and an 'incitement' clause to enforce the government's policy of segregation (Simons 1968: 53-8). The application of customary law for Africans was authorised (or made obligatory in certain circumstances) in a newly-constituted hierarchy of courts. In these courts a sizeable body of case law has evolved, reflecting the particular attitudes of the judicial officers (who are usually drawn from the ranks of the civil service). In consequence, both legalisation and case law have produced a codification of the administration's view of acceptable aspects of customary law as it operated in 1927, with modifications to suit government policy.

Accordingly, the customary law, which guaranteed the subordinate position of African women within the extended, economically self-sufficient, patrilineal family, was institutionalised but translated into the terminology and concepts of the dominant white society with its individualistic ethic. This distorted the position of women under customary law as it had originally operated. In terms of decisions made under the act, African women are defined as permanently under the guardianship of a male relative, such as father, husband or son. They cannot own or inherit property in their own right, act as guardians of their children, or, without the assistance of their own male guardians, enter into contracts or sue or be sued. However, also built into the system are protections for women to prevent extreme abuse and destitution at all stages of their lives. Some man is always responsible for providing for a woman and her children, and while the head of the family may control the product of 'his' woman's labour, he does not own it absolutely. He is more in the position of the manager of a joint estate. He has obligations to protect the interests of each 'house' formed by a wife and her offspring (for such unions are, at least potentially, polygynous) [5] and even to consult the 'house', and his heirs inherit his obligations to provide for widows remaining under the heirs' control.

Under the act, an essential feature of customary law unions is the transfer of bridewealth or lobola to the woman's family by the husband. In reality the transfer frequently takes place over many years, the lobola of daughters born of the union sometimes being used to pay that of their mother. Among its other uses, lobola in the past acted as an insurance for the wife's future support if the couple broke up through the husband's fault. Should the wife leave the husband as a result of his conduct (though 'mild' chastisement and adultery were not grounds for her to divorce him [6]), he would lose both his wife and the lobola already paid. If the union terminated as a result of her misconduct (including her persistent adultery), the lobola would have to be repaid - which could result in much family pressure being exerted on the woman to behave and, if she had left, return to her husband. She represented a sizeable investment for her husband's family, to be recouped in labour and biological reproduction. For them the lobola was both a lever to ensure that they got a suitable return on their investment, and an insurance policy against loss if they did not through some fault on the other side. The children of the union belonged to the husband's family once lobola had been paid, at least in part, and a reduction in the amount of lobola repayable on divorce was made once the woman had borne children, increasing with the number of children. Customary law unions were arranged, solemnised and dissolved entirely at the discretion of the families, as they still are, though outside intervention in the form of a judgement by an accepted court might be called on if (as frequently happened) a dispute over a lobola refund arose on the dissolution of a union. It may be argued that as a result of this practice women themselves and their offspring were placed to some extent in the position of property (or objects), transacted in exchanges between men and therefore not fully 'subject'; but before the inroads of the capitalist economy led to the present disintegration of the self-sufficient, extended family, women in practice usually had some control over their fate and some guarantee of protection from extreme abuse and destitution.

Whether a woman is placed in the position of an object which a man may transact is mainly of importance in so far as African societies accept that an owner has the right to transact his or her property without regard to its desires, even where it is animate, such as a dog or horse. Obviously African women are not and never have been entirely in this position, but the question addressed in this paper is whether the changes taking place in urban South African society, and its attitudes to property, are placing women more or less in this position of inability to control their own lives when opposing the wishes of the men in their families and the wider society in which they live.

As Africans became increasingly urbanised and absorbed into the capitalist economy and society, the institutions enshrined in the 1927 Act become wholly or partially irrelevant to the life-style of more and more Africans, as they had indeed been for many even in 1927. However, certain aspects of customary law unions have proved very persistent, and under the act such unions, their consequences, and any resulting disputes are dealt with under customary law. The customary law and many of its concomitant attitudes have therefore continued to play an important role in the African community even in modern South African urban society.

Legal Conflict: Customary Unions and Civil Law Marriage

The legal position as regards African marriage in South Africa today is highly complex, the practical situation even more so. Africans may, if they wish, still marry by customary law as outlined above, or they may marry by civil law before a marriage officer, who may be a duly appointed minister of religion, a magistrate or a commissioner (an official with magisterial-type powers appointed to deal with African cases). Where a minister of religion is not appointed as a marriage officer, as is the case with many of the independent black churches, the marriage is not a civil law marriage unless the couple are subsequently married by a marriage officer. Most churches exert strong pressure on members to marry in church, which in the majority of cases constitutes a civil law marriage, and in addition urban African women appear to be opting for civil marriages increasingly, partly for the legal protection it gives against other marriages by the husband. Civil law marriage must be monogamous and supersedes any prior customary union, except for some protection for the inheritance rights of the children of such unions. Moreover, during the subsistence of a civil law marriage, neither party can legally enter into a subsequent customary union with a third party. The civil law wife is recognised as the only wife, with consequences which may be illustrated by the case of P.N., an elderly woman whose customary union husband began to run a shebeen (illegal bar) in a township in 1979, with the aid of a woman employee. As the shebeen operated at night, he frequently slept there. One day in 1981 he collapsed and was rushed to hospital, but died en route. When P.N. went to collect the body, she was informed that the man's wife had already claimed it. It transpired that her husband had married the shebeen employee by civil law some time before. As the recognised wife, the civil law wife was entitled not only to his body (the burial of which is very important in African custom) but also to his pension, although P.N. had been married to him by customary law for over fifty years and had four children by him.

Civil law marriages are not, however, entirely to the benefit of African women. When a civil law marriage takes place in South Africa, the couple always have a choice, though a limited one, of how they wish their property to be owned and controlled during the marriage. For everyone but Africans the choice is between community of property and antenuptial contract. In the case of the former, everything owned by each spouse at the time of the marriage or acquired during the marriage falls into a joint estate, which in theory is usually divided equally on the termination of the marriage. The husband controls the joint estate. This system operates automatically for all non-African population groups in South Africa unless they make an antenuptial contract to the contrary – a common practice among middle-class whites, largely to remove the wife from the control of the husband, who otherwise controls not only the joint estate, but all her business transactions as well. For African civil marriages, however, the law states that unless a declaration is made by the parties, before the wedding, that they wish community of property to operate, the marriage is automatically <u>out</u> of community of property but with the husband controlling all the wife's property as well as his own. This leaves the African woman with neither the financial protection of a joint estate with her husband, nor the freedom to control her own property, even though she is recognised as having the legal capacity to own it. Yet by marrying by civil law, the African woman also loses the protection of the customary law. Civil law introduces into the centre of African family life the concept of outright ownership, rather than the African customary law concept of the head of the family as manager of a joint family estate, with rights and obligations to other family members, providing them with guaranteed economic support in need [7]. Thus, while in theory the civil law gave women more control over their own fate, it may be argued that in practice their position was, if anything, worse during the marriage (and sometimes after it ended) than if they had been married by customary law. Given the reluctance of many African men to pool their earnings with their wives, and the low earning capacity of most African women, this introduction of absolute ownership into the marriage can leave the woman in a very disadvantageous position. It is therefore interesting to note that community of property marriages are increasingly frequent, appearing in about 50 per cent of marriage certificates. Antenuptial contracts among Cape Town Africans are so rare as to be virtually non-existent: in a sample of 400 divorce cases, not one had an antenuptial contract, and both lawyers and the officials of the (African) Southern Divorce

Court confirm this fact.

There is a further way, however, in which a civil law marriage out of community of property without antenuptial contract may work to an African woman's economic disadvantage and leave her unable to decide about her own movements. If her husband dies without making a will, his estate will be distributed under customary law. She therefore nominally has the same rights to his estate as the widow of a customary law union, who is to be maintained out of the property earmarked for her 'house'. But a civil law marriage does not establish a 'house' in the customary law sense of a special legal entity of the wife and her children, so no property will have been earmarked in the same way for her and her children. It is quite possible that if her husband had a customary union wife, everything substantial he owned will have been allocated to her 'house'. But even if the civil law wife is the only wife, as a woman she cannot inherit under customary law. Her husband's property will devolve to the next male relative listed in the Table of Succession drawn up under the Black Administration Act (as the Native Administration Act is now called), and she may be obliged to live with him in some remote and unknown rural area in order to obtain any support at all if she has no property of her own, irrespective of whether her work or earnings contributed to her husband's estate. The civil law wife in this case is in a worse position than the customary union wife. Oddly enough, if she and her husband were married out of community of property but by antenuptial contract, her husband's property would devolve as if she were White, even if he died intestate, in which case she would inherit all or a large part of his property.

The Ambiguities of Modern Marriage Payments

Recent figures for customary unions and civil law marriages for Africans are not available and the former would be difficult to compile, since they are registered only in the province of Natal. Customary unions still occur in Cape Town, particularly in Crossroads, but it is not uncommon to find a couple marrying by customary law and some years later getting married by civil law, often after coming to settle in town from the country. In addition, in practice Africans have continued to insist on the giving of lobola even for civil law marriages. The property transaction is still regarded very widely as essential to mark the legitimation of the sexual union, but nowadays when a payment takes place it may be unclear in at least one of several different ways why the payment has been made.

First, it is no longer necessarily obvious to the community in which the couple live what consequences are expected to result from the payment. Whether a customary union has taken place followed by a civil law marriage, or whether lobola payments were made in anticipation of a civil law marriage before which the couple merely lived together, is not always clear, even to all the parties concerned.

Second, it may be unclear to outside observers (and even sometimes to the parties themselves) whether a payment constitutes lobola at all. Sometimes a substantial gift of cash or goods is made by the prospective bridegroom to the wife's parents prior to the marriage, which may not be intended (by some of the parties involved) to form part of the lobola payments. This may become a source of subsequent bitter disagreements, as became evident in interviews with divorcees. It may also be unclear, even in the case of a long-term relationship, whether a customary union has taken place accompanied by lobola payments, or whether a couple are simply living together (as frequently happens in the towns), with the man paying seduction damages to the woman's family on the birth of each of the children. Indeed, seduction damages are often converted into the first lobola instalment if the parties agree to marry by either customary or civil law rites. In customary law the damages were to recompense the girl's guardian for the lowering of her lobola price as a result of her seduction, since she became 'soiled goods'. There was no concept of payment for insult to the girl's feelings, as in civil law, so she had no interest in the payment, which could therefore reasonably be converted straight into lobola.

If such a conversion does not take place, the children remain members of the wife's family, according to customary law. However, this raises a third ambiguity, for it is no longer clear what purposes lobola is in fact meant to serve. Not only has its ritual significance marking a change in a relationship become less clear, as indicated above, but also actual payment, even if long delayed, would still not appear to be essential for securing the children to a man's family. The birth or conception of children before civil law marriages is common (in a sample of 65 recent African divorce cases heard in Cape Town, all of marriages with children from the marriage, 40 couples had either had or conceived the children before the civil law marriage). Some of these would be children of acknowledged customary unions, others of more ambiguous relationships. A number of informants admitted that the man had made only a token payment towards the lobola at any time, and in one case it appeared that promises to pay the lobola had not been fulfilled at all. Nonetheless, most of these informants were adamant that when the divorce occurred both they and their families had regarded the children as children of a legitimate customary union and therefore as belonging to the man's family. Disagreements on this point had sometimes surfaced, however, on the breakdown of the marriage, or where the husband's family subsequently tried to claim the lobola of the daughters after the wife had brought them up. Part of the ambiguity is created by the fact that in practice, unlike a civil law marriage, a customary union does not necessarily take place at a given moment but is concluded over a period of months or even years. Conflict between township practice and South African court rulings on the consequences of lobola payments before or after civil law marriages further complicate the situation.

Ambiguities which have developed concerning marriage payments have thus left the woman in particular in a vulnerable position in borderline cases. On the one hand, where no civil law marriage has taken place, she fears being discarded and left destitute if the man denies that a customary union existed. On the other hand, if after the birth of her children she married their father by civil law, she often fears that his family will insist that a customary union took place and demand the children as of right arising from this, despite South African court decisions to the contrary. Reasons given by informants for not resorting to the courts for assistance were family pressure, ignorance of the law, and mistrust of the State's courts. A woman is still frequently in practice at the mercy of family negotiations on the status and consequences of the union to a large extent, but without the concomitant economic security.

Further, although lobola has continued to be paid, it has lost most of its functions for insurance and social cohesion, both inter- and intra-familial. This can be traced largely to the changed means of payment. Money is replacing cattle, and tends to be spent and vanish rather than produce calves, leaving nothing on the dissolution of the marriage either to be returned to the man's family or with which to support the ex-wife. For this reason there is a steep decrease in urban areas in claims for the refund of lobola when marriages break up, even when there are no children and the marriage has been of fairly short duration. The substitution of money for cattle is not a new development – missionary records mention it as beginning to occur in the nineteenth century – but the process has been accelerating throughout this century. Lobola in Cape Town is currently still expressed in terms of cattle (in contrast to Johannesburg, where there appears to be a growing tendency to refer to it in monetary amounts), but is rarely fully paid in animals, which are kept only in rural areas. The value of lobola beasts is unrelated to the market value of real cattle. Rather, it is determined in every case, within conventional margins, by a bargaining process between families, and 'calves' are sometimes said to 'grow', as money is given in instalments.

Thus virtually all women informants claimed at least initially that between eight and ten cattle had been paid on their marriages [8], but the monetary amounts these represented varied by hundreds of rand. Agreements to pay lobola of several hundred rand are common, with amounts rising to R1000 or even more. An educated wife commands more lobola, since the cost of her education and loss of her future earning capacity to her family are taken into account. The average African non-agricultural wage per month in South Africa in the second quarter of 1981 – the latest available figure – was R215 (Quarterly Bulletin of Statistics, December 1981). Little of this is available for saving. The August 1981 Minimum Living Level figure for an unmarried African man living in a hostel in Cape Town was R80.48, and for those supporting an average African household (as unmarried sons sometimes are), R195.76 (Nel, 1981). Thus lobola still represents a very sizable investment by a man and those of his family who assist him with payments (most men interviewed had in fact earned their whole lobola alone). Africans have always stressed that lobola is not a sale price. Nonetheless, with the increasing absorption of Africans into the wage economy and the dwindling of the ritual, social cohesion and insurance functions of lobola, little is left of its multifaceted elements except the payment of valuables to acquire a wife. This increasingly makes women objects in transactions, the initiation of which they may now more often be able to influence than in the past, but the consequences of which remain largely outside their control.

In the light of this development, it is particularly interesting to note that the flow of money to the bride's family is nonetheless increasingly being reversed. In customary law the bride took to her new family her own cooking utensils and sleeping mat – originally homebaked pots and a woven mat, of little material value compared with her lobola cattle. However, with the changes urban life entails, a trousseau will now, ideally, include full bedroom and kitchen suites, or at the least a bed, chest of drawers, and cooking utensils. The wedding, if a church ceremony, will be open to all and may cost the bride's family a considerable amount in food and drink for the guests. It is quite common now for the bride's family to find itself in debt, including hire purchase payments, for more than the amount of the lobola paid and promised.

It is tempting to suggest that this type of dowry arrangement was a logical development, resulting from the change-over from the practice of the couple living with the husband's family in an extended household, as was the custom and still is to a large extent in rural areas, to that of setting up their own home in the city. The old arrangement generated the concomitant attitude of disapproval of any interference in the arrangements of the new couple, including major gift-giving by the bride's family after the marriage (which was taken as a slur on the husband's family). This attitude has proved to be persistent. However, the young couple now need more financial assistance and the bride's dowry today (though it is not referred to as such) frequently helps the young couple establish their home in much the same way as it does, for example, in Mediterranean countries. However, the practice is also being increasingly observed in rural areas, where this functionalist explanation of the development of 'dowry' carries much less weight, and informants stressed that it was a development of the bride's family wishing to help their daughter and demonstrate their status, rather than in response to demands from the groom's family. Furthermore, in the gross overcrowding common in the Cape Town townships, suites of furniture are often an embarrassment rather than an assistance, since the young couple usually live with the groom's family or as lodgers, quite possibly without even a room to themselves while waiting for a house, and the furniture has to be left with the store or distributed temporarily to friends and family. It does seem, rather, that with the great contemporary increase in the instability of marriage, the 'dowry' may be an attempt by the girl's family to replace the ongoing insurance of assistance to be provided originally by lobola cattle should the marriage be dissolved through the husband's fault. Given the legal situation, such insurance is now provided by the furniture to some extent, even in the case of marriages in community of property, since there is a frequently used provision in the law for a guilty party to forfeit the benefits he or she would have derived from the marriage. Quite possibly too, ideas of a trousseau given by the girl's family in 'western' style are becoming more widespread from magazine and other sources, and are playing a role in the growth of the 'dowry'.

Double Standards

Despite the increasingly high family investment in marriages, marital breakdown is steadily increasing, as it is in the White and Coloured communities too. The strains on urban African marriages are, however, considerably greater. Urban African men in Cape Town tend to apply blatantly double standards to sexual behaviour. It is very common after marriage for them to acquire girlfriends, whom they frequently flaunt in public, but they usually take strong exception to any boyfriends their wives may have. While women do not in general accept the fact of their husbands' girlfriends with equanimity, they have not challenged the attitude of masculine assertiveness much in public. As Bozzoli points out (1981), African nationalism has tended to identify national oppression with the erosion of independent, pre-capitalist African societies and to insist on the sanctity of the pre-capitalist family ideal, embodying though it did the subordinate position of women. Subordination within that context did, however, carry with it assurance of economic support, while in an urban low-wage economy, where monogamy is perforce (for economic, even where not religious and legal reasons) virtually universal, girlfriends not only draw away much-needed funds, but also, especially if unmarried, threaten the stability of the marriage in a way that extra-marital liaisons did not do in a pre-industrial society.

Thus economics and male sexual infidelity now interact to increase the strains on marriage in a way not experienced in pre-capitalist African society. Even apart from sexual infidelity, low wages and shortage of housing place enormous strains on even fully urban marriages, while those where one party lives in the country, or where one or both oscillate backward and forward between urban and rural areas, are under even greater strain from lengthy separations. Further, the dual marriage system can create a particularly difficult situation for civil law wives when endorsed out of the city or returning to visit their in-laws if they find themselves confronted by a customary union wife of their husband. In rural areas in particular, strong pressure is exerted on women to accept customary unions as valid marriages carrying certain given consequences. Whatever the official legal situation, in such a setting in practice customary law will tend to prevail and the customary union wife will take precedence as the first wife. One informant told of how, after marrying her husband by civil law, he had brought her and their children from Cape Town to a house in his village and left them there, whereupon his customary union wife, of whose existence she had been unaware, arrived and claimed the house as his first and therefore senior wife, a claim which the civil law wife felt unable to dispute.

The result of all these stresses from the interaction of the existing apartheid capitalist society and values stemming from a polygynous, extended family operating in a subsistence economy is a high and rising rate of marriage breakdown, though figures do not exist with which it can be quantified. For customary unions, divorce is an arrangement between families. In the case of civil law marriages, however, a decree of the courts of the South African state is required. What follows is a description of the property issues which arise at this intervention as it operates in the existing situation, and thereafter the significance of property for the position of African women in South Africa today will be discussed.

Divorce and Housing

There is a strong tendency for lawyers and laymen other than Africans to assume that, because Africans are by far the poorest section of the South African population, property plays no significant part in the issues arising for Africans on divorce. It is certainly true that many of the problems faced by Africans are very different from those which arise among the wealthier sections of the population, but it is the very uniqueness of their property and property institutions which creates the most serious problems. For African women the situation is further complicated by the tendency of both the customary law and, on occasion, the South African State, to treat them and their children as the property of their men.

Probably the most important rights in property for an African in Cape Town are those in the marital house, even though no African owns a house in the city: all housing is owned by the State. However, even if the man himself has the right to permanent residence in Cape Town, without being allocated a house, he cannot legally bring his wife and family to the urban area. With the length of the housing waiting list, the loss of the marital house loses an African far more than merely a roof over his or her head. In the system that the Administration Board uses to control the urban African population, the complications arising from the possession or loss of a house are both far-reaching and serious.

Houses are normally registered in the husband's name and if a woman has no children, on the breakdown of her marriage she will either have to move out into lodgings or stay on at the house, with all the unpleasantness that may entail [9]. There is a widespread problem of violence by husbands, who may periodically assault their wives and/or their children. Both drink and customary law sanction of 'chastisement' by the husband appear to play a role in this, as well as overcrowding. Informants of all population groups confirmed that the police were extremely loath to intervene in what had been defined as marital violence. For Africans the problem is complicated by the great housing shortage, which has resulted in many estranged couples being forced to live under the same roof, though not as man and wife, thus rendering the wife particularly vulnerable to assault. Several women asserted that a desire to be safe from their husbands' violence in such a situation was the major reason for their instituting divorce proceedings. Fortunately for them, they could do so at civil law, (whereas in customary law only their guardians could institute divorce proceedings) and with the increasing breakdown in urban areas of the return of <u>lobola</u>, they were more likely to be free of family pressure to return to their husbands.

If a wife has young children, her position is better. Custody of young children is now usually given to the wife, and in the last few years the Administration Board, which controls housing for Africans, has tended to give the house to the custodial parent, but only on sight of the divorce decree. This means that a husband with young children and an erring wife who has not abandoned them may well think twice before instituting divorce proceedings which will probably result in his being obliged to move out of the house to single quarters and to go to the bottom of the waiting list for a house [10]. Since the house is not owned by the parties, the divorce court will not intervene in its allocation and the wife may well find herself eventually in possession and in control of the most valuable asset she is likely to have in the city.

Possession of the house may, however, threaten an equally crucial asset – her pass (or permit to be in an urban area), if it is issued under section 10(1)(c) of the Black (Urban Areas) Consolidation Act of 1945. This gives her rights to be in the urban area only while married to a man with permanent rights of residence. While enforcement is not as rigorous as it might be, the legal (and often practical) result is that widows and divorced women are forced to return to the rural areas, which they may have left (apart from visits) twenty or thirty years before as children and where they may after all the intervening years have no family, friends or acquaintances. For a divorced woman awarded custody, the status of her pass is certain to become public when she goes to have the house transferred into her name, and may come out even if she seeks lodging instead, since a lodger's permit is required. One informant' husband had informed on her when her pass was not endorsed after the divorce, and the temptation to defend one's possession of a house in this way is obviously strong. If her pass is endorsed with her divorced status, she becomes an illegal resident in Cape Town and, if not forcibly bussed out to a 'homeland', she will face regular fines every time she is caught by a police spot check. As her pass will not be in order, she will have great difficulty in obtaining domestic or other wage labour: employers of Africans who do not have valid passes are liable for fines of up to R500, with the average first offence fine currently standing at R100. An African woman on a section 10(1)(c) pass is allowed into the urban areas very much as a possession of her husband, and if she ceases to be his, she is treated by the State as an object to be returned to the storeroom, irrespective of her blameworthiness. This leaves her even less in control of her fate than did the customary law where, if she was blameless, her subsistence at least was ensured.

Custody of Children and Maintenance

The combination of state policy, African men's attitudes generated by the customary law, and, above all, the housing shortages result in far more contested African divorces than among other 'population groups', mainly extremely bitter fights over the custody of children. African divorces of civil law marriages are heard usually in a special court (the Southern Divorce Court), where unrepresented plaintiffs are common, so that legal costs are not a deterrent to lengthy court disputes and lawyers have not had an opportunity to reach a settlement. Widespread attitudes among men dictate that payment of lobola should give the husband custody of at least the older children [11] and should preclude the payment of maintenance, since the children are his. This reluctance to relinquish custody to the mother and to pay maintenance is reinforced by the economic difficulties of paying maintenance out of a usually very low wage when maintaining the second family he is likely to acquire. Above all, his desire for custody is reinforced by the spectre of losing his house to the custodial mother.

The primary criterion of the court in awarding custody is the welfare of the child, with the assumption that with young children and with girls the mother is prima facie the best custodian. A great deal of mud-slinging is therefore usually involved in the attempt to prove the other parent is less suitable, and parents have to show that, if they work, someone suitable is available to care for the children. Since African wives very seldom receive maintenance for themselves in the Southern Divorce Court [12], and since maintenance for children is usually perforce very low as a result of the husband's other commitments, both parents will work in virtually all cases where work can be obtained. But child care provisions are minimal and most alternatives (such as help from relatives imported into the city for that purpose or sending children to rural areas) result in serious problems, especially for women who have little income or security when divorced. Throughout most sections of South Africa women's wages are lower than men's (there are no equal pay provisions) and African women are largely excluded from the more skilled or semi-skilled lucrative work and are, as outlined above, frequently in occupations particularly vulnerable to economic fluctuations. The result is that divorced African wives, more than any other section of South African society, are forced to rely on unpaid family and communal assistance for minding their children, ironically while they themselves are in many cases employed as nursemaids for white children. While a woman's affection for her children obviously plays a major role in her decision to fight for custody of them, the fact that she is 'subject' enough under civil law (in contrast with customary law), to become a custodian at all is again a somewhat mixed blessing [13].

Moreover, since the lobola system generally no longer operates to provide for an abandoned wife, the wife will probably have to go to the Maintenance Court to obtain a court order for child maintenance. A man unwilling to pay can, however, considerably delay the order, and make enforcement difficult or impossible after it is made. If he is unemployed, no order can be made against him, although theoretically he can be jailed if it can be shown he is refusing to work. However, this is difficult, as even allowing for those who choose not to work, the rate of unemployment among urban Africans with a right to be in Cape Town is very high; from a survey it was estimated as 13 per cent for only the three established townships in 1981 at the height of the economic boom in South Africa (personal communication, Steffan Schneier). And though many men earn some money in the informal sector, these earnings are usually difficult for the ex-wife to prove.

Even when he is employed, the amount a husband may be ordered to pay will depend on his income and other obligations. A number of men in this position have a customary union wife and family in the 'homelands', and the maintenance courts in practice will take these into account (including the customary union wife) when dividing his income to allow for dependants, though there is no guarantee that the money allowed for them is necessarily sent to them. As with other South African men, though more frequently, given the attitudes and pressures described above, an African man may also have a new wife and family, so that a higher number of men than in other South African population categories are in the position of having support obligations to not two but three families. Often, too, money must be sent to parents, since African pensions are very low (R89 every second month) and elderly parents in the 'homelands' or city often rely on their children for assistance, while attitudes within the society make refusal of such demands difficult. Given the mores of urban African society, it is also not uncommon for a man to be paying maintenance for one or more children of ex-girlfriends. Thus an exceptionally heavy number of support demands fall on the population category with the lowest salaries in South Africa. Several women informants said that with all these likely scenarios in mind, they had decided it was not worth pursuing a claim for maintenance, but where they do it seems likely that it is the customary wife who will be the ultimate loser.

There are small state child-maintenance grants for African women with two or more children if their incomes are below a certain (very low) level and if their husbands have completely disappeared. Non-payment by the husband whose whereabouts is known, however, will not qualify a woman for child maintenance, and an African woman with one child or none is most unlikely to obtain maintenance [14].

As has been noted above, urban claims for the refund of lobola are fairly rare, and informants indicated that in general such claims were considered a waste of time, as the money was usually spent before the divorce occurred. This at least partially relieved women of the urgings of their families to return to their husbands, unless there was still a possibility of further lobola payments. However, a frequent ploy in African marriage quarrels has always been for the woman to return to her family until a further payment is made, whether of or in addition to the original lobola. This is taken as an indication of how much the husband wants her back and an earnest of his good intentions. As a result, since the finality of a quarrel is not usually clear, families may urge a woman to return if the husband offers a further payment. Many informants relied on their families for financial assistance to pay for their divorces, and family pressure to return to the husband may result in this assistance being withheld. It may also result in the withholding of financial support by a family able to provide it, being in receipt of lobola which was meant to ensure support for the wife in the event of marriage breakdown. Thus the uses of property under civil and customary law may converge to leave the woman in need of more financial assistance than under the customary law, but subjected to all the pressures generated by the lobola system to act against her will.

Conclusion

The question that must be asked is: what does the changing relationship between African women and property in modern urban South Africa demonstrate about the society and the role of African women in it? The changing relationship is largely the result of the shift from a pre-industrial to a capitalist society, with a slower and uneven shift between the corresponding legal systems and attitudes. The two legal systems therefore currently co-exist side by side in modified form. Often the attitudes generated by each of them alter more slowly than the society in which each operates. Sometimes the two sets of attitudes clash with each other. This is particularly likely to happen where one system is deliberately subjected to domination by the other with the aim of bringing about change in African society. Add to these dysfunctions the further complication of apartheid administrative controls interacting with both systems of law to produce results not contemplated in the logic of either system. That the results are often unjust and disruptive of existing social bonds is therefore not surprising; rather it must be asked why they appear to work so consistently to the disadvantage of women, and what the relationship is between this and the already noted phenomenon in customary law of often treating women themselves and their offspring as a kind of property.

It may be argued that the position of African women should be steadily improving, since the use of civil law is increasing and the civil law is meant to give women more control over their own lives, children and property than was allowed under customary law. In customary law women and their children were to some extent in the position of objects to be transacted in exchanges between men, though protections in the system against extreme abuse and destitution, and ordinary affection, ensured that they had some control over various aspects of their lives. Their position was less vulnerable than might at first appear. But the interaction with a capitalist economy has tended to destroy the ritual, social cohesion, and insurance elements in this system, while in practice leaving women still very much open to pressures from their families to obey them despite the women's wishes. Women's own internalisation of the values that see them as 'goods of exchange' whose value can be reduced by 'spoiling' also play a role in preventing them from opposing an imposed fate. This is revealed, for example, in the refusal by women to accept back into the category of 'unspoiled girls' women who oppose their seizure in _thwala_ marriages. Customary law nowadays provides very little security for African women or control over their own lives. On the other hand the civil law has not proved particularly effective in these respects either. The civil law of marriage, as modified for Africans, while it does not treat women or their children as objects of exchange between men, has failed to give the majority of married African women either the status of being fully in control of their own property or the protection of a joint estate, since their property in the most common form of African civil marriage is held out of community of property but subject to the control of the husband during the subsistence of the marriage. Once the marriage is dissolved, the woman will have full control of her property. The increase in value of what I have termed 'dowry' is an interesting development in her protection; but in practice the marital property system may nullify even this provision for her future. Given the poverty of most Cape Town African families, household possessions and motor cars generally constitute all the property involved in most cases in the city. A common story in court and from informants is that the husband sells the furniture as soon as the woman has left the communal home (or sometimes even before) and spends the money. Even though it is often the woman who had made the hire purchase payments or brought the furniture with her on marriage, her chances of obtaining a refund of the money are very slight, given the low income of most Africans and the problems of debt collection.

Nor have the combinations of the customary and civil law systems of marriage proved better for women. On the contrary, the introduction of the civil law of marriage as a system taking precedence in a clash between civil and customary law marriage systems has left the woman who is married under customary law, and to some extent her children, vulnerable to destitution and humiliation. Alternatively, the grafting of the institution of _lobola_ onto the civil marriage appears to have produced an almost equally unsatisfactory combination for women, leaving them with most of the disadvantages of the customary law marriage but with very few of the protections against destitution, or the advantages of the civil law. The system does not appear to be working to men's material advantage either, whether husbands or fathers. The most frequently articulated reason for desiring it, given by even educated informants, is that it is custom and that it is very important to maintain one's African identity – which is no doubt particularly true in the face of the collapse or change of so much else in African family life. However, this still leaves unanswered the more fundamental question of why certain institutions survive despite few apparent material benefits, because of sentimental attachment and the attribution of symbolic importance, and others fall victim to changing ways of life.

Thus, while on paper the civil law marriage would appear to give a woman ownership of her property, the ability to become custodian of her children, and a maintenance claim both for herself and them without the necessity of living with her own or her husband's family, in practice these benefits usually fail to materialise or prove to be of dubious value. The woman's earning ability is likely to be low and her protections against her husband disposing of her property prior to the divorce practically non-existent. The problems of obtaining custody and a house in which to stay with her children are manifold. Her chances of obtaining maintenance for herself are extremely low. The attitudes deriving from the 'objectification' of women and their children in customary law have tended to persist to at least some extent among most sections of the African population. Resentment by men at loss of custody and the duty to pay maintenance is not uncommon in all population groups in South Africa, but the reinforcement of these attitudes, derived from the payment of lobola, is peculiar to African communities. The African woman is in a uniquely disadvantageous position compared with women of other population groups in South Africa.

Finally, in this context, the major effect of the Administration Board on African property, apart from limiting the amount of housing available, has been to exclude women from control of arguably the most important asset for Cape Town Africans - the marital house. The house of a married couple is always registered in the man's name, and in the case of divorce even a custodial mother's claim to it is secondary to that of the man's should he rapidly produce other dependants. As shown above, the ramifications of this system may include extremely bitter custody fights, and indirectly, the cancellation of the woman's pass. All these features demonstrate the extent to which African women are regarded as undesirable in urban areas, tolerated only as a necessity for the men whose labour is required and who will, it is hoped, form a stable working force.

In practice, the introduction of the civil law has not therefore generally improved the position of urban African women in relation to the control and ownership of property in South Africa, nor their ability to control their own lives. On the contrary, in many crucial aspects it has deteriorated. This is partially the result of persistent attitudes derived from the 'objectification' of women in customary law, attitudes aggravated by the changes in the institution of lobola brought about by the increasing impact of the capitalist economy. It is also partly a result of the lower status in general accorded by the civil law to women in marriage, particularly African women, and partly from the State's attitude that African women in the cities are acceptable only when attached to a man in an approved relationship, except where already regrettably entrenched with certain residence rights. The net effect of this is to leave African women less able to determine various aspects of their lives than African men or both sexes in other population groups. While direct family controls have decreased to some extent, economic and state pressures have intervened to limit the ability of women to resist control of their lives. They are particularly vulnerable economically in times of crisis. The original society in which the customary law operated cannot be reconstructed, and possibly few urban African women would in fact want it were that possible. But at present they appear to be caught in a singularly unfortunate convergence of economic and legal systems that interact almost entirely to their disadvantage. That they have not been crushed by them is largely a tribute to the survival and extent of communal assistance within the urban African community.

Notes

1. In South Africa there are officially 22 population groups (Department of Internal Affairs, n.d.) collected under the broad headings of 'White', 'Coloured', 'Asian' and 'Black'. However, those not in agreement with the apartheid policy tend to use the term 'black' to cover all groups other than the 'Whites', and where it is necessary to distinguish those people officially referred to as 'Black', the term 'African' is used instead. Cape Town townships contain mainly Xhosa-speakers, but also include Sotho and Zulu as well, and offspring of intermarriage between them. The term 'African' is therefore used in this paper rather than 'Xhosa'.

2. The data have been collected from various sources. Apart from interviews with a number of African divorcees and other informants from each of the established townships in Cape Town and Crossroads, the following methods were used: courtroom observation in the Southern Divorce Court in Cape Town and King William's Town and of the Commissioner's Maintenance Court in Cape Town; participant observation in the office of the Divorce Clerk in Cape Town and interviews with these officials; a sample of records and appeals from the Southern Divorce Court; interviews with the presiding officers and the Registrar of the Southern Divorce Court; interviews with the relevant Commissioner's officials at the court in Cape Town; interviews and participant observation with a sample of lawyers of all population groups (mainly in Cape Town but also in King William's Town and Johannesburg), social workers and legal advice centres, ministers of religion and doctors; a sample of cases drawn from the Athlone Advice Office; and a sample of all divorce cases where both spouses were African divorcing in the Supreme Court since July 1981, drawn from the Supreme Court Records. I am indebted for helpful comments on preliminary drafts of this paper from Ms S Ardener, Dr T Bennett, Ms S Frankenthal, Dr R Hirschon, Professor D Park, Mr A Spiegel, Ms V van der Vliet and Professor M West. Research for this paper was sponsored by the Social Science Research Council, the British Academy, the Nuffield Foundation, Lady Margaret Hall, the Harry Oppenheimer Institute for African Studies, the Anglo-American and De Beers Chairman's Fund and the Centre for Intergroup Studies, University of Cape Town.

3. However, foreign African diplomats (including those of the independent homelands) are permitted to live in white areas, and do.

4. Residential rights are acquired under Section 10 of the Black (Urban Areas) Consolidation Act of 1945, which, in outline, provides that no African may remain in a prescribed (urban) area for more than 72 hours unless he/she has resided there continuously since birth (Section 10(1)(a)), or has worked continuously in such an area for one employer for at least ten years or lawfully resided continuously in such an area for at least fifteen years (Section 10(1)(b)), or is the wife, unmarried daughter or minor son of a Section 10(1)(a) or 10(1)(b) permit holder and is lawfully residing with him/her (Section 10(1)(c)).

5. The Black Administration Act, as it is now called, uses the term 'union' for customary law marriages, since 'marriage' is defined as always monogamous.

6. Under the Pre-Union Natal Code, however, which still applies in Natal, either spouse may obtain a divorce by reason of the other's adultery.

7. Civil law marriage works to an African woman's advantage in cases of divorce (with certain exceptions) and where the husband suffers industrial injury, as well as on his death, provided he has made a will in her favour or they are married in community of property or by ante-nuptial contract.

8. One Xhosa informant, however, told me that she had been able to marry a Zulu against the wishes of her stepfather only after going to court to obtain the permission of a magistrate, and her husband had then made no lobola agreement. When closely questioned, several other informants admitted that their lobola had not actually been paid in full, or, in one case, at all.

9. Even in Johannesburg, where there are 30 and 99 year leases for African housing, practically all women are effectively barred from getting such housing because building societies will not lend them the necessary money, since women have no contractual capacity under customary law. Even if a woman can prove that she married under civil law, fear of a subsequent marriage by her under customary law should her existing marriage terminate prevents building societies from making the necessary loans (Cape Times, 8 Sept, 1980).

10. If a man can show within a few weeks that he has dependants, however, he will probably be able to keep his house. Both lawyers and other informants had stories of immediate remarriages by the ex-husband for this reason.

11. Under customary law settlements, very young children were sometimes in fact left with the mother for a few years, until considered old enough to begin to do chores for the father's family.

12. The Southern Divorce Court has a roll of approximately 20-25 cases each day in Cape Town (where it sits for 12 days in the year), which will include both opposed and unopposed matters. It is therefore very loath to go into questions of maintenance, which require much evidence and are time-consuming. All questions of maintenance for children can be (and usually are) referred to the

Commissioner's maintenance court, but South African law provides that a woman may obtain maintenance for herself only if it is awarded at the divorce hearing. As the Southern Divorce Court is so loath to consider maintenance questions, it is extremely rare for women to obtain it, unless it has already been agreed between the parties' lawyers and embodied in a consent paper, which the court will then make an order of court when granting the divorce - a fairly rare phenomenon in the Southern Divorce Court. In a sample of some 300 divorce and maintenance variation cases, only one case of maintenance for a wife (disabled, and abandoned after many years of marriage) was seen other than in a consent paper, and the forum of the award could not be ascertained. Africans can opt to divorce in the Supreme Court but it is much more expensive. While legal aid is obtainable for very low income groups, lawyers are reluctant to take African divorces to the Supreme Court on legal aid, as the level of their reimbursements is usually set at the much lower level applicable to the Southern Divorce Court. The Supreme Court, on the other hand, may award maintenance in an unopposed case to a woman who claims it in her summons, though for lower income groups (into which practically all Africans in Cape Town would fall) it would probably require good reason shown why the wife could not work.

13. Where the children are older, additional incentive to the parents to fight for custody may be provided in the short-term by the child's soon-to-be-realised earning capacity (legally at age 16). In the longer term children represent a form (though often imperfect) of insurance against destitution in old age. Short-term hardships to cement the parent-child bond may be regarded as a long-term investment.

14. Evidence on how long the grants take to be processed is contradictory (they all have to go onto a central computer in Pretoria), but depending on which official, social worker or recipient was the informant, the time cited varied from between about two months to 'never'. It would seem on balance that many grants take approximately twelve months to be processed. Grants in Cape Town are available only to those legally in Cape Town.

'FEAR WOMAN': PROPERTY AND MODES
OF PRODUCTION IN URBAN GHANA

Sallie Westwood

Theoretical Perspective

Ghana, like other post-colonial states, is a complex social formation
in which pre-capitalist and capitalist modes of production coexist. It
is not the aim of this paper to discuss the articulation between these
two modes of production at the level of the total social formation, but
to consider this articulation as it is manifest in the capital city Accra
among the urban Ga, who pride themselves on being 'real Accra
people' [1].

Despite the controversy surrounding the concept of mode of
production and the complexities of the debate concerning the
articulation between modes of production, it is my contention that if
we are to attempt a materialist analysis of the relationship between
women and property in urban Ghana our starting point must be the
mode of production [2]. My understanding of a mode of production
is close to Marx's original discussion, that is, a mode of production
is constituted by the forces and relations of production. The forces
of production comprise raw materials, techniques and labour power.
The relations of production comprise the ownership of the means of
production, distribution and exchange, the distinct form of exchange,
and control over the labour process. Thus, a mode of production is
both an economic and a social entity which has a specific historical
and cultural setting.

Property, therefore, is one aspect of the relations of
production and in the context of this paper it is set within a social
formation where the relations of production are both capitalist and
pre-capitalist. In this scheme property mediates the relationship
between gendered subjects and the mode of production and it is this
relationship which ultimately confers power through ownership and
control. By concentrating attention upon property we have opened up
the possibility of unravelling the complex relationship between women
and the mode of production. The complexities are linked to the fact
that it is women who have the major role in reproducing the relations
of production and this work of reproduction provides one set of
inter-relationships between women and the mode of production.

The problems with the concept of reproduction have been

discussed in the work of Edholm, Harris and Young (1977) and more recently in Beechey (1979) and Barrett (1980, pp.19-29), who have all pointed to confusions and contradictions in its meaning and use. In this paper reproduction is understood in three ways: the first is simple biological reproduction, the second is the reproduction of labour power, and the third is the area of social reproduction which I understand as the induction of new members into the dominant ideologies held within the social formation. The first two areas are most essentially the preserve of women's work and are located within specific practices in the domestic sphere. These areas necessarily form a major part of the analysis in this paper.

The articulation between pre-capitalist and capitalist modes of production within Ghana presents a complex totality in which property relations are differently characterised between the two modes, operating under two different systems of sanctions; the one related to custom and convention and upheld within indigenous institutions, and the other related to an imported system of legal precepts which uphold and protect private property. Allot notes that the most important source of law in relation to property, succession, family and marriage is still customary law which applies to particular communities (1970, pp.38-9). In addition, common law and a series of statutes relating to property, succession, marriage and the family are also important. The statutes are based on the initial legal definitions provided by English law.

Property relations within pre-capitalist social formations are embedded in structures of kinship and descent which allow or frustrate access to and control over property in the form of titles to land and resources and positions within prescribed hierarchies. Alongside these structures are the definitions of the jural status of members of the collectivity. These rights and definitions are not independent of the overarching ideologies which, among other things, define and construct the gendered subject, woman. Thus, a patriarchal ideology will have an important effect upon the institution of property.

In contrast with the pre-capitalist formation, under conditions of capitalism, property becomes synonymous with private property. Macpherson, following Marx, argues that the development of capitalism and the market economy necessitated the generalisation of private property as a system which allowed for the alienation and transferability of resources, including land and capital (1973, pp.120-40). Thus, property became bound to material goods rather than the income they secured. However, the ability to justify this extension of private property required a legitimation in a universal and this was found, writes Macpherson in 'labour' which '... was made so much a private exclusive property as to be alienable, i.e. marketable' (1973, p.130). In Marxist terms this heralds the arrival of labour power as a commodity and the commodity form is predicated upon private property.

But the arrival of labour power as a commodity in the colonial context was understood as a male property. As Boserup noted, women agriculturalists were neglected by the colonial administrators who, instead, 'promoted the productivity of male labour' (1970, p.54). This discrimination was repeated in the cities, where jobs in the urban sector, as the outcome of bargains on the labour-market, fell to men and not to women. This legacy survives today and is reinforced through the unequal chances between the sexes in relation to education. Very few women in Ghana are involved in the sale of their labour power in the labour-market. Instead, like the women in this paper, their rights to a livelihood and access to income are bound to their rights to land and their ability to acquire commercial capital. This situation means that in the context of urban Ghana very few women have a direct relationship with the capitalist mode of production through the sale of their labour power. Instead, as we shall see, women are integrated through the sphere of circulation, through the ideological level and through the forms of reproduction. However, the exchange relations which mediate the sale of labour power have had an impact upon the nature of property relations. Property rights and titles may be sold, whereas under pre-capitalist conditions they are not because, as I have noted, access to property rights and titles is located in the kinship network. Thus, our initial task is to understand the defining features of the indigenous Ga system and the way in which they structure women's access to property and, therefore, to control and power in the social formation.

Gender Relations and Ga Social Forms

Historically, the Ga social formation was a theocracy in which three mighty patriarchs controlled and managed the affairs of the state, aided by the lineage heads who were male. Today these men are chiefs and sub-chiefs and are incorporated into the Ghanaian state through a system of salaries. Colonialism created Ga chiefs and brought the Ga together in defence of their economic interests, both against the powerful Ashanti empire and the Europeans. As a coastal people the Ga have had over three hundred years of contact with the European powers: thus it is hardly surprising that 'pure' indigenous forms are difficult to locate [3].

Ga social forms are predicated upon the principle that the lives of men and women are irreconcilably opposed. The gender constructions of male and female that operate within the Ga context have their material form in the separation of men and women into male and female houses, into different religious and ritual roles and in different spheres of economic activity. This differentiation is not a separation of equals because Ga social forms are deeply patriarchal, not only at the level of ideology, but in the institutional expression of male dominance. (Ideology is here understood as a set of material practices, not as a system of ideas and beliefs divorced from the materiality of cultural forms [4].) I do not propose to deal with the debates surrounding the concept of patriarchy here, but to take as a starting point the conception of patriarchy offered by McDonough and Harrison which focuses on two key issues: '... the control of women's fertility and sexuality in monogamous marriage and ... the economic subordination of women through the sexual division of labour (and property) ...' [5]. Clearly, the material expression of these two areas will vary between cultures and it is our task to analyse the precise conditions of existence and modes of variation of patriarchy as they exist in different social formations.

Under the Ga system, women are offered the possibility of a power base of their own deriving from the collectivity and solidarity of their lives in Central Accra. However, while women may exercise authority in their own sphere they are jural minors in Ga society; women, it is said, are 'on the left hand'. Consistent with a patriarchal ideology women are conceived of as irrational and incapable of clear and concise thought, although not incapable of deception and deceit which they supposedly use to gain advantage in their relations with men. It is this construction of woman which forms one element of the phrase of Accra's graffiti, 'Fear Woman', which incorporates the notion of woman as witch, one who will attempt to emasculate the male population, thereby reversing the 'natural' order.

Patriarchal relations are constructed and reproduced through the system of kinship and descent that structures the ability of women to take control of property rights. The kinship system is a crucial site. It is within this set of relationships that women do their work of reproduction, and kinship also defines the relations of production in the pre-capitalist mode of production. It is not possible here to present a detailed account of Ga kinship. I will only focus upon elements crucial to the relationship between women and property. Thus, in the pre-capitalist mode of production, access to the means of production is held within the extended family, and the mode of production and forms of reproduction are brought together in the kinship system. Similarly, in considering the articulation between the two different modes of production, it is within the domestic sphere bounded by the kinship network that the work of reproducing labour power for capital is carried out by women; consequently the two spheres are intricately linked and these links are reproduced through property relations and the domestic labour of women.

Field's enthnographic account characterises Ga kinship as patrilineal whereas Kilson emphasises cognatic affiliations [6]. However, Kilson notes that Ga social forms are deeply contradictory, emphasising both cognatic affiliations and the patrilineage [7]. A cognatic descent system offers greater flexibility because it allows members to emphasise ties that they regard as most useful. But, as we shall see, men appear to be the major beneficiaries of this flexibility.

The most important descent unit is the we, which recruits members at birth and consists of both living members and ancestral shades. A council of elders, which consists of both a male and a female section but in which men have ultimate control, runs the affairs of the family, makes decisions about property rights and transfers, and exercises social control. Each family recognises a family house to which members return for the annual festival of

Homowo (the major Ga festival). Thus:

> We are corporate groups: every we has a name, an estate
> which includes land and titles to office, two sets of names
> which rotate between generations of the offspring of male
> members differentiating full siblings by sex and birth order,
> and often responsibility for the cult of a god which mediates
> relations between family members and the supreme being.
> Although membership in the we depends upon cognatic descent,
> Ga emphasise their patrilineal affiliations (Kilson, 1974,
> p.20).

The we brings together both cognatic and patrilineal affiliations,
expressed by the naming system and the desire to distinguish between
maternal and paternal links. Thus, names are inherited through men,
not through women. To be named is to enter Ga society and to
acquire legitimacy, and at the naming ceremony the child is put first
on the right shoulder of the officiating elder to demonstrate his or
her entry into the patrilineage. Only then is the child put on the left
shoulder, which signifies the mother's family. The child, therefore,
comes first and last into the control of the male line, thus
undermining the women's control over their own fertility, while
enhancing the importance of women as childbearers, and supporting a
definition of woman that is securely tied to her role in biological
reproduction. This is, in the famous account by Engels, the
establishment of father-right: 'The overthrow of mother-right was the
world historic defeat of the female sex' (1972, p.120).

The control that men exercise over female fertility is built into
the Ga definition of kinship and descent, but the expression 'Fear
Woman' suggests that male control is not as well entrenched as the
structures would suggest. Men, dependent upon women to reproduce
the lineage, constantly fear a withdrawal of female fertility. It is the
oldest weapon, given new meaning by the use of modern
contraceptive techniques. Ultimately, the men have little to fear;
women may want fewer children to provide resources for each, but
they do not want to be childfree.

The we not only provides the context for female fertility, but
also distributes titles. The Ga emphasise the patrilineal nature of
succession to office, although Kilson discovered that 60 per cent of
the male members of the Ga council of elders were occupants of these
positions through female and not male affiliations (1974, p.24). The
cognatic principle is, therefore, important and acted upon, but in
the interests of whom? Ga women are an important source of access
to offices that are, however, monopolised by men. Thus, as with
biological reproduction, women are an important vehicle for the
advancement of men.

Succession to office and thus the possibility of access to a state
salary is one area of descent consideration; but the we also
determines access to property rights and titles. Usufruct rights to
land and buildings, which are of major importance to the urban Ga
(alongside the importance of fishing boats and nets for the fishing

community) are distributed among family members on the basis of kinship, seniority and gender. Kilson argues that gender is a secondary consideration, but this needs to be set within the context of a society that gives higher status to men and in which, in the matter of personal property, gender is paramount (ibid., pp.22-4).

Although many urban Ga have family links with the villages outside Accra, they do not see themselves as farmers; they are more interested in acquiring land close to the city to erect buildings for their own use or for letting [8]. This is important to both Ga men and women, but men and women do not build houses together. The stated aim of many trading women is to build their own house and although they can afford building materials, they recognise that land is easier to acquire through usufruct rights than on the open market in Accra. The significance of houses to the urban Ga is underlined by Kilson:

> The social significance of building a house is far greater than the economic implications of converting movable property into immovable property or of deriving fluid capital from rents. It is a means of perpetuating one's identity within the otherwise highly fluid cognatic descent system (1974, p.30).

In relation to personal property, and this may include a house, the gender division among the Ga assumes pre-eminence. Trustees for the property of a deceased person are usually siblings of the same sex. For males the principle governing inheritance of personal property is primogeniture, the eldest son (that is the senior son of a man's senior wife) having the major claim upon the estate. A senior daughter inherits the estate of her mother. However, she does so in competition with her maternal aunts and her female siblings who also have claims on the estate. If the estate is large and includes property such as a house, the claims of siblings are likely to be upheld.

Nowadays, the traditional pattern of inheritance is complicated by modern legal definitions in the form of wills. A will may divide property on a basis different from that outlined above. Legal definitions in Ghana have been influenced by English law and tend to uphold the principle of primogeniture which is traditional for Ga males. A will, based on the notion of private property, is upheld against the conventions of descent. As a system of access to property rights and titles it is clear that Ga kinship is gender specific. If Ga women are to inherit, it is through their mothers or their sisters. Their access to property through men is very limited, but the converse is true for men. As we have seen, their access to titles and salaried state-positions may be through women. Thus, cognatic affiliations may be seen as another area which is used by men to increase their power. This is consistent with the patriarchal nature of Ga social forms and the subordination of women.

Faced with this situation it is hardly surprising that Ga women have sought sources of wealth and power outside the extended family system. In addition, they have attempted through the institution of modern western marriage to increase their access to property and wealth.

The customary form of marriage in Ga society, as we shall see, is deeply penetrated by commodity relationships and the cash nexus. Marriage is understood as an alliance between families and not individuals, and thus cross-cousin marriages which consolidate already-existing alliances are not discouraged; but other kinsmen and kinswomen may not marry. A marriage is contracted by the elders of the two families involved on the basis of a series of gifts and ceremonies which extends through six stages. The impetus for the marriage is the coming of age of the young man when he is given a room in his father's house, that is, access to property. Approaches are then made to the father and elders of a would-be bride. The young woman has no control over this process [9].

It is not the ritual process which is our major focus (although this symbolically reinforces the subordinate status of the women) but the way in which the marriage is transacted through the cash nexus. At each stage of the proceedings, from the 'knocking fee' to the wedding, money and alcohol pass from elders of the groom's family to those of the bride's family. This is the bride-price and the young woman has no access to this money. Marriage payments vary with the status of the families involved; they may be as low as £50 or as high as £200. The mediating role of the cash nexus suggests that a commodity is involved and can, therefore, be alienated freely by those who have control over it. Money is exchanged for the domestic labour of the bride and for her ability to provide the patrilineage with new members.

The bride receives a dowry of cloth and beads from her family. However, there are no strict controls on what her dowry should be as there are for the marriage payments. That her dowry is not given in cash could be said to symbolise her subordinate status.

According to customary practices it is only on the occasion of the first marriage of a Ga male that the complicated series of six stages will be followed; subsequent marriages may be simplified for junior wives. Indeed the Ga language distinguishes between a first wife kpeemoyoo, 'wedded woman', and other wives who are called yoongo 'taken woman'. On the death of the male, the marriage contract may be extended by the subsequent marriage of his wife to one of his full siblings. In such cases the children of the second union are counted as the children of the first husband, if he was an elder sibling. The naming system continues as though he were still alive, revealing again the patriarchal basis of Ga kinship.

Ideally on marriage a Ga man has a responsibility to provide a means of livelihood for his wife in the form of capital with which to trade. A woman is thereby given the means to financial independence and her husband may make no claims on her income. In reality it may be a father, mother, or later in life, her children who provide the means to economic independence for a Ga woman. Clearly, such a system provides a legitimate basis for financial independence which gives women absolute control over their own earnings (cf. Field, 1940, p.56). It does not mean however, that women will not be economically subordinate to men. In many cases, earnings from trade are very small and women have, as noted, only limited access to the labour-market. However, it presents a situation which is in direct contradiction to the patriarchal basis of Ga society. Women will do everything in their power to maximise their trading advantage, as will be discussed in the last section of this paper.

On marriage a woman is obliged to cook and care for the domestic needs of her husband and children, and this defines female responsibilities in producing, nurturing and servicing the present and next generation of workers. A married man gains the exclusive rights to the sexual services of his wife. This exclusive right reinforces his control over female fertility and polygamy extends this control to more than one woman. Ga men are expected to treat all their wives equitably; however, the ground rules are themselves unequal.

Men are supposed to provide the economic support for their wives and children domestically. This 'chop money' provides a focal point for the antagonisms between men and women. Quarrels are frequent between the sexes and the subjects of the quarrels are twofold; the men accuse the women of infidelity while the women accuse the men of irresponsibility in their provision for their wives and children (cf. Azu, 1974, p.102). The subject that each chooses to focus upon is important; the men are evermindful of the sexuality of women and the manner in which it must be controlled.

Women, on the other hand, centre their attention upon the economics of marriage and their access to the earnings of men. Very often Ga women have no option but to maintain the domestic unit, contributing more than their allocated share towards the costs of reproducing labour power. Latterly, women have recourse not simply to the tribunals held by the chief but to a system of law (The Maintenance of Children Act 1965) which applies penalties to men who do not support their wives and children [11]. The women employ both sets of sanctions in an attempt to exercise some form of control over their marriage partners. Thus, even in the case of marriages not sanctioned by the state, the state may intervene directly in the marriage contract to uphold the rights of women to economic support and therefore, to a share in the rewards of the labour power that they reproduce.

Many Ga women express a preference for a western legal marriage. (I use the term legal marriage as the Ga do, to distinguish it from the customary form of marriage which is no less legal but which does not require the sanction of the Ghanaian state.) Ga women expect better economic support from a legal marriage and a share in their husband's property. As one women expressed this: 'No one will steal what is yours and what the man gives you is legal.' The importance of legal marriage for Ga women is, therefore, securely tied to its implications for access to property. However, it is also possible that Ga women may lose through such marriages by becoming economically dependent upon their husbands or because their husbands make claims upon the property that they themselves control. In addition, women may face harassment and intimidation from their husband's relatives after his death, because the suggestion that a husband and wife may share rights in property is, as we have seen, completely alien to the traditional Ga system.

It cannot be assumed that partners to a legal marriage will cohabit: the Ga residence system separates men and women and supports this separation with mystical sanctions, conceived of in terms of the belief that menstruating women would pollute ritual objects in the male compounds. Such a rationale forms part of the expression of a patriarchal ideology (cf. Kilson, 1974, p.14).

Men's houses are less crowded than the women's because each man has his own room, whereas women reside with other women or with their children. Men, therefore, have control over larger areas of physical space through their rights to property in the form of housing. Cooking, washing, and other domestic tasks are carried on in the women's house; thus women have less space and less privacy than their brothers or husbands.

The consequence of this form of residence is to divide men and women, but to offer to each sex the possibility of solidarity. The women especially, living and working together within the compound and the market, offer support and assistance to one another in matters of domestic organisation and child-rearing. Boys are sent to their father's compound at the age of ten, but a mother and daughter grow closer as their life experiences become more shared. Marriage, child-birth, trade, all of these contribute towards a high level of solidarity between women based upon interdependence and reciprocity (cf. Field, 1940, p.8).

Fish, Mediums and Merchandise

Thus far I have shown the complexities of Ga social forms: in the first instance, the kinship system provides the parameters for the forms of reproduction that take place within the Ga social formation. These forms are not independent of the mode of production, or the state, which intervenes in family life, most importantly in relation to the distribution of property rights. On the other hand, for the pre-capitalist mode of production, it is the kinship system and related forms of organisation that constitute the relations of production and define who has access to and control over the means of production, distribution and exchange. I now want to consider the ways in which women are more directly integrated into the mode of production and I will discuss this in relation to three cases; the women of the fishing community, the priestesses and the traders. These cases provide an insight, not only into the relationship between women and property, but also the way in which the capitalist and pre-capitalist modes of production are articulated.

The Fishing Community

The women most securely tied to the pre-capitalist mode of

production are those who are part of the fishing community in central Accra. The Ghanaian fishing industry is divided into a capitalist sector, complicated by the intervention of the state, and the remnants of a pre-capitalist sector [12]. Fishing in the pre-capitalist communities remains an occupational specialisation based upon a community of lineages, not the labour-market. There is no open access to those outside the community to train in fishing. There are acknowledged owners of nets, the 'Big Men' of the fishing community. However, as with traditional land rights, members of the fishing crews are not simply employees, but have rights through lineage affiliations to the use of equipment and a share of the catch. Thus, patrilineal links prevent the existence of wage-labour in a pure form.

The fishing community, although not fully integrated into the capitalist mode of production, is hierarchically organised both on the basis of traditional roles, and on the basis of the ownership and control of the means of production. Net owners receive a share of the catch proportionate to their status, and the crew leader receives a larger share than the younger novices. Often nets and boats are jointly owned by brothers, and skills and property are transmitted from father to sons, although this inheritance is mediated by the interest of all male members of the family in the continuance of the crew.

Women have no access to nets or boats and are thus divorced from the major means of production and subsistence within the community. There are strong taboos against the presence of women at sea, and it is the men who accumulate great wealth from fishing, investing it in housebuilding. However, women do play an important role. First, they reproduce the generations of fishermen, both in the simple biological sense and in the more complex sense of providing domestic services for the labour-power essential to the catch.

Second, the women have the crucial task of selling the share of the catch which falls to their husbands or their father and brothers, and maximising prices in the market-place to secure cash for the community. Thus, they are important in integrating the products of labour into the market system. Usually the women take a proportion of the income for themselves, but this relies upon the ability of men to secure the catch. It is not founded upon the independence of the women, but upon the way in which the spheres of reproduction and production interact. Nevertheless, an astute woman with the assistance of her daughters can accumulate money in her own right over a period of time.

Their involvement in the distribution and exchange of petty commodities means that women are also linked to the dominant capitalist mode of production and it is this which allows them to accrue money, the basis for their independence. The capital that they accrue cannot be invested in the means of production because they cannot own boats and nets. It is rare for a woman from the fishing community to be wealthy, either in terms of the community or beyond it. Women are subordinate and their role in distribution, rather than production itself, reinforces their subordination.

Ga Priestesses

The community of priestesses in central Accra also exemplifies the complex nature of the urban formation and the intersection of capitalist and pre-capitalist forms. The basis of their recruitment, knowledge and training is located in pre-capitalist relations. The priestesses are mediums who interpret, within the framework of the traditional Akom and Kpele cults, the work of the gods of these cults in the material world [13]. But their success owes much to their ability in interpreting events beyond the lineage and within the world of market society, and in providing protection against its malice and apparent anarchy. The priestesses, therefore, are not simply a 'survival', but are integrated into the capitalist system through the ideological work they perform. In a social formation that is still deeply fatalistic, their conception that events are the work of extra-terrestial forces is a powerful legitimation for the existing system. Their discourse has no concepts with which to analyse the real power of capital or the market: unemployment, failure in business, or grinding poverty are seen as individual problems which are the outcome of malevolent forces beyond the control of the individual [14].

The priestesses interpret the world through an arcane knowledge acquired through a period of training. This knowledge and the skills associated with it may be conceived of as the property of the priestesses, or, alternatively, as a certain cultural capital which assumes a commodity form as part of the services that the priestesses exchange for cash [15]. Their knowledge and their craft are given a new value through the cash nexus. Thus they are integrated into the capitalist mode of production through the exchange relationship that mediates their ideological function.

The intervention of the cash nexus also has repercussions for the production and the reproduction of their knowledge. The acquisition of arcane wisdom is also mediated by the cash nexus, in the form of often large payments made to the elders of the cult. This money is usually raised by the women through the extended family network. It is this group of male elders who ultimately control entry into the knowledge and practices of the cult. However, it is the priestesses who decide if a woman is being called by the gods, who train her and who decide when she is ready to leave training. Evidence of a calling may be found in the successive deaths of children, failure in trade, prolonged ill health, or in fits and seizures, especially in the context of ritual occasions.

As a community of women with a common knowledge and practice, the priestesses express a very high level of solidarity as do women in the trading sphere and in the compounds. Their solidarity is expressed through the vocabulary of kinship: they are sisters to each other and daughters to mothers, the latter being older experienced women who train the younger women and hold positions of authority in the hierarchy. To the wider community they present a picture of strength based upon one voice that seeks to support their interests against criticism or derision. Internally, however, the community of priestesses is not an egalitarian one, but one in which the lives of the 'sisters' are closely circumscribed by their 'mothers' from the time that they begin their training. This situation is comparable to the trading sphere where a caucus of powerful traders controls the lives of many other traders.

The novice emerges from her training with a wide variety of skills and knowledge which includes divination techniques, a knowledge of herbal medicine, and a thorough knowledge of the rituals that regulate the relationships between the human world and the world of the gods. She must know the history of the gods and a great variety of songs and dances. The priestess also acquires in training a social and psychological sensitivity that is constantly deployed in interactions with her clients and the wider community.

Following her training a priestess has to establish a place in the community and the trust of her clients, who come in confidence for effective remedies to their problems. She has, therefore, to build a reputation for the accuracy of her divination and predictions as well as her effectiveness as a healer. This requires that she has a firm knowledge of the people among whom she will work. It is thus important to her fortunes that she is able to penetrate the community in some depth. Thus, despite the radical change in their lives the priestesses return to the compounds to live alongside other members of the community.

The priestesses are feared by many who believe that they can promote good or evil in the world, a fear reinforced by the fact that they have a great deal of confidential knowledge about their clients. It is also their proximitity to death that strikes fear into the populace. The priestesses are unanimous in their desire to be disassociated from 'ju ju', the common term for magical practices in Ghana [16]. They consistently stress that they are mediums for the gods and that they themselves cannot work mischief or miracles.

The priestesses are remarkable women. They are astute, perceptive and powerful. Some of them, through their knowledge and the ability to use this knowledge in conjunction with personal qualities become wealthy women. But I would argue (Westwood, 1978, p.252) that a simple economic explanation for their motivation, persistence and power, as advanced by Kilson (1971, pp.171-7), ignores both the complexities of the situation and their own interpretation of these complex phenomena. It is true that the cult leaders and 'executive' priestesses exact a high price for training, and some priestesses I knew commented that if a trainee had a great deal of money her training would be less prolonged. But they also noted that to train quickly the initiate needed 'a big brain'. Thus, if this is the economic rationale to which Kilson refers, it does not affect all the priestesses, but only a few.

Kilson argues strongly that the priestesses are motivated by money and status based on market criteria. Clearly, such a view would be convenient for this paper, but as I have suggested this would ignore the internal coherence of the discourse within which the priestesses operate and, most importantly, it fails to grasp their ideological role in establishing capitalist forms as normal and natural.

Kilson poses the problem at the level of individual gain and entrepreneurship; she has nothing to say about the complex structural position the priestesses occupy. The woman who seeks economic gain above all else will take up a career in trade. It is to this sphere of activity that we now turn.

Ga Traders

Ga women are astute enough to equate independence with economic freedom from men, and trading is fundamental to the realisation of female autonomy. Trading is _the_ female vocation and the major means by which Ga women may accrue wealth and power and through which they are incorporated into the capitalist economy [17]. But the level of their incorporation varies widely with the scale of their operations. Many traders operate on the basis of very small-scale commercial enterprises which only allow them bare subsistence.

Traders are integrated into the capitalist mode of production at the level of circulation, exchanging petty commodities for money. They are part of merchant capital: money is required for an initial outlay of commodities and it is accumulated and invested in order to secure greater rewards. As one trader commented, 'When you have money you do not let it lie idle but buy more goods with it.' Many women start their trading careers with very small amounts of money that they use as capital:

> 'I started when things were not costly, with just £1 that I saved from hawking goods with my mother. I made £1 make £3 and then I made £3 make £6; so, little by little I made money. Sometimes the money fell off, other times I made money.'

In both cases the money to start trading did not come from husbands. In the first case, a very successful trader, the money came from her father which reflected his own commercial background. In the other it was her own initiative which provided her initial capital.

However, capital itself is not sufficient to embark upon a successful trading career; the woman must have access to the organisations of the trading women and, most importantly, access to the major Accra marketplace, Makola market. Sellers are organised on a commodity basis into loosely-structured organisations that seek to protect market prices, for example, the Bread Sellers Association. In contrast to these commodity-based organisations, the Makola Women's Association is highly structured with a formal committee that negotiates protective measures for the traders of Makola market. As one trader commented on the organisation, 'It is important because then people cannot tread on you so easily.'

This organisation has an impact beyond Accra because it attempts to affect the nature of imports and thus what is available throughout the country. In addition, membership has important implications for the allocation of market-stalls and thus entry into the market. Officially, stalls are allocated by the Accra-Tema city council, but the informal contacts between the women are more powerful in deciding who gains access to Makola market [18]. This network, which effectively makes it very difficult for women outside Accra to gain entry, is maintained by Ga women. Thus, Ga women have important advantages offered by their position in Accra. It offers them the possibility of much greater rewards than are available to women traders in other parts of the country. Ga women are clearly aware of this and they protect their rights over the market-place. In a sense, Makola market is regarded as their property and they control access to this property and its division among themselves. Beyond the market-place the solidarity of Ga women is further reinforced by their membership of voluntary organisations that provide economic security for women in cases of hardship, and a system of organised savings which may enable a woman to expand her trading activities. These associations have a predominantly female membership but they do have male members, often in executive positions.

The Makola women, it has been argued, were important to the success of Kwame Nkrumah. Accra was crucial to Nkrumah's survival and the market women were important in disseminating political messages and producing political allegiance for him. This does not mean that the Makola women always gave him unequivocal support. For example, his intention to 'smoke out hoarders and profiteers' did not endear him to the Makola women [19].

Conflicts between the Makola women and the government bring them into direct confrontation with the state. The conflicts are always related to the protection of the market and the freedom to buy and sell for profits and super-profits if possible. Restrictions, centralisation of the distribution of goods and the import of commodities are the key issues that will fire a protest from the traders. In addition, they organise the hoarding of goods and consequently the supply of commodities in an attempt to control the market. The issues, therefore, are property-based and do not threaten capitalism. They reflect a demand for more power for the seller of goods in the market-place. Such action is not based upon an alternative ideological commitment, but securely upon bargaining a better position within the present system.

The links between the wealthy traders and the foreign firms reinforce the dependence of Ghana on foreign interests [20]. An example of these links is provided by the chairwoman of the Makola Women's Association who is a direct link between the United Africa Company (UAC) and the trade in cloth in Ghana. She is part of a caucus among trading women who have important links with the metropolitan firms and who mediate the distribution of goods in Ghana. These women owe their pre-eminence within the market-place to the dominance of foreign capital and they strengthen the grip of these firms over the Ghanaian market. This particular woman had been amply rewarded by UAC who in 1973 gave her the title 'Queenmother of UAC' taken of course, from traditional discourse and holding with it money rewards, and trips to Britain and Holland.

Thus, the opposition by the powerful traders to the government's attempts to control the import and distribution of goods produced in effect a lobby for the multi-nationals.

Despite the advantageous Accra location very wealthy women, having incomes in excess of 10,000 dollars a year, are few in number. Some are middle-level traders whose scale of operations allow them the means of livelihood and additional resources to invest in the education of their children. Many are poor traders who often find themselves in opposition to the powerful market women who control supplies of goods and freedom of entry into the market-place. Although they may aspire to positions of power they recognise that they have only a small chance of success. They could see 'no way forward, no way to prosper' and this was explained by the closed nature of the group who controlled the market-place; 'The big traders, they help each other and they profit by this ... They help one another and they sit on our heads'.

Successive governments have sought to control the Makola women, and committees such as the 1973 Logistics Committee have been set up with the express purpose of providing trading licences to control the flow of goods into Ghana. One of the women I knew well was a wholesaler of provisions who spent a great deal of time negotiating with the government on the matter of import licences. The Committee was finally disbanded due to substantiated evidence of favouritism towards certain traders. This information had been given by a trader prosecuted for hoarding a variety of goods. Her access to these goods by virtue of her liaison with a member of the Logistics Committee had incensed many of the market women [21].

Following the 1979 coup by Rawlings, the army closed down Makola market, or large sections of it. It is a measure of the power of the trading women that, in order to do so, the army had to employ force. This operation was intended to purge racketeers from the distribution network. What followed were massive shortages and a breakdown in the distribution of goods in Ghana which still persists. But the market-place was reinstated under new controls. However, in 1981 Rawlings again seized power. Declaring a campaign against 'profiteering', he continued to institute policies which threatened the power of market women.

Makola women who are successful are not content simply to manage the market-place. They seek other ways of furthering their control over distribution by investing in businesses, very often in the field of transport. Trucks, lorries, taxis and other passenger vehicles declaring the names of trading women are part of the transport system so essential to Ghana. It is these lorries that sometimes carry the message 'Fear Woman', a comment in this context on the economic power of Ga women. One woman I knew had started a contracting company at a time when she was one of the few in Ghana who had any access to building materials. The company, she explained, was for her daughter. Makola women with the resources invest heavily in the fortunes of their children, but very clearly on a gender basis. Boys are to be educated for the professions; girls, on the other hand, are to be businesswomen. In addition, they invest their money in houses in Accra that realise rents and will be inherited by their children. Thus, they are women of property who are fully integrated in the capitalist mode of production as 'merchant princesses'.

The wealthy trading women delight in their ability to exercise power in the local community. At public occasions such as funerals and traditional ceremonies they appear in groups, often dressed alike and they swagger through the crowds, ignoring most people and acknowledging only the powerful. They are an impressive sight with their arms linked and their expensive cloth. They are never to be seen in the company of men. It is these women who are feared and admired and who are the basis of the legendary tales of the autonomy, wealth and power of Ga women. It is they who have fired the popular imagination and there is no doubt that they exercise considerable power, most especially, it must be noted, in relation to the economic lives of other women.

In conclusion, it is possible to underline certain crucial areas in the relationship between women and property. The first of these is the role that Ga women play in simple biological reproduction in which their fertility becomes the property of the patrilineage and consequently they lose, in Engels' terms, their mother-right. Second, due to the system of residence that separates men and women, the process of reproduction of labour power is within the control of women; it is their responsibility and very often they carry the economic burden of the reproduction. Third, women in Ga society are jural minors and consequently they have less access than men to positions of responsibility and control in the Ga context. They cannot be chiefs or patriarchs, but they can provide access for men to these positions which give men greater power and a salary paid by the state. Similarly, they have less access to rights to property and land through the lineage. This is clearly demonstrated in the case of the women within the fishing-community who have no access to the means of production. As a consequence women have to look to the market-place as a source of economic power and the possibility of acquiring property. Some women are very successful in this sphere and they become wealthy owners of land, houses, trucks, large stocks of goods. But for most the market-place is simply a means of livelihood independent of men. Men and women do not share their resources and this tradition has been used by Ga women as a basis for acquiring power and influence both within the Ga community and beyond it. In addition, some Ga women exercise power and influence through their control over a certain arcane knowledge and their ability as priestesses to interpret the world and protect people against its vicarious nature. In these ways, therefore, women are a threat to the over-riding patriarchal nature of Ga forms.

Notes

This paper is partly based upon research carried out in Accra in 1973. I am grateful to Ali Rattansi for reading and commenting upon an earlier draft of the paper, and to Jyoti Chotai for typing the paper.

1. The 1970 Population Census of Ghana gives the total population of Ghana as 8,559,313 with 2,472,456 in the urban areas. The urban population is nearly equally divided between males and females. The Greater Accra region accounted for 824,133 of the urban population. The 1980 Census does not include a volume comparable to the 1960 Tribes in Ghana. From the 1960 data it is possible to obtain a figure for the Ga population of 235,210, that is 3.5 per cent of the population. The Ga of Central Accra represent 15 per cent of the total Ga population. Due to their coastal location the political and economic strength of the Ga far outweighs their numerical strength.

2. For a review of current debates and an interesting discussion see the Introduction by Wolpe in Wolpe (1980). Other relevant discussions may be found in Meillassoux (1981) and Sacks (1979).

3. For a more detailed history and ethnography of the Ga, see Reindorf (1966); Field (1940); Kilson (1974); Bruce-Myers (1927-8, pp.69-76, 167-73).

4. Cf. Althusser (1971, pp.123-73); Hirst (1976).

5. McDonough and Harrison in Kuhn and Wolpe (1978, p.40). For a review of the debates surrounding the concept of patriarchy see the article by Beechey (1979).

6. Field (1940). Kilson notes, in relation to Ga kinship, 'I consider it is cognatic not only at the level of ideology but at the level of social transaction', (1971, p.7).

7. Cf. Azu (1974, p.18).

8. The urban Ga may, however, be interested in becoming absentee landlords or 'capitalist' farmers who will pay a labour force to work the land. Women are interested in marketing agricultural products.

9. For a discussion of the exchange of women between men see Rubin in Reiter (1975, pp.171-85).

10. For the wealthy Christian sections of the community the customary marriage system has become integrated with the western form of marriage, incorporating an engagement ring and an elaborate white wedding.

11. For a more detailed discussion see Lowy (1977).

12. For an extended discussion of the fishing industry in Ghana see Lawson et al. (1974).

13. For an extended discussion of Ga religion see Field (1961) (originally published in 1937) and, in relation to the Kpele cult, Kilson (1971).

14. This discussion is based upon a more detailed analysis to be found in Westwood (1978, pp.250-71 unpublished PhD thesis, University of Cambridge).

15. The idea of knowledge as property is not new; for a recent example of work using this idea see Murphy (1980, pp.193-207). The notion of cultural capital is borrowed from the work of Bourdieu, see for example, Bourdieu (1974, pp.71-112).

16. The priestesses are anxious to dissociate themselves from witchcraft and malevolent magic. There is an interesting comparison here with the work of Ngubane on Zulu medicine where she notes that night sorcerers and malevolent practices are male phenomena. See Ngubane (1977, pp.31-2).

17. Boserup notes in relation to West Africa that women may constitute as much as 80 per cent of those involved in trade and commerce (1970, p.88). Nypan (1960) recorded that 85 per cent of stall holders in the Accra markets were women. It is interesting to compare the Ghanaian situation to that of the migrant women of East Africa described in the work of Nelson (1978).

18. This is confirmed by Roberston (1974, p.662).

19. For a comment on this see Woddis in Gutkind and Waterman (1977, p.267).

20. For a discussion of the process of underdevelopment in Ghana see Howard (1978), and for the post-independence period Killick (1978).

21. This committee was set up under the National Redemption Council which was in power in 1973 under the leadership of Colonel Acheampong, who was deposed in a palace coup in 1978 by Colonel Akuffo.

9   SUBJECT OR OBJECT? WOMEN AND THE CIRCULATION OF VALUABLES IN HIGHLANDS NEW GUINEA [1]

Marilyn Strathern

> There is an economics and a politics to sex/gender systems
> which is obscured by the concept of 'exchange of women'. / We
> need... an analysis of the evolution of sexual exchange along
> the lines of Marx's discussion in Capital of the evolution of
> money and commodities. (Rubin, 1975, pp.204-5 sentences
> transposed)

Many people in the Highlands of Papua New Guinea today (late
1970s) enjoy a substantial cash income, primarily from the proceeds
of coffee. Certainly in the central Highlands areas almost every
household has plantings in this lucrative crop. Cash sometimes buys
food, but by and large is channelled into non-subsistence ventures of
an often ceremonial nature (cf. P. Brown, 1970; Finney, 1973; A.
Strathern, 1979). In fact how money is spent is more interesting
than how it is earned – and reveals a dramatic contrast between
certain societies of the region. This concerns the differing
involvements of men and women.

The Highlands were first explored in the 1930s, and have been
subject to 'development' since the late 1950s. Nearly everywhere
coffee is planted by households along the pattern of food production,
that is, by the joint labour of husband and wife. Nearly everywhere
men monopolise the major portion of earnings, and use money for
ceremonial gift-giving. Money is also diverted into non-traditional but
prestigious forms of purchase, such as trucks or business
enterprises with an investment appeal. However, relations between
the sexes over the disposal of income has not followed similar lines.
On the contrary, the extent to which women handle large sums of
money varies. In some areas women have set up banking and finance
corporations on a public scale; yet in spite of easy communciations
along the Highlands Highway and in spite of very similar
'development' conditions in other areas, the response has so far been
localised and is not a general one. This is more than a matter of
history. At least in part explanation must be sought in the structure
of relations between the sexes.

Such relations are concerned with the power that men and
women hold over one another in specific roles, with the organisation

158

of production, and with the definition of sex-based activities. They are also embedded in a symbolic structure which invests what men and women do with certain meanings. These meanings are not simply derived from or representative of day to day interaction; rather, they may make that interaction a metaphor for other things. Throughout the Highlands a sexual division of labour makes women responsible for daily horticultural tasks, men for intermittent ones and for the conduct of public life. Gender everywhere provides a powerful source of symbolism, so that contrasts between what women and men do may stand for contrasts between domestic and political action or between mundane and spiritual states. There has in fact been considerable confusion in the ethnographic record over the relationship between symbolic constructions that turn on gender and the 'position' of men and women vis-a-vis one another. The analytical distinction is important in the present case.

People's reactions to innovation are partly influenced by the significance they read into particular items or events; thus the spending of money is invested with meaning. These meanings may or may not be directly concerned with status or the perception of power relations. They will however constitute a cultural logic to be taken on its own terms. Paradoxically, following this dictum will involve running counter to those analyses that take as their starting point women as actors on the social stage.

Two Contrary Cases

Central Highlands horticulture is based on sweet potato and other root crop cultivation, and on the domestic pig. People may live in homesteads scattered through clan territories, or else in villages. Clans which for certain purposes define themselves as a body through common patrilineal descent are generally middle-order units in a hierarchy of bounded groups (tribes, clans, subclans, lineages). They may act as units in fighting and in contracting marriages. Sometimes members of a clan live together. In other parts, villages more heterogeneously composed - perhaps containing representatives from several clans - emerge as the salient political entities. Political leadership rests with self-made big men, who gain prestige through their prominence either in warfare or in oratory and large scale cermonial exchanges of wealth between groups.

Proper cross-societal comparison is beyond my scope (cf. P. Brown, 1978). Initially I reduce comparison to a simple contrast between two cases: the Daulo region in the Eastern Highlands Province and Hagen in the Western Highlands, some eighty miles along the Highlands Highway.

Lorraine Sexton (1982; in press) has described Daulo women's reactions to men's deployment of cash in ceremonial exchange and business. There women have developed their own savings and exchange system called in Pidgin <u>wok</u> <u>meri</u> ('women's work/enterprise'). Small groups drawn from the co-resident lineage wives of a village protect their savings from the depredations of their husbands by banking them collectively. They use the capital for business ventures and for exchanges with similar women's groups.

An extensive network of 'mother' groups sponsoring 'daughter' groups (as they are called) has spread over the last twenty years into several districts and thus into different language groups of the Eastern Highlands and Chimbu Provinces. In Daulo the organisation of a wok meri group is based on a collectivity – the wives of lineage mates – that traditionally works together on other occasions also. There may be more than one such group in a village, each under its 'big woman' (a new title used in the movement). Established groups sponsor 'daughter' groups in other villages by making them loans that are eventually repaid when they become 'mothers' themselves. A complementary set of symbols turns on affinity, so that 'mothers' and 'daughters' also see themselves as bride-givers and bride-receivers to each other, the bride being the wok meri expertise itself.

An important point to be drawn from Sexton's fascinating analysis concerns the way this activity is conceived. Women regard themselves as garnering and safeguarding their incomes – men are cast as spendthrifts, concerned only with short term consumption. There is some competition between spouses' demands on a household's income, and men have investment interests of their own. Nevertheless Daulo men also respond to women's efforts; they respect women's claims to dispose of some of the cash income [2], and further support groups with expert advice, acting as bookkeepers and truck drivers. A male 'chairman' may act as a group's public spokesman, although the focus of such occasions remains the women's exchange transactions, and money is given and received in their name. Sexton reports (in press) that after one women's ceremony in which thousands of participants and thousands of kina (PNG currency; 1k = c.75p) were mobilised, men of one clan were so impressed that they urged all their wives to join the movement. Through such ceremonies a group calls in its loans, and with the accumulated capital may purchase wholesale stores, trucks licensed to carry passengers and cargo, or contemplate buying a section of an expatriate-owned coffee plantation.

Superficially, 'development' in Hagen appears similar. The same small tradestores mushroom overnight; men and women come to the roadside to sell coffee; ten-ton trucks and numerous passenger vehicles are mobile evidence that Hageners, like the people of Daulo, spend on investment projects. Yet in the late 1970s there was nothing to parallel wok meri. Whether from the money of men or women, those trucks are invariably purchased in the names of subclans or lineages, conceptually male.

Like Daulo women who support men's businesses, as well as their own, Hagen women contribute to men's enterprises. Yet Hagen women are also typified – especially by men – as spendthrifts. Whereas Daulo women's stereotype of men as squanderers of resources seems a piece of contextual rhetoric invoked in wok meri ideology, the similar stereotype Hagen men hold of women seems to support the fact that Hagen women engage in no major financial dealings of their own. Here men take the lion's share of coffee proceeds, arguing that large sums of money are tantamount to 'valuables' and thus fall into the male domain; women are further urged to contribute what small savings they have scraped together towards specific ventures being organised by their husbands. That on the whole women do so quite willingly is analytically beside the point. The point is that money is taken off them in two rounds – first when large sums are categorised as male wealth, and second when their modest savings are seen as swelling men's collective enterprises. In the context of group prestations or vehicle purchase it is men's 'names' that are displayed.

An immediate framework for analysis suggests itself: that what crucially differs here is women's participation in public affairs, the amount of control they exercise over wealth and thus also the very relationship between the product of their labour and rights to its disposal. This suggests examining the nature of ownership and mechanisms of appropriation, and thus claims to property as an index of the extent to which women act in their own right.

Indeed, one stimulating reappraisal of Highlands kinship (Lindgren 1978) focuses on relations of production between the sexes, that is, how women's labour is appropriated (1978, p.6). It is addressed to situations of the Hagen rather than Daulo type [3].

> Exchange transactions become a way to appropriate women's surplus labour and reproduce the whole agnatic structure and ideology... (having) as their effect the recruitment of children to their father's clan and the rights of women to confer property on their offspring are never structurally recognized. The role of surplus is the recreation of the agnatic ideology and not to give women equal rights in property and people (Lindgren, 1978, p.11, my emphasis).

Women's claims to property thus appear as a function of the success to which men appropriate wealth to perpetuate hegemony through agnation. Kinship (specifically descent constructs) is not an autonomous system, he argues, but must be examined as an ideology 'which serves to legitimate and hide relations of inequality and exploitation in the process of the material and social reproduction' (Lindgren, 1978, p.1) [4]. Yet he is replacing the autonomy of kinship with the autonomy of property relations. The concept of property remains unexamined in his account.

Lindgren is absolutely right to point to women's labour as a major constraint on Highlands production, while the conceptualisation of male interests leads to this labour being devalued. Lindgren's concern is with ceremonial exchange, but in Hagen at least there is obvious continuity between traditional prestations and non-traditional group projects insofar as in both cases boundaries are drawn around men's collective interests. And it is also clear that in modern Hagen, with women's earnings appropriated twice over, the introduction of cash has in some ways perpetuated the apparent devaluation of their labour. Yet this whole analysis raises questions. How can we conceive of women being 'deprived' of 'rights' over the disposal of property when such rights appear not to have been allocated them in the first place [5]? More crucially, what do we mean by 'property'?

In fact, it would be misleading to imagine that the difference between Hagen and Daulo is to be grasped only in terms of women's control over resources. At the same time I also want to indicate why we find this style of argument compelling (cf. Holy and Stuchlik, 1981). The problem these two cases appear to raise for the analysis of women and property relations may well include problems of our own making.

Property and Persons

What compels us to talk of labour being undervalued or of rights not recognised? Embedded in our notion of 'property' is that of 'rights' exercised over others or at the expense of others, constructs I have used myself (e.g. M. Strathern, 1972). But it carries certain assumptions. Such a western concept of property [6] entails a radical disjunction - property relations are represented not as a type of social relations but as a relationship between people and things (cf. O'Laughlin, 1974; Bloch, 1975). The disjunction between people and things can also be merged with that between subject and object [7]. As subjects people manipulate things; they may even cast others into the role of things insofar as they can hold rights in relation to these others. In the western folk antithesis between treating someone as 'a person' and 'as an object', a person is defined as an acting subject, recognisable therefore by his or her rights, which should properly include control over the products of labour. Lindgren consequently takes as axiomatic women's right to confer property, so that prevailing Highlands ideologies are a 'misrepresentation of the objective fact' of women's labour input (1978, p.7, my emphasis). Discussion of social relationships in terms of control over property, I would argue, is also a covert discussion of how far this or that category can act as 'persons'.

This conflation may work for us, and for other cultures too [8]. In the Highlands, however, ideas of personhood are not necessarily bound up with a subject-object dichotomy nor with its attendant issues of control. This is a topic already discussed in detail for Hagen (M. Strathern, 1980; 1982; A. Strathern, 1981). I want to proceed to its corollary.

It is the western dichotomy between subject and object which often informs the anthropological desire to make women the proper subjects for analysis, to treat them in our accounts as actors in their own right. We are terrified of rendering them as mere 'objects of analysis' because this diminishes our own humanity. It makes us uncomfortable to come across ethnographic contexts in which men or women - it is usually women - appear to be treated as objects. The analysis of bridewealth arrangements in which women are exchanged for wealth struggled with this issue for years, and the methodological solution, that it is after all only rights in women being exchanged, reveals the premise of the debate. Such a solution allows of course that women's status as persons remains intact. The point is that when women – or some aspects of their social personality – are exchanged for objects, we fight shy of indigenous equations between women and wealth.

Central Highlands marriages are accompanied by bridewealth. Clan groups, sets of men bound by patrilineal ideology, may define themselves through the exchange of women as they do through the exchange of wealth in general (Rubel and Rosman, 1978). Reciprocity may be direct (women for women) or indirect (wealth is initially given in the stead of women whatever the subsequent transactions). Items used in bridewealth are also used in periodic prestations between clans or villages – pigs, shells, money, perhaps plumes. People themselves may see women moving between groups exactly as wealth moves. It was systems of this kind that preoccupied Lévi-Strauss (1949), and he has been criticised for an androcentric treatment of women as mere objects in his analysis. Restoring women to a proper place frequently comprises converting them back into subjects – looking at their active participation, considering their decision-making powers. Van Baal's (1975) otherwise brilliant essay on women as 'objects or behaving as objects' takes this perspective.

The assumption behind such a restoration is that if women are passed between groups of men, equated with the wealth that flows between them, then they are being treated as objects themselves. As objects they must be a form of property, an instrument in the social relations created by those with rights in or over them. As objects women are denied subjective status, and to rescue them from occupying a comparable place in our analyses we have to describe those situations in which they do act as subjects. This validates our prior distinction between subject and object – one can deny that women are really objects (things) by pointing to their acting as subjects (persons).

Whatever the advantages of such an approach in drawing attention to neglected areas of data, it does not help the interpretation of cultural equations between women and wealth. Such an equation is explicit in Hagen. Some of the commonest female names are terms for shell valuables; in the 1960s I heard fathers refer to their daughters as tradestores – that is, business ventures; women are also acknowledged sources of sustenance, likened to the sweet potatoes they grow. Men may thus compare women with valuables they exchange with one another; with the investment potential that lies in the ties created by a woman marrying from one clan into another; and with the very products of female labour. Nor do women find anything odd or objectionable in such equations. It is important to add that, as the agents who manipulate wealth, men are not envisaged in this manner. It is not people in general who are likened to wealth, but women in particular. We would seem to have an obvious case for considering that Hagen women are classified as 'property'. Moreover, men give as a rationale for the power they claim over women the fact that males are the 'owners' of land, pigs and shells (as in the case O'Laughlin (1974) discusses). Yet for all that, the western corollary does not follow: these Hagen concepts are

<u>not</u> tantamount to a conceptualisation of women as 'objects'.

One reason has already been given: whatever the outcome for power relations, men's role as transactors does not compromise women's personhood, for the definition of personhood is not tied up with manipulation of things. It is the second reason that I want to pursue. What do we mean when we refer to a cash income or to exchange valuables as 'property'? Are these wealth items 'objects' in the western sense? Because if wealth items are not objects, then a vernacular equation between wealth and women does not make them into objects either. That is why 'things' cannot be isolated from the context that gives them meaning (cf. pp.158-9). Highlands valuables, including money, are not always treated as objects in the western sense, and are not to be understood as 'property' if property entails objectification. Rubin (1975, p.174) makes the point in general; indeed this piece of anthropological insight has been part of our analytical repertoire for over fifty years.

Property as Gift

However passive a role women play in his models (MacCormack, 1980), Lévi-Strauss never meant to imply that because women were exchanged between sets of men they were less than persons (1969, p.496; cf. Schwimmer, 1973, p.187). As Wilden puts it: 'It is not the male or female persons who are exchanged... What is exchanged is the <u>sign</u> they <u>re</u>-present' (1972, p.250; original emphasis). As such they are to be analysed along with other information-bearing exchange items. To know what messages are carried by the items used in transactions, we need to understand the nature of transaction itself.

Here I take up Gregory's (1979; 1980) position that in modern Papua New Guinea we are dealing with a political economy of a type where relationships are characterised by both gift-debt and commodity-debt [9].

> A gift is nothing more than the social form of a thing or a worker in much the same way that a commodity is a social form of a thing or worker. But a gift is different from a commodity in that whereas a commodity exchange establishes a relation between the objects of a transaction, gift exchange establishes a relationship between the subjects (Gregory, 1979, p.404).

The contexts in which women are equated with wealth are primarily those of ceremonial exchange, and these set up relationships based on gift-debt. Gift exchange establishes a relationship between subjects because 'gifts are inalienable whereas commodities are not' (1979, p.404).

Gregory (1980, p.640) quotes both Marx and Mauss to this effect. Analyses of exchange relationships have repeatedly returned to Mauss's essay of 1925 [10], and we are well used to his proposition that exchange items create bonds between persons 'since the thing itself is a person or pertains to a person. Hence it follows that to give something is to give part of oneself (1954 (1925), p.10) [11]. An 'identification' is set up between the person and the thing (Schwimmer, 1979) [12]. If a thing exchanged may stand for an aspect of a person, it follows that when people are exchanged they may at that point stand not just for themselves but for aspects of personal substance or social identity located at another level. They are equated with 'things', yet their symbolic referent is not a thing in the sense of an object, but aspects of personhood.

Exchange systems are elaborated throughout Melanesia [13], and it appears generally true that the manner in whch such aspects are 'located' or symbolised takes one of two forms. The one involves metaphoric symbolisation and the other metonymic. In the former, wealth or assets (a clan estate, valuables of certain kinds) stand for an aspect of intrinsic identity, for agnatic status or 'name' for example. They cannot be disposed of or withdrawn from the exchange system without compromising that identity. In the latter, over a second class of things (other valuables, personal possessions) people exercise proprietorship to the extent that they have personal rights of disposal. Such items are frequently regarded as the products of the person's labour, creativity or energy. But although disposable, they are not 'alienable' in the way that commodities are alienable. Labour remains forever part of the person; disposal of such products is construed as a loss to the producer, in the sense that the labour is not purchased but rather the person compensated.

In some systems different items may fall into these two classes - non-disposable clan land may be contrasted for example with disposable personal possessions (cf. Salisbury 1962, pp.61-65). But it is also the case that the same valuables may operate as now one type, and now the other. In an exchange a gift may metaphorically stand for the donor's 'name', or it may metonymically represent his or her labour. In this second context the quality of detachability (the disposable 'part' of a person) makes these items look on the surface like 'objects'.

But this object-like appearance may be deceptive. As part of a person, the removal of these things involves a loss: compensation is paid to the person, not a price for the thing. It follows that in this situation there need be no subject-object dichotomy of the western kind [14]. There are 'things', but people are not differentiated by the extent to which they act as subjects or are treated as objects (cf. Giddens, 1971, p.11). Although individual items can be permanently disposed of, the system requires that the item is replaced by some token of equivalence that takes its metonymical place, standing for the input of labour or creativity. Relationships may be created by the movement towards compensation this entails, as they may by the metaphorical messages about the person carried by other valuables. In either case things stand for aspects of the person - for their actions or their name - and through exchange alter the respective standing of partners in relation to one another. They cannot be opposed to persons, as our own subject-object matrix postulates.

In what follows I suggest that when Hagen women are equated with wealth and become gifts in exchanges between men, their symbolic referent is an understanding of personhood metonymically constructed. That 'the person' appears to be a male subject is to be noted. For the moment let me stress Gregory's point.

> Where the producer is a clan and the produced are people, the inalienable gifts are people. This point is the essence of Lévi-Strauss's argument that women are the 'supreme gift' ... Women as gifts are the inalienable property of the clan that produced them (1980, p.641).

We should not be particularly disconcerted if women are compared with shells or tradestores. To imagine they are being treated as objects is based on our own antithesis between persons and things, a false premise in the circumstances. Falsity lies not in the equation between women and wealth, but in the implicit equation between wealth of this kind and 'property' as we understand the term.

The Circulation of Women and Valuables

The circulation of women and the nature of reciprocities set up by marriage, bridewealth and payments to maternal kin continue to figure in accounts of Highlands societies (e.g. D. Brown, 1980; Feil, 1980; 1981; Le Roy, 1979a; Sillitoe, 1979).

These accounts generally - with the exception of Feil 1980 - take their cue from the ideological context - that it is groups of men who exchange between themselves valuables/women. This does not mean that all wealth objects are classified as female; on the contrary men may exchange overtly 'male' as well as 'female' items. Nor is the source of wealth only conceptualised as male; in some maternal payments, for example, it may be seen as female. The full issue of what Herdt (1980) calls the 'genderising' of valuables and of donor-recipient relationships is too complicated to go into here. The specific issue to consider is the exact nature of the equation between wealth and women.

When Hagen clansmen celebrate their achievement in giving away pigs and shells to a recipient clan, they are not only presenting themselves to an audience but through the mediation of the gifts forcing on the recipients recognition of their renown. The purchase of a truck has similar implications, though here the full exchange sequence may be incomplete: the truck may display the wealth and strength of its owners without being used as a direct instrument of social relationships with others. In both cases however clan resources have been converted into items that act as visible carriers of messages about its success.

Conversion implies appropriation, and appropriation there certainly is. In one sense Hagen men convert women's labour in growing vegetables and looking after pigs into wealth items over which they have ideological control, and this conversion is done through separating ceremonial exchange (transactions) from the domain of production. But this appropriation does not entail alienation as such [15]. When a woman acquiesces in her husband's demands that a pig be given to some partner of his, the pig may be looked at from three points of view. The original pig was a result of the husband's 'transactions'. It was also 'produced' – it fed off the husband's clan land. Finally, it was cared for by the wife, and her labour requires compensation. The simple removal of the pig from her care to its display on the ceremonial ground, where it is marked as a wealth item, does not remove the consequent obligation between husband and wife. At some point the husband must acknowledge his wife's labour – generally through seeing that some of the returns on that specific transaction reach her. Pigs are much more visible repositories of women's labour than gardens, and women's prestige is measured in part by the number of pigs they have to care for. Although the husband's 'name' is on them, he should replace the animals he has taken from his wife's stalls. In this sense her labour is not alienated.

The manufacture of shell valuables is not counted as labour in the same way: the input of effort is in terms of how men manage to attract them to themselves. They stand much more prominently than pigs for men's 'names' (cf. A. Strathern, 1979, p.534). Nowadays men try to make money, whose production in respect of their relations with women is like pig production, into something closer to the procurement of shells. Nevertheless they cannot ignore the demands of women, who expect a return on any money they contribute. Women thus do not look for financial profit – the increment that raises men's names [16] – from the running of trucks and passenger vehicles; they do expect help with transport for themselves to go to market or visit connections of their own.

In spite of tension between the sexes over the deployment of wealth, then, 'alienation' as such is not at issue. In spheres of exchange pigs, shells and money stand for aspects of the person. But what precisely are these aspects?

To follow through the logic of the gifts: if women themselves may act as wealth, then what persons are they representing? Traditional Hagen exchanges that combined both pigs and shells constructed the personhood of the donors somewhat ambiguously. The clan body could be looked on as a primarily male entity, represented in transactions with shells, or as composed of both men and women, as in the transaction and production of pigs. When women, as sisters and wives sharing substance or identity of interest with men, move between clans, we may argue that it is part of themselves that men are exchanging. Women may be likened either to shells or to pigs, and the self that is being exchanged refers to the clan either as a set of men or as a collectivity of men and women. In the same way as things act as mediators in gift exchange, Hagen women sent or received in marriage may thus stand for aspects of what I call the 'clan person'. From the viewpoint of women, aspects of themselves are bound to their identification with their clan brothers.

Clan groups that share a common substance thus see themselves as linked to one another through the marriages of women. Women are 'roads' for exchanges, and elaborate group prestations follow the pattern of marital alliances. The antithesis between and necessary conjunction of internal and external sources of fertility and strength (cf. Weiner, 1978, pp.182-3) is expressed in a contrast between 'male' and 'female' contributions. Ambivalence surrounds the notion of external sources – they are regarded as both intrusive and expansive. Yet clan identity is ultimately constructed prior to its exchanges with other clans, through its association with its clan territory for example [17], and exchanges confirm rather than alter the nature of this identity.

When men give wealth to one another, under the rubric of war compensation or child payments, or simple ceremonial exchange, the donor is giving himself. As a transactor the donor is male (women as such do not transact with valuables; when they do, they are 'like men'). This self, I have argued, may be constructed either as purely male, or also as taking into account the combined efforts of husbands and wives together. The difference between shells and pigs stands for these different emphases in identity. A complementary logic turns on a distinction inherent in all Hagen wealth objects. It is in essence similar to that Damon (1980) has described for Woodlark Island ceremonial (kula) objects, some of which carry a person's name and others of which represent his labour. The distinction is between that aspect of a wealth item which metaphorically stands for one's (and one's clan's) name, for inherent resources, and that aspect of the same item that is metonymically acquired by and attached to the person but is also detachable and can be given to others [18]. This latter characteristic is expressed in the Hagen phrase that wealth is 'on the skin'.

At several points reference has been made to clan land. Hagen land is much bound up with the male person, a given, non-disposable fact of identity. But it is made productive through labour (A. Strathern, in press). Women symbolise that labour. In this sense clan strength is necessarily composed of the efforts of men and women together. Hagen wealth objects represent (metaphorically) a capacity for exchange itself which is male: it is inappropriate for women to handle wealth publicly – the male person's transactor status is bound up with identity and prestige derived from clan connections. But to the extent that wealth items are also (metonymically) 'on the skin', they can be differentiated from the actor as 'things' – objects in his possession which actually constitute part of his resources but which he can also dispose of. They are thus both part of the clan person (the male actor) and differentiated from him (on his skin).

Wealth items – both pigs and shells – thus refer at the same time to given, ancestral, land-based sources of strength, and to the efforts and creativity of people, their own 'efficacy' (Goodale, 1978). In the first sense wealth indicates attributes intrinsic within the donor (M. Strathern, 1979); in the second sense wealth is detachable, 'on the skin'. In so far as the first set of attributes are conceptually 'male', this detachability is in turn symbolised as 'female'. Thus whereas the production referent of pigs is a constant reminder of combined male and female effort, shells ordinarily thought of as exclusively 'male' are also given 'female' attributes at the point of exchange. They are decorated, for example, with the red colour associated with women (cf. A. Strathern, 1979, p.535). As a metaphor, shells are unambiguously male; at the point of detachment their metonymical relationship to the person is signalled. As for the trucks purchased with money, they are 'male' insofar as they represent (metaphorically) clan prestige; the women's effort that went into raising the money is recognised in their rights to usufruct. Yet it is only men's names that the vehicles can carry: men's and women's productive efforts are separately constituted.

On a different scale women make small gifts to one another of netbags and ornaments. Here they give part of themselves (eminently female things in the case of netbags, associated with the womb) yet there are covert connotations of maleness (netbags are receptacles for valuables, food grown on the clan land).

The dual gender [19] of all these items rests on a perceived contrast between their referring to intrinsic attributes of the donor, and to things differentiated from him or her. It is their cross-sex attributes that signal that they are to be conceived as separate from the actor. The symmetry between men's objects (pigs and shells publicly transacted) and women's (netbags, ornaments) is not perfect, however, because women's items do not constitute 'wealth' in the same way. Instead, as we have seen, women themselves may be regarded as like wealth objects. When women are exchanged as wealth they could stand for the 'name' of their own clan, but this metaphorical possibility is heavily overlaid by their metonymical status. They are both members of their natal clan, an identity never relinquished, and leave it to reside elsewhere. They who grow up on the land of one clan but feed their children on the land of another, mediate between the two. In this they have the character of a disposable 'thing'. Females do not substitute for or stand for males in this sense, but like wealth 'on the skin' are to be differentiated from them.

The symbolic construction of wealth as detachable as well as intrinsic has probably been of great importance in the development of exchange institutions on the scale found in Hagen and its immediate neighbours. At a general level Hagen also shares features here with several Highlands societies. In the circulation of valuables symbolising aspects of the person, people themselves may stand for particular social entities (cf. Wagner, 1977; 1978). The mechanism which separates signifier and signified is often that of gender discrimination. Thus it is common in these patrilineally-oriented societies for special attention to be paid to maternal sources of nurture [20]. The woman is a source of nourishment and stands for the productive relationship between her clan and her husband's. In this sense she may be truly likened to the valuables that flow between them – either as compensation for her or to follow the road she has opened up. To women travelling along this road, men may stand for rootedness, for the soil that is another base for nurture. Women are 'persons' in these systems; yet the extent to which their personhood as represented in exchanges is tied to that of men in fact varies, and Hagen will not do as a general model for the Highlands as a whole.

Idioms of Investment

Nash has analysed the impact of money on the traditional currencies of Bougainville, where 'shell money stands for people' (1981, p.118). 'Once shell valuables lost their exclusive reference to 'person' and became substitutes for objects, the inclusion of them into a single system made people like objects' (1981, p.118). She describes the changing meanings of payments associated with marriage and sexual services. While this process may have begun in certain aspects of Highlanders' lives, to a large extent money has been absorbed into a gift-debt system. Although it is used as an instrument of commodity exchange, in the context of ceremonial prestations it acts as an instrument of gift exchange. Here gifts retain their reference to persons; my argument is that the way in which the person is symbolically constructed has considerable bearing on the nature of men's and women's participation.

If Hagen women are like valuables, both part of and detachable from the clan body, then there is no ideological locus for them to act as public manipulators of wealth, any more than they can act as full representatives of (metaphorically identified) clanship. Their very detachability points to a source of nurture and productivity separate from men's. We can consequently make sense of the fact that by and large Hagen women concur in the male disposition of wealth. They do not organise themselves and money is taken off them, to be channelled into male enterprises. Yet when these enterprises are collectively defined, it is with pride that women make their small contributions, reveal what they have managed to save, and thus their own significance as a separate source of wealth.

Metaphorically constructed identity thus makes the Hagen 'person' male. In this sense women as well as men have a male identity. They are nurtured (mbo) clan members. Their efforts and achievements, however, are to different ends. Whereas men augment this maleness through their transactions, women make the increment detachable. In this metonymic sense men's 'on the skin' attributes are female. Whereas women are pre-eminently detachable, men become so only in specific contexts. Hageners draw analogies between life-time bridewealth gifts for women and death compensation for men (A. Strathern, 1982). Until he subsequently becomes a clan ghost, the dead man loses his metaphorical status in relation to clan identity, and must be treated metonymically, as a detached 'thing'.

These constructions are not, however, found throughout the Highlands. On the contrary, inspite of the general claims I have made in relation to notions of personhood as such (p.165), it does not follow that gender distinctions will be used in only one symbolic way. Elsewhere, for example, female elements may stand not in a metonymic relationship to male, but be metaphorically placed. In one

170

such system (the Southern Highlands Wiru) wealth is regarded not as 'on the skin' but as the very skin itself. The distinction between transactor and producer does not apply to the same extent, and women may give and receive valuables in their own and their children's name. I would not argue that Daulo must be like Wiru; I would argue that it is to such differences in the way wealth symbolises aspects of personhood that we must understand the differing responses Hagen and Daulo people have had to money and investment.

To a greater extent than Hageners, Wiru women initiate small exchanges on their own account and are recipients of wealth items. Wealth is exchanged in the context of Wiru affinal-maternal prestations in the form of 'child payments' or payments 'for one's skin'. The referent is not a clan body but the personal body embedded within a matrix of kin relations. People manipulate wealth to stand for both maternal and paternal aspects of themselves, different items carrying different meanings. Yet as the cycle of exchange develops these differences are merged, so that, when a couple receive payments as the maternal kin of their grandchildren, mother's father becomes identified with mother's mother. Women create their substance in the bodies of their children, and at the same time are ideologically cast as givers and receivers of the wealth which stands for this. Here wealth can stand for bodily substance ('skin'), and if there is an equation between women and wealth it is because wealth is a metaphor for what is regarded as the feminine origin or nature of that substance. In this context [21] gift exchange ties persons back into the relationships that produced them: it does not construct the 'female' parts of the person as detachable. If anything, other aspects of the exchange system present detachability as a male not female quality.

The women of Daulo today manage, save and invest considerable sums of money through operations ceremonially staged on a vast public scale. The accompanying idioms are significant. Women's groups propagate a specific set of notions that revolve around the concept of nurture. Each new group stands as 'daughter' to the 'mother' sponsor. 'Mothers' give loans to make the work of their 'daughters' grow, transactions accompanied by birth and marriage rituals. For Daulo 'mother', like 'father', is a term for 'owner':

> As a mother cares for her child, so does an owner look after her property; ... Pigs grow and reproduce; coffee trees mature and bear fruit; money is invested to earn a profit. By the use of the term <u>oraho</u>, 'mother, owner', <u>wok meri</u> women not only base their relations with other groups on fictive maternal ties, but they also claim control of money by describing themselves as its 'owner' (Sexton, 1980).

The ownership exercised by mothers is of a special kind, with strong parthenogenetic overtones, reminiscent of Gillison's description of the Gimi to their south-east. There 'the vigour and fruition of all nurtured life is believed to depend upon exclusive attachment to, or symbolic incorporation by, individual female caretakers' (1980, p.147). The Gimi identification between the nurtured thing and its maternal source is resolved through symbolic and actual cannibalism (Gillison, 1980; in press). Problems of detachment lie with men, who both separate themselves from the implications of being female (and cf. Poole, 1981), and sustain the depiction of women as cannibals who will envelop them. Possibly the attitude of Daulo men towards women's investment associations revolves around a similar tension between extracting the products of nurture and encouraging women's continuing nurturant role.

At the outset I stressed that participation in transactions is to be understood in the context of relations between men and women. Daulo men significantly cast themselves as supporters of wok meri. Although much deployment of wealth remains in men's hands, they also respond to the wok meri's nurturing claims. There is a potent equation between the tending and producing of wealth and women's maternal roles. Since money invested is seen to grow, it is appropriate that women, promoters of growth, both should be supported by men and should see themselves as guarding resources that in the end are part of the productivity of their husbands' lineage. Sexton writes:

> In rituals like the symbolic marriage ceremonies ...wok meri women claim responsibility for the communal welfare ... Traditional male cult activities in the Highlands ... enable men to take on symbolic responsibility for the fertility of women, crops and pigs, and for the well-being of the human and animal populations ... In the Daulo region, as in many other areas in the Highlands, male cults have not been practised for some time. It is of major importance that women have developed wok meri rituals in which they symbolically shoulder the burden of insuring the 'fertility' or reproduction of money which has become a requisite (as a major component of bridewealth) for the reproduction of society.(1982)

Both Hageners and Daulo make certain equations between women and wealth. But I would argue that these have little to do with 'property', in the sense of rights over objects. They are related instead to the way in which wealth items signify aspects of the person. I have suggested that if Hagen wealth and women have the character of 'things', this is derived from the manner of symbolisation. The referent remains the 'person'. Such 'things' are not to be understood as objects alienable from the subjective actor: they are part of the person, with that further quality of detachability which makes them powerful instruments in gift exchange. There may well be between the Daulo and the Hagen case a difference in the manner in which women are thought of as 'things'. Yet in a gift-exchange system, 'things' are still parts of persons, though they may metonymically refer to an aspect of personhood separately constituted from those identities realised through metaphor.

I would be cautious, then, about applying the concept of

'property' to the wealth items and new currencies of the Papua New Guinea Highlands, if the term has to carry the distinctive western dichotomy between subject and object. This caution arises from a comparative exercise which has dwelt on the manner in which identifications are set up between persons and things. The theory which informs this perspective is an old one. I have merely extended it in reference to those situations where a class of persons, women, are in turn equated with wealth items, and thus come to stand for other persons or for aspects of themselves. As a limited exercise it has ignored power relations and the sociological contexts in which decisions are taken about the deployment of wealth. My particular concern has been to put something in the place of our western paradigm of property ownership which is itself so very much bound up with a special view of the person. In following Mauss's dictum that the thing given is personified, we have of course discovered that it matters also how the person itself is constructed.

Notes

1. I am more than grateful to Lorraine Sexton for letting me consult her then unpublished papers (1982; in press), and for corresponding over the issues raised here. I thank Fred Damon, Gillian Gillison, Chris Gregory, Lisette Josphides, Marthe Macintyre, Buck Schieffelin, Andrew Strathern and Roy Wagner for their comments and encouragement; Annette Weiner for the benefit of her unpublished study, Women's wealth and political evolution in the Pacific; and Debbora Battaglia for the stimulus she has provided through her own work on exchange and constructs of the person in the Southern Massim. Gratitude is due to the members of the Oxford Women's Studies Committee for their comments on my presentation; to the Departments of Social Anthropology in Edinburgh and Sydney, who heard a version; and to the Australian National University who enabled me to present part of the paper to the A.A.S. (1981). Shirley Ardener and Renée Hirschon have been invaluable critics.

2. The coffee crop is divided according to the processing stage, and men and women may make different claims here; women also dispose of proceeds from the sale of vegetables and such. Ideally, however, husband and wife are regarded as 'sharing' in the profits from such products.

3. Lindgren had not of course got the Daulo material to hand, but refers to older Highlands reports on Hagen and on Daribu, Huli, Mae Enga, Tsembaga, Siane. His own contrast is with the Dani of West Irian. Here, he suggests, the ideological rationale for exchange is not the reproduction of patriclans, and consequently men do not appropriate women's labour to the same degree. I have not, in the present account, followed through the implications of his analysis for 'reproduction' through child bearing.

4. Weiner would extend my critique in another direction; she has consistently argued that the concept of 'reproduction' needs to be dislodged from its current androcentric theoretical position (e.g.

1976; 1979; 1980).

5. He sees evidence of such 'rights' in the fact that sisters sometimes pass on property or status from their natal clan to their own children. These rights, he suggests, stem from woman's position in the sphere of production that the ideology of agnation contradicts. (I do not mean to suggest by implication that the concept of property is unexamined in Sexton's account – on the contrary, she analyses in detail concepts of ownership and disposal.)

6. Western culture is not of course itself undifferentiated, and these ideas about property that I take to stem largely from capitalist relations do not operate in all contexts (Schwimmer, 1979). They do, however, arguably inform certain intellectual approaches to the analysis of women, their 'rights' and control over resources, with which I am concerned. Bloch (1975) describes a non-western approach to property very similar to our own in its treatment of 'things'.

7. Cf. Giddens, 1971; also Godelier, (1972, p.120 ff.) in the context of discussing Marx's formulations (e.g. 1973 (1875-8) pp.452-3).

8. James (1978, p.152) describes Uduk abhorrence to bridewealth on the grounds that they would regard it as equating women with animals.

9. Gregory acknowledges (1980, p.639) Godelier's insight that often 'the precious objects we encounter in primitive societies have a dual nature; they are both goods and non-goods, 'money' and gifts, according to whether they are bartered between groups or circulate within the group' (1977 (1973) p.128, original emphasis). Beyond the internal exchange-system goods may thus traditionally have had the character of commodities.

10. For example: LeRoy 1979b; Schwimmer 1973; Weiner 1978; and outside Melanesia, Parry 1980; Good 1982.

11. We do not always have to understand the equation as between the gift and the donor; a gift may stand for either donor or recipient, so that one party either extends him or herself, or else renders to the other what is appropriately considered an aspect of the other (Schwimmer, 1973; 1974). For a Southern Highlands case see LeRoy, 1979b.

12. If Mauss himself drew attention to the fact that goods in a gift economy are not the alienable objects of the west (1954, p.74), he also drew attention to areas of western life where this notion of alienation does not apply (cf. Note 6). I have not here done justice to Schwimmer's (1979) scheme in its contrast between alienation and identification, and the use to which production is put.

13. I bring in the comparative frame to insist that the present analysis, otherwise largely confined to Hagen, does not rest on the elucidation of a single ethnographic case. The rather cryptically presented argument here is a condensation of considerations importantly raised by Damon (1980) and Munn (1977) in reference to kula valuables, by Schieffelin (1980) in reference to Kaluli notions of reciprocity and compensation, and by Salisbury's (1962) original presentation of the Siane case.

14. This underlines Mauss's original formulation that we are dealing with items standing in a special relationship to persons, not satisfactorily subsumed under the western notion of 'ownership' (cf. 1954, p.22). In a capitalist economy the market allows things to be exchanged for things, and people to be classed by their ownership of things. Such objects are seen as external to or surplus to the person, as labour may also become, so that there is no problem about removing them provided a fair price is paid for the object. An identification may be set up between the person and the class of things he or she possesses - as 'property', 'estate' - or a family's name associated, for example, with a class position, that is, with their resources. But it is the set of things which is regarded as the crucial source of this identity - land, capital or labour as a commodity - and not these things as creating social ties between oneself and others.

15. The labour of low status men is a separate issue (Schwimmer, 1979).

16. Cf. Damon, 'Rank and relations: names on Woodlark Island' prepared for A.S.A.O. Symposium 1982.

17. Gregory has emphasised the significance of land in relation to the nature of Hagen transactions (pers. comm.).

18. In M. Strathern, 1981 the concepts of metaphor and metonym are applied to a rather different area of symbolisation, the construction of 'womanness' itself. Munn's (1977) superb account of Gawa canoes turns precisely on the contrast between what is regarded as attached to and what is detachable from the person; she indicates the value generated by detachability. LeRoy (1979b, pp.30-32) refers to the metonymical relationship between men and pigs in Kewa.

19. The 'gender' of these items is highly context specific. M. Strathern, 1981 gives them a different analytical placement.

20. The essentially non-Highlands Etoro (Kelly, 1974) of the Papuan Plateau provide a provocative negative case. The (often externalised) sources of nurture that so frequently in the Highlands are visualised in terms of maternal origins in this society are located in the role of the senior inseminating man of the opposite 'moiety' from ego ('sister's husband').

21. There is not space for a full discussion. On the Wiru see A. Strathern, 1971, 1978, 1980.

10 WOMEN AND MEN; KINSHIP AND PROPERTY: SOME GENERAL ISSUES [1]

Ann Whitehead

The Social Character of Property

The starting point of this paper is the apparently simple, but actually extremely perplexing, question of what is it that we are interested in when we are interested in property and property ownership. If we can demonstrate differences between men and women in either the amount of property that each sexual category has access to, or in their forms of property ownership, in what ways could these be a significant aspect of gender relations? Why is it important to specify property ownership and distribution in relation to the sexes? Are they interesting in themselves, in so far as they document another area of sexual differentiation, or is there a deeper significance? Are we, for example, subscribing to a view that property ownership is somehow determinant of other areas of cross-sexual behaviour, and that we can explain aspects of gender asymmetry in these other areas in terms of the differential access of the sexes to property? This raises in turn the question of what is the theoretical status of property in terms of explanations about social behaviour, and in this case, in terms of explanations about gender relations? It seems obvious that one way or another the relatively empirical starting point of women and property leads to some profound theoretical and conceptual problems.

My paper argues that what examining 'women' and 'property' demonstrates above all is the social character of property. The particular aim is to show how legal and ideological practices, which are very often located within kinship and family structures, construct men's and women's ability to act as fully independent subjects in relation to property quite differently. The general form of my argument however is to reassert what anthropologists have long held, at least at the level of rhetoric, that property is not primarily a relation between people and things, but a relation between people and people – a social relation, or a set of social relations. Implicitly at least, this reassertion suggests a view that British social anthropologists have somehow insufficiently examined social relations in dealing with property. Given our self definition that what we study, par excellence, is social relations, this charge is either

176

distinctly odd, or rather serious - depending of course upon how convincing is my case.

My own view is that there has long been a relatively unexamined form of materialism in some of the influential schools in British social anthropology. It is unexamined in the sense that some of its conceptual and theoretical premisses are taken for granted. In an earlier review of Goody (1976) [2], I emphasised the important part that 'property' played in the explanation that was offered for differences in kinship which were being examined between two blocks of society - those of Europe and Asia, and those of sub-Saharan Africa. I pointed out that quite detailed, and apparently dissimilar differences in kinship behaviour and the kinship sphere were explained by the effects on the forms of transmission of property from one generation to another of the economic and social stratification occurring in one of these sets of society. 'The link between the economy and stratification is through the system of inheritance which organises the transmission of property from generation to generation, at death, at marriage or at some other point in the life cycle' (Goody, 1976, p.65). In examining Goody's case for the distinctive elements between the two kinds of society, I queried his argument that the technological basis of an economy constituted its most important determining feature, and asked whether in all economies it was the ownership, command and control of material resources which were the most significant aspects. Examining individual themes in his dichotomy and his explanations for their source I commented that the form of materialism adopted appeared to be accompanied by recourse to 'psychologistic' forms of explanation. I gave as examples explanations in terms of the desire to retain resources within the nuclear family, or in terms of the apparently inbuilt tendency of men to accumulate wives unless restrained by material considerations.

I would now argue that psychologistic explanations of one kind or another are logically connected to forms of materialist approach in which there is a common-sense view that what the economy is all about is the distribution of resources and how to get more of them. Although there has been consistent critical debate in social anthropology about various of the theoretical premisses prevalent in the Cambridge department in the early sixties, there is evidence of the continuing influences of this paradigm of the economy. It can be found for example in many of those studies which describe economic systems in terms of the distribution and inequality of resources and discuss such themes as the relationship between control of economic resources and power and/or status. In this form of materialism the model of man (sic) is <u>homo economicus</u>; that is to say man motivated to gain control over as much or as many of the valuable <u>things</u> in an economy that he can. In this model the concept of property becomes synonymous with the ownership of things by people. The anthropological axiom of the 'embeddedness' of the economy is effectively jettisoned in making an assumption that for the purposes of analysis the material can be separated off from the social. The social relations implicit in the production and exchange

177

processes of the economy and the social character of property are qualities which, if dealt with at all, are added on rather than intrinsic to the analytical perspective. It is of course rage and bafflement at the supposed processes by which things control people in this kind of determinism which lies at the root of many objections to it.

It is worth also pointing out that other unexamined assumptions about the character of relations between people and things enter into British anthropological theorising about kinship not only because of this paradigm of the nature of the economic, but also through the dominant influence of jurisprudence. Fortes (1969) has explored the historical continuity between his work and that of the nineteenth-century jurisprudentialist Sir Henry Maine, among others. The consistent use in African anthropology of the rights 'in rem' and rights 'in personam' formulation to describe marriage transactions springs to mind as an everyday example of this influence [3]. It is clearly based on the legal separation of subject and object, and in this case some of the objects are actually subjects ('personae'). I am not by any means alone in querying some of these underlying assumptions. Strathern's contribution to this volume raises the question of ethnocentricity in the concepts of property used by anthropologists. The radical perspective that she introduces is that the implied distinction between subject and object which lies at the root of our concept of property is not a universal one. Indeed she argues forcibly that to adopt such a notion of property is to misunderstand seriously the meaning of the relation between women and wealth in the New Guinea Highlands.

The economies with which she is concerned are characterised by ceremonial exchange of gifts. It is men who transact these gifts, and the significant transactions occur effectively between clan groups. The role of the sexes in and the organisation of production is such that men depend on the labour of their wives for their capacity to be successful in gift exchanges. At the same time relations between clan groups are marked by the transfer of women between the men, specifically as marriage partners, and this transfer is accompanied by a flow of gifts in the opposite direction to that in which the bride travels. These goods are often the same kinds of goods that are involved in ceremonial gift exchanges. In emphasising the specificity of the split between subject and object in Western concepts of property, Strathern criticises those who try to equate these systems of exchange, so that they end up stressing the material character of the relation between the genders, and conceptualise people being exchanged for things. She very cogently argues that, in the systems of thought of some societies in the New Guinea Highlands, what resides in the exchanged thing is part of the person, which cannot be alienated, and, moreover, that when women are exchanged they have a similar status as thing/person, and that in some senses they are also aspects of men when being exchanged. Thus in arguing that the boundaries between subject and object are not immutable, she also argues that the boundaries between men and women are not always clear cut.

In discussing her ethnographic data, Strathern thus, most properly, raises in a particular form those very old and important questions in anthropology which the issue of women and property, and women as property, raises. Far from being a stick to beat materialists with, Strathern demonstrates that, not only are Mount Hageners truly Maussian in their thought processes and conceptual baggage, but that they are resoundingly Marxian as well. For, as I would now like to show, Marx's materialism is not based on an ahistoric concept of property, nor does it prejudge the issue of the character of the subject/object relation.

The best place to begin to examine Marx's materialism for an understanding of the notion of property is in the idea of the fetishism of commodities. In Capital Volume I this is expressed in the following way: 'In the commodity form ... a definite social relation between men ... assumes, in their eyes, the fantastic form of a relation between things' (Marx, 1954, p.77). What we are to understand by the fetishism of commodities first and foremost is the nature of the production processes which underlie commodity exchange. What we see are objects exchanging through the medium of money. However the quality which is being exchanged – their value – is concealed labour time deriving from socialised production. Moreover, it is the set of social relations implied in the capitalist form of socialised production which is concealed by the commodity form.

However the fetishism of the commodity form refers to another way in which the commodity represents a set of social relations as an object – that specific set of social relations concealed by the notion of private property. Marx argued that the ownership of capital and labour power essential to capitalism requires a specific legal form of property – private property. One of the major themes throughout Marx's historical work was to trace the rise of this specific form of property and its implications for social life. Marx's concept of private property has been discussed by Pashukanis [4] who argues that capitalist property is basically the freedom to transform capital from one form to another. Capitalism, he points out, thus requires the assertion of an individual's rights as against all other individuals. It requires, that is, the separation of property out of social relations so that it becomes a characteristic inherent in the object which can be disembodied from the individuals who now stand in relation to it. The right of some individuals to own property entails the corresponding propertylessness of some other individuals. In addition to the separation of property as an object divorced from social relations, Pashukanis reminds us that Marx also argued the corresponding transformation of the legal concept of the person: 'At the same time therefore that the producer of labour becomes a commodity, and a bearer of value, man acquires his capacity to become a legal subject and a bearer of rights' (1978, p.112). The concept of the subject is twinned with the concept of property, as essential elements in the fetishism of the commodity form:

Simultaneously with the development of generalised commodity production social life disintegrates on the one hand into ... the kind of relations in which people have no greater significance than objects (e.g. labour power as a commodity, relations between persons as owners of things, A.W.) and on the other hand into relations of a kind where man is defined only by contrast to an object – that is a subject (Pashukanis, 1978, p.113).

This legal subject/object property complex is confined to the generalised commodity economy and it is to be contrasted with economic forms which are not dominated by production relations characterised by abstract labour (labour power). Thus in addition to having characteristically different legal concepts of property Marx argued that in the feudal social structure

all rights were considered as appertaining to a given concrete subject or limited group of subjects. Marx said that in the feudal world every right was a privilege. This epoch completely lacked any notion of a formal legal status common to all citizens (Pashukanis, 1978, p.119).

This view then fully accords with those of Strathern. Western (or 'capitalist' or 'bourgeois') concepts of property are highly specific ones which embody firstly the legal separation of subject and object, and secondly the legal separation of subject from subject in his or her capacity to have control over the disposal of a thing which has been designated his or her property. It is critical to bear in mind the opposite of this historically specific set of concepts: situations in which the separation out of each person from his social relations and thus his social statuses such that each is related to the other as conceptually and legally equivalent does not occur. There are also ones in which the capacity to own things in the sense discussed above does not occur. I find this suggestion, that bound up with the concepts of property are concepts of the person, and that these concepts of the person in turn can be characterised by their degree of individuation within social relations, an extraordinarily powerful one to begin thinking more generally about women (and men) and property. My contention is that the evidence from studies of women's relation to property, including the essays in this volume, suggest that whatever the nature of the economic system described in terms of the nature of its production and exchange relations, women's capacity to act as fully acting subjects in relation to objects (property), or the aspects of persons which may be being treated as objects (rights in people), is always more circumscribed than that of men. It is my further contention that in a very general sense, it is the kinship or family system which serves to construct women as less able to act as subjects than male subjects are able so to do.

In order to illustrate this contention I want to examine aspects of men's and women's relation to property in pre-state non-class societies. I have chosen this category of societies precisely because they are economies with the least developed commodity exchange. As a consequence they have relatively undeveloped concepts of private property, and are the ones in which we would expect little subject/object separation of the kind discussed above. They are also ones which are exceedingly familiar, both because the corpus of classic British anthropological work is made up of studies of this kind of society, and because they have recently been scrutinised as 'primitive communist' or 'lineage mode of production' societies by anthropologists adopting the marxist paradigm.

Kinship, Property and Gender in Pre-State, Non-Class Societies

By pre-state or non-class societies I am referring primarily to societies which are either of the foraging type or which practise forms of technologically simple agriculture. Most of my anthropological knowledge derives from Africa but other areas in which these kinds of economy are situated include Australia, New Guinea, parts of South America, especially the Amazon Basin, and so on. There are very important differences in the forms of social organisation within this general category. However the first part of my argument will assume the possibility of generalisation amongst them [5].

In these societies, although the numbers of people calling themselves by a common ethnic name may have been small, nevertheless their economies supported societies numbering in total hundreds of thousands. In them, production was for use, or for use values, and although in addition forms of economic exchange were significant, these were not forms of commodity exchange. Typically they lack forms of centralised political and economic institutions, and in one way or another kinship provides the major basis for the framework of social organisation. The groups tend to occupy the land at relatively low levels of population density.

The technical basis of the production system is very simple and, where the land is worked by human agency, productivity is low. Access to major productive resources is communal in nature. Although there is individual ownership of certain productive resources (e.g. tools and seeds), access to the major means of production is based on the membership of a group. Land in particular is occupied by virtue of membership of the group, which may be ideally a kin group, but which may also be a collectivity defined in a number of other ways. In fact, land ownership in its detailed form in these kinds of society is very complex, in that there is normally a hierarchy of ever more inclusive claims to land rights and the membership criteria for the land-allocating groups may be quite complex. Typically, however, an important element in these land rights is either the notion that a particular kin group has the rights to certain areas of land, or that by virtue of working the land (e.g. slash and burn systems) a residential group of a village type has rights over it. In the latter case the village/hamlet or locality unit may not be a corporate kin group but is instead composed of households or domestic groups linked by a variety of kin and other ties and sharing a common locality. The important aspects of the communal nature of this property ownership are: although land is abundant, there are usually identifiable 'owners' i.e. a group whose authority has to be sought to establish use rights; these rights are granted on the basis of certain links many of which are kinship, quasi-kinship, or residence; they are not granted to individuals qua individuals, but in the statuses as members of kin or neighbourhood groups. However the meaning of this communality has to be explored in other senses, since it does not necessarily mean collective working, and collective consumption.

In all cases, direct exploitation of the land is invested in smaller units than the communal group in which ownership is invested, and this is shown both in the forms of labour process and in the forms of disposal of the product. For simplicity I shall confine myself to the agricultural type in discussing the forms of labour process, which vary widely from case to case. In most cases there are divisions of labour based on age and sex which imply interdependence between the genders and the generations. In say, the African literature, there are numerous cases of areas of highly individualised forms of production, which often go together with fragmented and small residential units, in which men and women exploit plots of land as individuals, providing the bulk of the labour for it themselves and having considerable say in the disposal of the product. In other cases the household forms a significant production unit, and the labour of household members may be pooled under the direction of the household head to provide the crops for a common food store. In yet others, groups of households with close kinship links may co-operate closely in the labour processes, and there will be rules about the allocation of labour to fields and plots which are owned separately, and about the ownership of the crops thus grown.

However, from the point of view of the specification of the nature of these production systems I would highlight the critical importance of the following. In the first place there are always some forms of labour organisation and labour process which operate at a much wider community and group level. Although some of these may be very informal, they may include particular forms of exchange labour obligations; or work parties of a group kind; or they may include the obligation to work on the fields and farms of those who are afflicted by crisis such as sickness or death. Thus although much production might be based on the smaller units, the entire round of agricultural production, and the survival of individual members, depends on co-operation in labour use at this community level. When we come to consider the distribution of consumption of the products two things stand out. Firstly there may or may not be considerable individual control over direct consumption, depending usually on the household form, and the degree of individualisation of the labour processes. Where there is a relative individuation in the social practices of disposal and distribution, the actual patterns are often highly normative in character, and various ideologies have a bearing on the direction of disposals and the extent to which a person benefits from his/her own work. So too, and secondly, where there are production units of a more corporate or collective character, the distribution of products is based on ideologies of sharing and collectivity. Consumption levels here are not based on the amount of work done, such that consumption is the reward for work done, rather the ideology is that all the individual members are maintained by this group. Individual consumption levels are based on the assessment of general need and of competing claims for resources.

When we come to consider gender, characteristically these societies are ones in which both women and men have important productive roles. Women (and men) may or may not produce the primary agricultural products or staples, and each sex typically has acknowledged rights to communal property including land. These rights are rarely, if ever, strictly speaking the same: often because of the way in which the outcome of critical options at marriage (residence, ritual status, 'group' membership) has to affect men and women differently. Although they cannot be precisely the same, these rights may be expressed as equivalences, as for example in Caplan's account in this volume. Both women and men may be quoted as having rights by virtue of a variety of kinship and residential statuses and there is little evidence of such rights having a form in which they are denied to women by virtue of their gender. However my own researches in Ghana tend to suggest that these ideologies of equivalence in the genders' access to land and other tangible resources have to be understood in the context of the implications of other aspects of the communal property system.

Gender and Inequality Among the Kusasi

The Kusasi of North East Ghana [6] are sedentary hoe agriculturalists with a formerly leaderless political organisation and a strongly patrilineal kinship organisation. They are a large ethnic group occupying the dry savannah countryside around Bawku which they share with several other less numerous groups. Their district borders on that occupied by the Tallensi, and they speak a similar language. The densely settled land is intrinsically quite fertile, but is subject to local depletion and exhaustion. The staple crop is millet, and groundnuts and a little rice are grown for cash. Agriculture is still largely unmechanised, although about twenty per cent of households own a plough, and many households own a handful of cattle which are used for farming and bridewealth. In farming activities large and complexly organised households in which there is often more than one married man are a significant production unit, but exchange of labour between households makes an important contribution to the farming input. It is men who provide most labour for the millet and groundnut crops although women have important tasks in the growing cycle.

Land is not bought and sold, nor is it strictly speaking rented, although certain forms of temporary use do occur. All land has its ultimate ownership vested in some kin group or is linked to a political office, but since there is an historical dimension to the establishment of these rights, land may be subject to competing claims of ownership. The most important ownership rights to land are usufruct ones, and from this point of view both men and women can and do own farms as individual farmers. In addition to these 'private' farms, heads of households 'own' household farms and direct the work of household labour on them to provide staple food for the household. For all these farms, whether the farmer is a man or a woman, household head, or household dependant, their usufructory rights can be obtained in a number of ways. Examples include land obtained through patrilineal inheritance, through lineage membership, through clan membership, through in-law-ship, through being a wife of the lineage, through 'begging for' and so on. The major factor affecting a household's resource base is where its head stands in the social and political relationships of community and clan. The same is true of individuals. This helps to explain why, in addition to there being a complete discrepancy in the size of men's private farms and those of women (several acres for men compared with one acre for women), women, who are almost all in-married from other communities, most often report that they cannot get land in the area.

Perhaps even more radically, the meaning of land-use rights ('property ownership') has to be interpreted carefully in a technologically poorly-developed agriculture in which human labour is the most important transforming input. In particular, the usefulness of land rights is limited by the extent of rights in labour. Rights to ~~land~~ are more or less meaningless without the labour power to work it. In the course of the farming cycle Kusasi farmers make extensive use of the work of household members and of exchange labour parties within the community. My study of labour use among 60 households showed that the use of exchange labour was particularly unequal. Those farmers with high status in terms of their position in the household and domestic group, or those with dominant political status in terms of clan and community, had a larger share. Those who fared relatively badly were, for example, married men living as household dependants, poor household heads from politically unimportant clans and married women. The use of the labour of other household members was also unequally patterned according to position in the household hierarchy. For example, young unmarried boys could not command the labour of their married elder brothers, and adult women could not command the labour of adult men. In terms of gender, the net effect is that Kusasi women utilise both household labour and exchange labour differently from men. It is difficult for a woman to command the labour of social superiors, either within the immediate polygynous family unit or within the set of neighbouring agnatically related households. They rely on very junior men, often young boys. They never mount the large exchange work parties which are so important for male farmers, especially household heads.

Equally relevant to the meaning of land ownership is the form of ownership of crops produced on it. The Kusasi conceptualise the crops on private farms as being owned by the farmer who has grown them. There are a few obligations to be met in the form of gifts as rewards for help during the farming cycle. All kinds of privileged claims for some share in the harvest are made on farmers by junior household members, and by closely related kin inferiors and these are occasionally met. But, as I have pointed out elsewhere [7], it is significant that Kusasi conceptualise men and women as behaving differently in relation to the disposal of food crops. Built into the idea that mothers care for their children is a strong ideology that they do not let their children starve. Thus stereotypically women grow groundnuts 'for the children to chop' (eat); men grow groundnuts for cash. Thus, while both men and women farmers own their crops, within the terms of the value system about crop disposal women have less opportunity to realise them for cash.

The cash that individual farmers get from selling farm produce is wholly owned by the farmer, whether man or woman, and like other cash income no other person has rights to it. The right of individuals to spend their money how they like is tempered by the practice of and value placed on 'helping others'. When other household members, close kin, or needy neighbours and political allies 'beg' for help, I observed differences in being able to hold out against such claims. It is much easier for a household head, married man, senior wife, unmarried son or brother, and junior wives and daughters, in that descending order, to hold onto their income. This order reflects the generalised status hierarchy within the complex Kusasi household.

As I have described it, kinship conceived in some rather broad sense, organises access to land, organises the labour processes in agriculture, and the meeting of subsistence needs and the distribution of product. Work is done and needs are met within structured social relations which are mediated by kinship ideology, of which a dominant theme is notions of sharing, collectivity and generalised reciprocity. These ideologies of sharing and the notion of collectivity, while they are strongly located in the small-scale units of the residential household and minimal lineage, also provide the ideological underpinning for forms of sharing which take place across immediate production units. That these forms of sharing take place at all is a measure of the communal nature of the production system.

However, the fact that kinship may operate and does operate as a system of sharing, does not imply equality nor the absence of power in kinship relations. Thus they are just as much characterised by hierarchy and by inequality and these have their own ideologies – for example those of authority, of submission and of respect. We are familiar enough with certain aspects of these hierarchies in action in descriptions of the role of elders in for example the adjudication of cases, in the deference accorded to the old and older by younger men and by women, and in the ritual buttresses to kinship-ascribed authority in ancestor worship. Respect and power associated with age, gender and genealogical status are as characteristic of kinship relations as are norms of generalised reciprocity. My description details how manifestations of superordination and subordination are apparent in the activities which kinship relations organise. I have for example described how kinship statuses determine the individual's access to land, so that resources held may be markedly inegalitarian, especially between men and women, and how unequal command over labour is determined by position in the household and kinship system. In addition the allocation and distribution of communally-held produce on the basis of domestic, household or kinship relations is not egalitarian; it is based at the very least on normative assessment of need, which is manipulable.

These findings are not new. In one sense they are an elaboration of the idea of the 'embedded' economy. Each and every of the several elements of my description can be found in most of the British rural anthropological studies of Africa in the 1940s and 50s. In the earlier section of this paper I drew attention to Marx's contrast between the freely-acting individual subject of capitalism with rights as against other individuals, and the feudal person embedded in his social relations and within a set of social statuses, such that there is no concept of identical rights for all persons regardless of the social category to which they belong. If the freely-acting individual subject is not the legal concept of the person in feudalism then it is even less so in the economic forms under consideration here. In this situation the absence of a material form of abstraction - money - was allied to the absence of a conceptual abstraction - the individual. It is perhaps particularly misleading then that British social anthropology has not only tended to examine the economic component of the kinship system in terms of property, reciprocity as the principal mechanism of distribution, but that concepts of rights derived essentially from British jurisprudence should be so basic to its analysis. In situations where communal ownership is the basic land-people relationship we have to change the terms in which we think not only about property, but also about a number of dimensions which we habitually conceptualise as individual rights. We do this in part because our legal system constructs them as such, but also because many aspects of our major ideologies are founded on the concept of the human person as 'the individual'.

I would argue that Kusasi customary law and Kusasi custom definitely do not construct access to natural resources, access to harvested products, access to labour, or access to the disposal of usufruct in terms of the rights of individuated subjects. Kusasi concepts of 'ownership' do not convey that each person has an abstracted and definable capacity to assert a dominion over things (and people) which can be separated and distinguished from the dominion of other persons similarly constructed. Rather, as I have tried to argue above, 'rights' are contextual, determined primarily by kinship status and that kinship status has an irreducible collective dimension. They are manipulable by those with kinship-ascribed power and subject to ideologies which may be formally equivalent but in practice they confer, confirm and construct differences. Kusasi law and Kusasi metaphysics do have constructs which refer to persons as acting subjects but I would argue that these should not be thought of in terms of 'individuals' with 'rights'. These labels carry historically specific conceptual weight.

All this may seem a long way from the predominant objective of my paper which is to explore the issues of women, or more properly, gender and property. It is my contention that centering on the way in which each society constructs the acting subject is a useful way of looking at this problem. In particular it helps me to get at the often elusive quality of women's disabilities in relation to property in Kusasi-like societies. Nowhere is this more apparent than when we come to consider another kind of property within them – that property which figures in marriage payments, and the genders' relation to this.

There are a number of writers who from various theoretical perspectives, interpret societies of the Kusasi type as ones of relative sexual egalitarianism. In contrast to this I find that one of their most compelling aspects is that they embody an apparent paradox: women often have a considerable role in production and have certain kinds of property rights, yet these are also societies in which women's status in marriage exchanges often takes on a highly objectified character. Again one ought not to over-generalise amongst the very many forms of marriage with many different kinds of social implications within such a broad sweep of societies. A highly common situation is one in which marriage is an affair of kin groups, or neighbourhood groups, such that one or both of the marrying individuals is conceived as moving between collectivities. For Kusasi these kin groups are patrilineal localised descent groups which are named in terms of their clan affiliations (the clan is the exogamic unit). It is women who are conceived of as moving between them. Marriage sets up important ritual obligations of in-laws to the clan from which wives have come, for example at funerals [8]. (Strictly speaking, these obligations are between the localised descent group sections but they are stated in terms of clan. There are many behavioural ways in which Kusasi women appear to be subservient and the segregation of male and female activities and concerns is striking, and I found the area in which gender subordination was most marked was that surrounding the management of marriage.

Marriage is clearly a highly important preoccupation of Kusasi men. Many senior men are polygynous although the total number of wives for each individual is not great. Men marry late and women early. Indeed girls may be sent at an early age to households into which they will marry at puberty. Marriages are not very stable in the early years but this is for a variety of reasons, many of which are not personal preference. One symptom of this is that 'woman' cases, i.e. cases about divorce, elopement, brideprice and child custody, are by far the majority of cases heard by chiefs and elders. Although the affiliation of children is an important theme throughout these cases – children belong to the group of the husband who has paid the brideprice – the disposition of women themselves, as wives, is also of great concern. A woman's interests in her children are barely acknowledged in these cases, and her interest in her marriage is only one amongst many interests which are raised by, for example, a second divorce or elopement. These interests in marriages operate at many different levels of which space precludes discussion. What is significant for the present discussion is that women are barely represented in 'woman' cases. As principals to a case they speak little when called, and as a category they are jural minors. No senior women are included in the company of chiefs and elders who try cases and women cannot initiate cases on their own behalf.

The so-called management of marriage, which in this terminology concerns relations between men and especially the political relations of the locality, also 'manages' women. Many of the activities which I have referred to already embody or carry statements about women's subordination, but this is epitomised in the character of the exchange which critically constitutes the marriage. Kusasi marry with bridewealth of five cows, which is given from the senior agnatic men of the husband's immediate family to the similar relatives of the bride. Amassing, getting the promise of, and distributing brideprice are also subjects which occupy much time in Kusasi social life. As has been frequently observed there is something critical about the character of such marriage prestations, which are conceived of in terms of exchanges, and the position of women in societies of this type.

In some societies the character of the exchange is suggested by the economically substantial character of the bridewealth payment. The items which figure in marriage payments are often those goods which in some terminologies are called the surplus product. These are products of one kind or another over and above subsistence requirements which are often called prestige goods. They may be such items as cattle or pigs, or kolanuts or yams, or they may be manufactured items such as cloth or necklaces or bracelets. Surplus product as a whole is disproportionately distributed amongst those with the most senior kinship or community statuses and its use in specific ways is controlled by them [9]. It may be used for forms of political, religious, or ritual activity, and may be particularly used in activities which involve alliance and solidarity between groups. It is also used in marriage transactions of the kind I have been considering. From the point of view of the specificity of women's position in these societies then, a defining characteristic is that the surplus product is disposed of by socially-powerful men in sets of marriage prestations (ceremonial gift-like payments).

In many societies where bridewealth is paid (cf. Burman, Strathern, Westwood, this volume), there is often an ideology in which women are more or less directly equated with the other items for which they are exchanged in the marriage prestations. In so far as these other items are not people (not the husband, nor other exchanging women, for example) but material things, the women appear to be being exchanged for objects, and this may be spoken of within the culture in terms very similar to buying and selling. Women may, that is, appear to be property, and this is enhanced by such customs as the 'levirate', the inheritance by the agnatic heir of the deceased's widow as well as his material property. However, it is made clear through other aspects of the ritual behaviour on marriage and from other culturally-specific ideologies that women are not in any simple sense things. In my view it is not the exchange of women for objects which is the most difficult aspect of this problem. Many feminists have argued that the conceptualisation by Lévi-Strauss of marriage systems as systems in which women are exchanged between men is the most general form of this argument. They may also argue that conceptualising women as having the capacity to be exchanged, at all, between persons, necessarily implies the objectification of women. Without being property, there are many circumstances in which women, in some senses, are what is transferred between men, or between men as members of kinship or other forms of collectivity.

The critical point here of course is in what sense? If what is being exchanged in marriage is not women as property, is there some other sense in which their status as persons is encroached upon? As a category, their status as subjects is clearly different from that of the male subjects who are transacting them, in so far as, for example, they never, in these exchanges, act to transact men. In special circumstances women can transact each other (woman to woman marriage) but by and large the kinship system, which embodies a set of rules about marriage as well as a set of symbols and values about the meaning of prescribed acts, constructs men's and women's ability to act differently in relation to marriage. My own view is that in these societies what kinship does, through ideological and legal practices, is to construct men and women as subjects differently so that one gender may transact the other at marriage. In so far as we are right to describe women as objectified by the form in which they are transacted by the marriage system, we can describe men as full acting subjects, and women as considerably less than full acting subjects.

The Construction of Gender Differences Through Kinship

Although I have discussed this proposition through the example of pre-state non-class societies, it is, I think, much more generally applicable than this. What I find noticeable about women's relationship to property in many other situations is that a recurring motif is that of how 'individuated' from social relations men are compared to women. Women are less often able to act in socially unencumbered ways than men. One can, for example, think of the differences in the carry-over effect of the parental statuses of mother and father into the occupational sphere in contemporary Britain. The specific set of social relations which time and time again have to be taken into account are those of kinship and family. The general tenor of my argument is that a woman's capacity to 'own' things depends on the extent to which she is legally and actually separable from other people (as does a man's). Put very crudely, the issue raised is the extent to which forms of conjugal, familial and kinship relations allow her an independent existence so that she can assert rights as an individual against individuals. In many societies a woman's capacity to act in this way may be severely curtailed compared to a man's. Conjugal, familial and kinship systems appear often to operate so as to construct women as a subordinate gender, such that by virtue of

189

carrying kinship (or familial or conjugal) status women are less free to act as full subjects in relation to things, and sometimes people. This I would argue is the general form of their relation to property.

Two illustrative examples may be briefly touched on. Although there are several different forms of dowry system, dowry seems to me to be a very characteristic form of female property. Sharma's discussion (this volume) centres on the way in which family and marriage relations organise a rather indirect relationship of women to dowry property in India. Bearing the dowry, women act as conduits or channels for the transfer of resources between families. In so far as they own property, it is in trusteeship - it is conceptualised as being to pass on to other female members of the family into which she has married. In the Hindu conception of the joint family the interests of the incoming wife and daughter-in-law are fully submerged with those of the husband's family. Under these circumstances 'getting your hands on', i.e. asserting some form of ownership over the incoming resources, for a wife whose dowry it is, depends on a large number of factors. Sharma has argued that some of these concern the incoming wife's relation to the structure of family relationships - as for example the size of the household group, the standing of the family, and the degree of development of forms of hierarchy, seniority and authority within the joint-family based household. However, the general character of the wife's relation to dowry property is clear. It is property which she receives only by entering a certain status in relation to a man as his wife, or to the joint family as an incoming daughter-in-law. The primary character of her relation to the dowry property she brings in is mediated and indirect. The dowry may come to be held by other female members of the family; if it is disposed of in other marriage transactions or in other ways, this is a 'family' decision in which she has a voice whose de facto strength is quite variable.

Quite different themes emerge if we now turn to consider the contemporary position with regard to women's property in Britain. Here the critical kinship status is that concerned with the conjugal family and specifically the relationship of marriage. I would argue that it is through the legal construction of the economic elements in the husband-wife relation that men and women are constrained and enjoined to act differently as subjects. In the past the unity of husband and wife was expressed in the legal merging of her property interests with his. Today a married woman retains property within the conjugal unit and has enforceable rights to conjugal property and the matrimonial home by virtue of her marriage, rather than by virtue of the property she brought into the marriage. However, the significant dimension in terms of my argument turns less on the gender's relation to property at the dissolution of marriage than on the mode in which the economic obligations of extant marriages are constructed. It has been amply demonstrated in recent feminist work that aspects of marriage which are legally critical are on the one hand sexual obligations and on the other asymmetrical financial obligations. The construction of the financial dependence of one partner on the other is at the core of legal treatments of husband/wife statuses. Apart from the well-known issue of the treatment of a married couple's income for taxation purposes, the other everyday example of this is the state income-maintenance schemes. Land's work (1978) has demonstrated that these enjoin earning on husbands, and housework on wives/mothers. A recurring theme in the feminist analysis of women's position in Britain can be interpreted as being an elaboration of the way in which the ideology and legal actuality of wifely dependence within marriage in capitalist society constructs women as less able to act as full subjects than men.

This paper began by considering the social character of property. Essentially my argument was that the concept of property in the sense of the relation of persons to things itself takes historically specific forms. I drew attention to the circumstances in which legally and ideologically the property relation takes the form of an individual's rights over things. I went on to consider the property rights of men and women in a situation where no such concept of individually-owned property exists. Once the person-thing (subject-object) relation becomes embedded in concrete social relations I argued that many ideological factors operate to give de facto inequality in the genders' capacity to act in relation to material things. I identified the kinship and family system as important sites for ideological and legal practices which construct male and female subjects with a differential power to act. In conclusion I tried very briefly to sketch ways in which this proposition illuminates women's relation to property in other circumstances.

Notes

1. My thanks to Renée Hirschon, for unbounded editorial tolerance, and especially to Nira Yuval-Davis and Felicity Edholm for serious and insightful discussions of an earlier draft.
2. Whitehead (1977).
3. Comaroff (1980) has an interesting discussion of this.
4. A Bolshevik legal theorist whose major theoretical work was first published in the 1920s.
5. I feel extremely diffident about the method of work in this article. I do not wish to present a primarily ethnographic study and hence my treatment of the Kusasi is not very comprehensive. However, while I think that generalisations are possible across many pre-state, non-class societies, the secondary work required to make sensible generalisations across such a broad sweep of societies is so large that my project of doing so is hardly begun. I am conscious that the presentation of a stereotype will offend many ethnographers.
6. This fieldwork was funded by a grant from the SSRC ⁺ whom grateful acknowledgement is made.
7. Whitehead (1981).
8. Hershman (1980) draws some very interesti⁻ between the relations set up on Tallensi marriage w⁺ Punjabi Hindus for whom marriage patterns

configurations of relations between groups. These parallels hinge in part on the funeral obligations of in-laws.

   9. There is a well-developed literature on the genders' relation to surplus product. See <u>Critique of Anthropology</u> (1977) as a beginning.

BIBLIOGRAPHY

Abadan, N. Social Change and Turkish Women, Publications of Faculty of Political Science, University of Ankara, no. 171-53, (1963)

Abadan-Unat, N. 'The Modernization of Turkish Women', The Middle East Journal, vol. 32 (1978), pp.291-306

_____ 'Turkish Migration to Europe and the Middle East: Its Impact on Social Legislation and Social Structure'. Paper presented at Conference on Social Legislation and Social Structure in the Contemporary Near and Middle East, Rabat, Morocco, (Sept. 25-9, 1981)

_____ (ed.) Women in Turkish Society, (E.J. Brill, Leiden,) (forthcoming)

Abel, R. 'The Rise of Capitalism and the Transformation of Disputing: from Confrontation over Honor to Competition for Property', UCLA Law Review, vol. 27, no. 1 (1979), pp.223-55

Allen, H. The Turkish Transformation: A Study in Social and Religious Development (Greenwood Press, New York, 1935)

Allot, A.N. Judicial and Legal Systems in Africa (Butterworth, London, 1970)

Althusser, L. 'Ideology and Ideological State Apparatuses: Notes Towards an Investigation', in idem, Lenin, Philosophy and Other Essays (New Left Books, London, 1971), pp.123-73

Ansay, T. and Wallace, Jr. Introduction to Turkish Law (Güzel Istanbul Matbaası, Ankara, 1966)

Ardener, E. 'Belief and the Problem of Women', in J. La Fontaine (ed.), The Interpretation of Ritual (Tavistock Press, London, 1972), reprinted in S. Ardener (ed.), 1975

Ardener, S. 'Introductory Essay', in S. Ardener (ed.), Perceiving Women (Dent, London; Halsted, New York, 1975)

_____ Defining Females: the Nature of Women in Society (Croom Helm, London, 1978)

Ariès, P. Essais sur l'histoire de la mort en Occident du Moyen Age a nos jours (Seuil, Paris, 1975)

Asad, T. 'Anthropology and the Analysis of Ideology', Man (N.S.), vol. 14, no. 4 (December 1979), pp.607-27

Aswad, B. 'Key and Peripheral Roles of Noblewomen in a Middle Eastern Plains Village', Anthropological Quarterly, vol. 40 (1967), pp.139-52

_____ Property Control and Social Strategies: Settlers on a Middle Eastern Plain, Anthropological Papers no. 44 (Ann Arbor, Michigan, 1971)

_____ 'Visiting Patterns Among Women of the Elite in a Small Turkish City', Anthropological Quarterly, vol. 47 (1974), pp.9-27

_____ 'Women, Class and Power: Examples from the Hatay, Turkey', in L. Beck and N. Keddie (eds.) Women in the Muslim World

(Harvard University Press, 1978), pp.473-81

Aziz, K.M. Kinship in Bangla Desh (Institute for Diarrhoeal Disease Research, Dacca, 1979)

Azu, D.G. The Ga Family and Social Change (African Studies Centre, Cambridge, 1974)

Barrett, M. Women's Oppression Today: Problems in Marxist and Feminist Analysis (New Left Review Editions, London, 1980)

Barth, F. Nomads of South Persia: The Basseri Tribe of the Khamseh Confederacy (George Allen and Unwin, London, 1961)

Beck, L. 'Women Among Qashqa'i Nomadic Pastoralists in Iran', in L. Beck and N. Keddie (eds.), Women in the Muslim World (Harvard University Press, 1978)

Beechey, V. 'On Patriarchy', Feminist Review, vol. 3, no. 3 (1979), pp.66-82

Beijing Review, 'Chinese Women Discuss Life and Work', 9 March 1979

Bloch, M. 'Property and the End of Affinity', in M. Bloch (ed.), Marxist Analysis in Social Anthropology (Malaby Press, London, 1975)

Bohannan, L. 'Dahomean Marriage - a Revaluation', Africa, vol. 29 (1949)

Boserup, E. Woman's Role in Economic Development (St. Martin's Press, New York, Allen and Unwin, London, 1970)

Bossen, L. 'Women in Modernizing Societies', American Ethnologist (special issue, Sex Roles in Cross-Cultural Perspective), vol. 2, no. 4 (1975), pp.587-601

Bourdieu, P. 'Celibat et Condition Paysanne', Études Rurales, 5-6 (1962)

_____ 'Les Stratégies Matrimoniales dans le Système de Reproduction', Annales (July, 1972), pp.1105-27

_____ 'Cultural Reproduction and Social Reproduction', in R. Brown (ed.), Knowledge, Education and Cultural Change (Tavistock Press, London, 1974), pp.71-112

Bozzoli, B. 'Feminist Interpretations and South African Studies: Some Suggested Avenues for Exploration', African Studies Seminar Paper (University of Witwatersrand, Oct. 1981)

Brown, D.J.J. 'The Structuring of Polopa Kinship and Affinity', Oceania, vol. 50, no. 4 (June 1980), pp.297-331

Brown, P. 'Mingge-money: Economic Change in the New Guinea Highlands', Southwestern Journal of Anthropology, vol. 216, no. 3 (Autumn 1970), pp.242-60

_____ Highland Peoples of New Guinea (Cambridge University Press, Cambridge, 1978)

Brown, R. (ed.), Knowledge, Education and Cultural Change (Tavistock Press, London, 1974)

Bruce-Myers, J.M. 'The Origins of the Ga', Journal of the African Society, vol. 2 (1927-28), pp.69-76, 167-73

Bujra, J. 'Production, Property, Prostitution: Sexual Politics in Atu', Cahiers d'études Africaines, vol. 65, no. 17 (1976)

_____ 'Introductory: Female Solidarity and the Sexual Division of Labour', in P. Caplan and J. Bujra (eds.) Women United,

<u>Women Divided</u> (Tavistock Press, London, 1978)
Cailler (later Cailler-Boisvert), C. 'Soajo-une Communauté Féminine Rurale de l'Alto Minho', <u>Bulletin des Études Portugaises</u> (N.S), vol. 27 (1966), pp.237-84
Campbell, J.K. <u>Honour, Family and Patronage</u> (Clarendon Press, Oxford, 1964)
Caplan, A.P. <u>Choice and Constraint in a Swahili Community</u> (UCP/IAI, 1975)
____ 'Girls' Puberty and Boys' Circumcision Rites Among the Swahili of Mafia Island, Tanzania', <u>Africa</u>, vol. 46 (1976)
____ 'The Swahili of Chole Island', in A. Sutherland (ed.), <u>Face Values</u> (BBC Publications, 1977)
____ 'Developmental Policies in Tanzania — Some Implications for Women', <u>Journal of Development Studies</u>, vol. 17, no. 3 (1981)
____ 'Gender, Ideology and Modes of Production', in J.de Vere Allen and Thomas T.H. Wilson (eds.), From Zinj to Zanzibar: Studies in History, Trade and Society on the Coast of Eastern Africa. <u>Paideuma</u> 28 (Frobenius Institute of Goethe-Universitat, Frankfurt, 1982)
____ 'Family and Household as Concepts on the Coast of East Africa', (forthcoming)
Castelo Branco, C. <u>Maria da Fonte</u> (Civilização, Porto, 1885)
Chen, J. <u>A Year in Upper Felicity</u> (Harrap, London, 1973)
<u>China Reconstructs</u>, 'Why the New Marriage Law was Necessary', March 1981
Comaroff, J. (ed.) <u>The Meaning of Marriage Payments</u> (Academic Press, London, 1980)
Cooper, F. <u>Plantation Slavery on the East Coast of Africa</u> (Yale University Press, New Haven, London, 1977)
Cosar, F.M. 'Women in Turkish Society', in L. Beck and N. Keddie (eds.) <u>Women in the Muslim World</u> (Harvard University Press, 1978)
Coulson, N. <u>A History of Islamic Law</u> (Edinburgh University Press, 1964)
Coulson, N., and Hinchcliffe, D. 'Women and Law Reform in Contemporary Islam', in L. Beck and N. Keddie (eds.) <u>Women in the Muslim World</u> (Harvard University Press, 1978)
Creighton, C. 'Family, Property and Relations of Production in Western Europe', <u>Economy and Society</u>, vol. 9, no. 2 (May 1980), pp.129-67
<u>Critique of Anthropology</u>, Women's Issue vol. 3, no. 9-10, (1977)
Croll, E.J. <u>The Women's Movement in China: A Selection of Readings 1949873</u> (ACEI, London, 1973)
____ 'Chiang Village: a Household Survey', <u>China Quarterly</u>, (Dec. 1977) pp.786-814
____ <u>Feminism and Socialism in China</u> (Routledge and Kegan Paul, London, 1978)
____ <u>The Politics of Marriage in Contemporary China</u> (Cambridge University Press, 1981)
Damon, F.H. 'The Kula and Generalised Exchange: Considering Some

Unconsidered Aspects of The Elementary Structures of Kinship',
  Man (N.S.), vol. 15, no. 2 (June 1980), pp.267-92
Davis, J. People of the Mediterranean: an Essay in Comparative
  Social Anthropology (Routledge and Kegan Paul, London,
  1977)
de Planhol, X. 'Geography, Politics and Nomadism in Anatolia',
  International Social Science Journal, vol. 11, no. 4 (1958),
  pp.525-31
du Boulay, J. Portrait of a Greek Mountain Village (Clarendon
  Press, Oxford, 1974)
_____ 'The Meaning of Dowry: Changing Values in Rural Greece', in
  A. Mackrakis and P. Allen (eds.), Women and Men in
  Greece: a Society in Transition, (in press)
Edholm, F., Harris, O., and Young, K. 'Conceptualising Women',
  Critique of Anthropology, vol. 3, no. 9-10 (1977) pp.101-30
Eglar, Z. A Punjabi Village in Pakistan (University of Columbia
  Press, New York, 1960)
El-Busaidy, Hamed bin Saleh Ndoa na Talaka (Marriage and
  Divorce) (East African Literature Bureau, 1962)
Elias, N. The Civilizing Process, vol. 1, The History of Manners.
  Originally published as Uber den Prozess der Zivilisation
  (1939), (Blackwell, Oxford, 1982)
Engels, F. The Origin of the Family, Private Property and the State
  (New York, 1884). Also (ed.) E.B. Leacock (Lawrence and
  Wishart, London, 1981)
Farsy, Kadhi Sheikh Abdulla Saleh Ndoa na Maamrisho Yake
  (Marriage and its Rules) (Mulla Karimgee Mulla
  Mohammedbhai, 1966)
Fee, Elizabeth "The Sexual Politics of Victorian Social Anthropology,
  in M. Hartman and L. Banner (eds.) Clio's Consciousness
  Raised: New Perspectives on the History of Women (Harper
  and Row, New York, 1974), pp.86-103
Feil, D.K. 'When a Group of Women Takes a Wife: Generalized
  Exchange and Restricted Marriage in the New Guinea
  Highlands', Mankind, vol. 12, no. 4 (December 1980),
  pp.286-99
_____ 'The Bride in Bridewealth: a Case from the New Guinea
  Highlands', Ethnology, vol. 20, no. 1 (January 1981),
  pp.63-75
Field, H.M. The Greek Islands and Turkey After the War (Sampson,
  Law, Marston, Searle and Rivington, London, 1885)
Field, M.J. The Social Organisation of the Ga People (Crown
  Agents, London, 1940)
_____ Religion and Medicine of the Ga People (Oxford University
  Press, Oxford, 1961)
Finnegan, R. and Horton, R. 'Introduction' in R. Horton and R.
  Finnegan, Modes of Thought (Faber and Faber, London, 1973)
Finney, B.R. Big-men and Business: Entrepreneurship and Economic
  Growth in the New Guinea Highlands (Australian University
  Press, Canberra, 1973)
Fisher, W. The Middle East: A Physical, Social and Regional

Geography (Methuen, London, 1963)

Fortes, M. Kinship and the Social Order (Routledge and Kegan Paul, London, 1969)

Freedman, M. Chinese Lineage and Society, Fukien and Kwangtung (Athlone Press, London, 1966)

Friedl, E. Vasilika (Holt, Rinehart and Winston, New York, 1962)
_____ 'Kinship, Class and Selective Migration', in J.G. Peristiany (ed.), Mediterranean Family Structures (Cambridge University Press, Cambridge, 1976)

Furtado Coelho, E.C.C.P. Estatistica do Districto de Vianna do Castelo (Imprensa Nacional, Lisboa, 1861)

Galanti, A. Bodrum Tarihine Ek. (Bodrum's History) (Tan Basi Meri, Istanbul, 1946)

Genel Nüfus Sayımı (Population Statistics), 'Province of Mugla. City and Village Population, Area, and Density by Ilce' (Government of Turkey, Idari Bolunus, Ankara, 1965)

Giddens, A. Capitalism and Modern Social Theory (Cambridge University Press, Cambridge, 1971)

Gillison, G. 'Images of Nature in Gimi Thought', in C. MacCormack and M. Strathern (eds.), Nature, Culture and Gender (Cambridge University Press, Cambridge, 1980)
_____ 'Cannibalism Among Women in the Eastern Highlands of Papua New Guinea', paper read to 79th Meeting of the American Anthropological Association (1980), n.d.

Godelier, M. Rationality and Irrationality in Economics (New Left Books, London, 1972) (Translated by B. Pearce from the 1966 French ed.)
_____ Perspectives in Marxist Anthropology (Cambridge University Press, Cambridge, 1977) (Translated by R. Brain from the French of 1973)

Gongren Ribao (Workers' Daily) A Selection of Letters on Age of Marriage, 11 September 1962; 27 September 1962; 9 October 1962

Good, A. 'The Actor and the Act: Categories of Prestation in South India', Man (N.S.), vol. 17, no. 1 (March 1982)

Goodale, J.C. 'Saying it with Shells in Southwest New Britain', paper presented to American Anthropological Association meetings (1978)

Goody, E. Parenthood and Social Reproduction: Fostering and Occupational Roles in West Africa, Cambridge Studies in Social Anthropology 35 (Cambridge University Press, Cambridge, 1981)

Goody, J. 'Inheritance, Property, and Marriage in Africa and Eurasia', Sociology, vol. 3 (1969), pp.55-76
_____ Production and Reproduction: a Comparative Study of the Domestic Domain (Cambridge University Press, Cambridge, 1976)

Goody, J. and Tambiah, S.J. Bridewealth and Dowry (Cambridge University Press, Cambridge, 1973)

Graaf, J. and Robb, N. 'Crossroads - the Facts', South African Outlook, vol. 108, no. 1280 (February 1978)

Gray, K.J. and Symes, P.D. Real Property and Real People, Principles of Land Law (Butterworths, London, 1981)

Gray, J.M. Report on the Enquiry into Claims to Land in Ngeza, Vitongoji, Pemba (Zanzibar Government Printer, 1956)

_____ History of Zanzibar (Oxford University Press, Oxford, 1962)

Gregory, C.A. 'The Emergence of Commodity Production in Papua New Guinea', Journal of Contemporary Asia (1979), pp.389-409

_____ 'Gifts to Men and Gifts to God: Gift Exchange and Capital Accumulation in Contemporary Papua", Man (N.S.), vol. 15, no. 4 (December 1980), pp.626-52

Grigsby, W.E. The Medjelle or Ottoman Civil Code (First English translation) (Nicosia, Cyprus, 1895)

Guangming Ribao (Guangming Daily) Wu Zhangzhan, 'The Principle of "Freedom of Marriage" Should Not Be Abused', 27 February 1957

Gutkind, P. and Waterman, P. (eds.) African Social Studies: A Radical Reader (Heinemann, London, 1977)

Hanson, F.A. Rapan Lifeways (Little, Brown and Company, 1970)

Harris, O. 'Households as Natural Units', in K. Young, C. Wolkowitz and R. McCullagh (eds.), Of Marriage and the Market (CSE Books, London, 1981)

Harris, O. and Young, K. 'Engendered Structures: Some Problems in the Analysis of Reproduction', in J. Kahn and J. Llobera (eds.), The Anthropology of Pre-Capitalist Societies (Macmillan, London, 1981)

Herdt, G. Guardians of the Flutes: Idioms of Masculinity (Stanford University Press, Stanford, 1980)

Hershman, P. 'Comparison of Punjabi and Tallensi Marriage Systems', Eastern Anthropologist, vol. 33, no. 4, 1980

Hirschon, R. 'Open Body/Closed Space: the Transformation of Female Sexuality' in S. Ardener (ed.), Defining Females: the Nature of Women in Society (Croom Helm, London, 1978)

_____ 'Under One Roof: Marriage, Dowry and Family Relations in Piraeus", in M. Kenny and D. Kertzer (eds.), Urban Life in Mediterranean Europe (University of Illinois Press, in press)

Hoben, A. Land Tenure Among the Amhara of Ethiopia: the Dynamics of Cognatic Descent (University of Chicago Press, 1973)

Holy, L. and Stuchlik, M. 'The Structure of Folk Models', in L. Holy and M. Stuchlik (eds.), The Structure of Folk Models (Academic Press, London, 1981)

Hooja, S. Dowry System in India (Asia Press, Delhi, 1969)

Howard, R. Colonialism and Underdevelopment in Ghana (Croom Helm, London, 1978)

Hurst, P.Q. Problems and Advances in the Theory of Ideology (Cambridge University Communist Party Pamphlet, Cambridge, 1976)

Italicus, S. Punica, 2 vols., translated by J.C. Duff (Heinemann, London, 1934)

James, W. 'Matrifocus on African Women', in S. Ardener (ed.), Defining Females: the Nature of Women in Society (Croom

Helm, London, 1978)

Jeffery, P. Frogs in a Well (Zed Press, London, 1978)

Justin, The History of Justin (taken out of the 44 books of Trogus Pompeius), translated by R. Codrington (William Whitwood, London, 1672)

Kandiyoti, D. 'Sex Roles and Social Change: A Comparative Appraisal of Turkey's Women', Signs (Special Issue, Women and National Development), vol. 3, no. 1 (1977), pp.57-73

_____ (ed.) 'Türk Toplumunda Kadın, Semineri' (Women in Turkish Society, Seminar) (Istanbul, 1978)

_____ (ed.) Major Issues on the Status of Women in Turkey: Approaches and Priorities (Çağ Matbaasi, Ankara, 1980)

Kelly, R.C. Etoro Social Structure: a Study in Structural Contradiction (University of Michigan Press, Ann Arbor, 1974)

Kenna, M. 'Houses, Fields and Graves: Property and Ritual Obligation on a Greek Island', Ethnology, vol. 15, no. 1 (January 1976), pp.21-34

Killick, T. Development Economics in Action: A Study of Economic Policies in Ghana (Heinemann, London, 1978)

Kilson, M. 'Ambivalence and Power in Traditional Ga Religion', Journal of Religion in Africa, vol. 4 (1971), pp.171-7

_____ Kpele Lala: Ga Religious Songs and Symbols (Harvard University Press, 1971)

_____ African Urban Kinsmen (Hurst, London, 1974)

Kuhn, A. and Wolpe, A. (eds.) Feminism and Materialism (Routledge, London, 1978)

Lamphere, L. 'Anthropology: Review Essay', Signs, vol. 2, no. 3 (Spring 1977), pp.612-25

Land, H. 'Who Cares for the Family?', Journal of Social Policy, vol. 7, part 3 (1978)

Landberg, P.W. 'Kinship and Community in a Tanzanian Coastal Village', Unpublished Ph.D. thesis, Davis, California, 1977

Laslett, P., Costerveen, K. and Smith, R. (eds.) Bastardy and its Comparative History (Edward Arnold, London, 1980)

Lawson, R.M. and Kwei, E. African Entrepreneurship and Economic Growth: A Case Study of the Fishing Industry in Ghana (Ghana University Press, Accra, 1974)

Leacock, E.B. 'Introduction' to Engels' The Origin of the Family, Private Property and the State (1884) (ed.) by E.B. Leacock (Laurence and Wishart, London, 1981) (first published 1972)

Leacock E.B. Myths of Male Dominance (Monthly Review Press, London, 1981)

Le Roy, J. 'The Ceremonial Pig Kill of the South Kewa', Oceania, vol. 49, no. 3 (March 1979), pp.179-209

_____ 'Competitive Exchange in Kewa', Journal of Polynesian Society, vol. 88, no. 1 (March 1979), pp.9-35

Lévi-Strauss, C. The Elementary Structures of Kinship (Eyre and Spottiswoode, London, 1969) (Translated by Bell, Sturmer and Needham)

Lewis, B. 'Arus Resmi' in Encyclopaedia of Islam, vol. 1, 1960, p.697

___ The Emergence of Modern Turkey (Oxford University Press, London, 1961)

Lindgren, M. 'Agnation and the Devaluation of Women's Labour - a New Guinea Example', Working Papers, (Department of Social Anthropology, University of Gothenburg, 1978)

Lisón Tolosana, C. Anthropologia Cultural de Galicia (Siglo XXI, Madrid, 1971)

Loizos, P. 'Changes in Property Transfer Among Greek Cypriot Villagers', Man, (N.S.), vol. 10, no. 4 (December 1975) pp.503-523

Lowie, R.H. Primitive Society (George Routledge and Sons, London, 1929, first imp. 1921)

Lowy, M.J. 'Establishing Paternity and Demanding Child Support in a Ghanaian Town', in S. Roberts (ed.), Law and the Family in Africa (Mouton, The Hague, 1977), pp.16-37

Lubbock, Sir John The Origin of Civilisation and the Primitive Condition of Man (P. Riviere, Chicago University Press, 1978 ed.) (first published 1870)

Lukes, S. Power: a Radical View (Macmillan, London, 1974)

Lu Yang Ruhe Duidai Lianai, Hunyin, Jiating Wenti (The Correct Handling of Love Marriage and Family Problems), (Shandong Publishing House, Jinan, 1964)

Mayer, P. and Mayer, I. Townsmen or Tribesmen (Oxford University Press, Cape Town, 1961, 2nd. ed. 1971)

MacCormack, C.P. 'Nature, Culture and Gender: a Critique', in C. MacCormack and M. Strathern Nature, Culture and Gender (Cambridge University Press, Cambridge, 1980)

McCreery, J.L. 'Women's Property Rights and Dowry in China', Ethnology, vol. 15 (1976), pp.163-74

McDonough, R. and Harrison, R. 'Patriarchy and Relations of Production', in A. Kuhn and A. Wolpe (eds.) Feminism and Materialism (Routledge, London, 1978) pp.11-41

McLennan, John Primitive Marriage: An Inquiry into the Origin of the Form of Capture in Marriage Ceremonies (A. and C. Black, Edinburgh, 1865)

Macpherson, C.B. 'A Political Theory of Property', in C.B. Macpherson Democratic Theory: Essays in Retrieval (Oxford University Press, Oxford, 1973)

Maher, V. 'Women and Social Change in Morocco', in L. Beck and N. Keddie (eds.) Women in the Muslim World (Harvard University Press, 1978)

Maine, H.S. Ancient Law: Its Connection with the Early History of Society and its Relation to Modern Ideas (John Murray, London, 1861, 1912 ed.)

Mair, L. African Marriage and Social Change (Frank Cass, London, 1969)

Maudelbaum, D. Society in India (University of California Press, Berkeley, 1970)

Mansur, F. Bodrum, A Town in the Aegean (E.J. Brill, Leiden, 1972)

Manushi (A journal about women and society) (Manushi Editorial Collective, Delhi, 1979)

Mardin, S.A. 'Some Explanatory Notes on the Origin of the "Mecelle"', The Muslim World, vol. 51 (1961), pp.189-96, 274-9

Marx, K. Capital: a Critical Analysis of Capitalist Production, vol. I (Progress Publishers, Moscow, 1954, first English edition, 1877)

_____ Grundrisse (Penguin Books, London, 1973) (Translated by M. Nicolaus from the German of 1939 (1857-58))

Mauss, M. The Gift: Forms and Functions of Exchange in Archaic Societies (Cohen and West, London, 1954) (Translated by I. Cunnison from the French of 1925)

Mayer, A.C. Caste and Kinship in Central India (Routledge and Kegan Paul, London, 1960)

Mbilinyi, M. 'Tanzanian Women Confront the Past and the Future', Futures (October, 1975)

Meillassoux, C. Maidens, Meal and Money: Capitalism and the Domestic Community (Cambridge University Press, Cambridge, 1981)

Menefee, S.P. Wives for Sale: an Ethnographic Study of British Popular Divorce (Blackwell, Oxford, 1981)

Middleton, J. Report on Land Tenure in Zanzibar (HMSO, 1961)

Mill, J.S. The Subjection of Women (MIT Press, London, 1970 ed.)

Miller, B. The Endangered Sex (Cornell University Press, Ithaca, 1981)

Munn, N. 'The Spatiotemporal Transformations of Gawa Canoes', Journal Société Oceanistes, vol. 33, nos. 54-55 (March - June 1977), pp.39-53

Murickan, J. 'Women in Kerala: Changing Socio-economic Status and Self Image', in A. de Souza (ed.) Women in Contemporary India (Manohar, Delhi, 1975)

Murphy, W.P. 'Secret Knowledge as Property and Power in Kpelle Society: Elder Versus Youth', Africa, vol. 50, no. 2 (1980), pp.193-207

Mwapachu, J.V. 'Operation Planned Villages in Rural Tanzania', in A. Coulson (ed.) African Socialism in Practice (Spokesman Press, Nottingham, 1979)

Myrdal, J. Report from a Chinese Village (Penguin Books, Harmondsworth, 1967)

Nader, L. 'An Analysis of Zapotec Law Cases', Ethnology, vol. 3 (1964), pp.404-19

_____ 'Choices in Legal Procedure: Shia Moslem and Mexican Zapotec', American Anthropologist, vol. 67, no. 2 (1965), pp.394-99

Nanfang Ribao (Nanfang Daily) 'Are Betrothal Presents a Means of Showing Gratitude to Parents?', 25 December 1964

_____ 'How I Refused to Observe the Old Customs for My Wedding', 18 January 1965

Nair, P.T. Marriage and Dowry in India (Minerva Associates, 1978)

Nash, J. 'Sex, Money, and the Status of Women in Aboriginal Southern Bougainville', American Ethnologist, vol. 18, no. 1 (February 1981), pp.107-26

Nel, P.A. The Minimum and Supplemented Living Levels of Non-Whites Residing in the Main and other Selected Urban Areas of the Republic of South Africa, Research Report no. 92 (Bureau of Market Research, UNISA, Pretoria, 1981)

Nelson, N. 'Dependence and Independence: Female Household Heads in Mathare Valley, a Squatter Community in Nairobi, Kenya', Unpublished Ph.D. thesis, University of London, 1978

____ 'Introduction to African Women in the Development Process', Journal of Development Studies, vol. 17, no. 3 (1981), pp.1-8

New China News Analysis, 'Present Conditions Relating to the Implementation of Marriage Law stated by Committee for its Implementation', 5 March 1955

Ngubane, H. Body and Mind in Zulu Medicine (Academic Press, London, 1977)

Nyerere, J. 'The Arusha Declaration', in Uhuru na Ujamaa (Freedom and Socialism) (Oxford University Press, Oxford, 1968)

Nypan, A. A Sample Study of Market Traders in Accra (University College of Ghana, Accra, 1960)

Obbo, C. African Women: Their Struggle for Independence (Zed Press, London, 1981)

O'Laughlin, B. 'Mediation of Contradictions: Why Mbum Women do not eat Chicken', in M.Z. Rosaldo and L. Lamphere (eds.), Women, Culture and Society (Stanford University Press, Stanford, 1974)

Oliveira Martins, J.P. Portugal Contemporâneo 2 vols. (Antonio Maria Pereira, Lisbon, 1925) (first published 1881)

Panigrahi, L. British Social Policy and Female Infanticide in India (Munshi Raun Manoharlal, New Delhi, 1972)

Papanek, H. 'Development Planning for Women', Signs, vol. 3, no. 1 (1977), pp.14-21

Parish, W.L. 'Socialism and the Chinese Peasant Family', Journal of Asian Studies, vol. 34, no. 3 (May 1975), pp.613-30

Parry, J. 'Ghosts, Greed and Sin: The Occupational Identity of the Benares Funeral Priests', Man (N.S.), vol. 15, no. 1 (March 1980), pp.88-111

Pashukanis, E.B. Law and Marxism: A General Theory (Inklinks, London, 1978)

Pauw, B.A. The Second Generation (Oxford University Press, Cape Town, 1963) (2nd ed. 1973)

Peking Review, Yang Liu, 'Reform of Marriage and Family System in China', 13 March 1964

People's China, Ling Meili, 'The Growth of a New Outlook on Marriage', 1 June 1951

____ Tso Sung Fen, 'New Marriages, New Families', 16 November 1957

Pereira, M.H. Livre Cambio e Desenvolvimento Económico - Portugal na Segunda Metade do Século XIX (Edições Cosmos, Lisboa,

1971)

Peristiany, J.G. (ed.) Honour and Shame: The Values of
Mediterranean Society (Weidenfeld and Nicolson, London,
1966)

Piault, C. (ed.) Regards sur les Familles et leurs Biens en Grece
(Hermann, Paris, forthcoming)

Pina-Cabral, J. de 'Cults of Death in Northwestern Portugal', Journal
of the Anthropological Society of Oxford, vol. 11 (1980),
pp.1-14

___ 'A Peasant Worldview in Its Context: Cultural Uniformity and
Differentiation in Northwestern Portugal.' Unpublished D.Phil.
thesis, University of Oxford, 1981a

___ 'O pároco rural e o conflito entre visões do mundo', Estudos
Contemporâneos, vol. 3 (1981b)

Pliny, Natural History, Book XXXV, vol. 9, Loeb Classical Library,
translated by H. Rackham (Heinemann, London, 1968)

Pocock, D. Kanbi and Patidar (Oxford University Press, Oxford,
1972)

Poole, F.J.P. 'Transforming "Natural" Woman: Female Ritual Leaders
and Gender Ideology Among Bimin-Kuskusmin', in S. Ortner
and H. Whitehead (eds.), Sexual Meanings (Cambridge
University Press, New York, 1981)

___ 'The Ritual Forging of Identity: Aspects of Person and Self in
Bimin-Kaskusmin Male Initiation', in G. Herdt (ed.), Rituals
of Manhood: Male Initiation in Papua New Guinea (University of
California Press, Berkeley, in press)

Quarterly Bulletin of Statistics, vol. 15, no. 4 (Pretoria, South
Africa, December 1981)

Quinn, N. 'Anthropological Studies on Women's Status', Annual
Review of Anthropology, vol. 6 (1977), pp.181-225

Radcliffe-Brown, A.R. 'Matrilineal and Patrilineal Succession', in
Structure and Function in Primitive Society (Cohen and West,
London, 1952)

Ramsay, W.M. Impressions of Turkey: During Twelve Years
Wanderings (Hodder and Stoughton, London, 1897)

___ The Intermixture of Races in Asia Minor, Some of its Causes
and Effects (Proceedings of the British Academy, vol. 7,
Oxford University Press, London, 1917)

Rapp, R. 'Review Essay: Anthropology', Signs, vol. 4, no. 3
(1979), pp.497-513

Reindorf, C.C. The History of the Gold Coast and Asante (Ghana
University Press, Accra, 1966)

Reiter, R. (ed.) Toward an Anthropology of Women (Monthly
Review Press, New York, 1975)

Renmin Ribao (People's Daily) Liu Jingfan, 'Purpose of the New
Campaign to Publicise the New Marriage Law', 20 March 1953

___ Yang Tawen and Liu Suping 'On the Reform of Our Country's
System of Marriage and the Family', 13 December 1963

___ 'Revolutionary Youths Must Take the Lead in Changing Old
Habits and Customs', 24 January 1972

Robertson, C. 'Economic Woman in Africa: Profit Making Techniques of Accra Market Women', Journal of Modern African Studies, vol. 12 (1974), pp.657-64

Rogers, B. The Domestication of Women (Kogan Page, London, 1980)

Rosaldo, M.Z. 'The Use and Abuse of Anthropology: Reflections on Feminism and Cross-Cultural Understanding', Signs, vol. 5, no. 3 (Spring 1980), pp.389-417

Rosaldo, M. and Lamphere, L. (eds.) Women, Culture and Society (Stanford University Press, Stanford, 1974)

Rubel, P.G. and Rosman, A. Your Own Pigs You May Not Eat: A Comparative Study of New Guinea Societies (University of Chicago Press, Chicago, 1978)

Rubin, G. 'The Traffic in Women: Notes on the "Political Economy" of Sex', in R. Reiter (ed.) Toward an Anthropology of Women (Monthly Review Press, New York, 1975)

Sacks, K. 'Engels Revisited: Women, The Organization of Production and Private Property', in M. Rosaldo and L. Lamphere (eds.) Women, Culture and Society (Stanford University Press, Stanford, 1974)

_____ Sisters and Wives: The Past and Future of Sexual Equality (Greenwood Press, Westport, Conn., 1979)

Sahlins, M. Stone Age Economics (Tavistock Publications, London, 1974)

Salisbury, R.F. From Stone to Steel: Economic Consequences of a Technological Change in New Guinea (Melbourne University Press, Melbourne, 1962)

Sanday, P.R. Female Power and Male Dominance: on the Origins of Sexual Inequality (Cambridge University Press, Cambridge, 1981)

Scheffler, H.W. Choiseul Island Social Structure (University of California Press, California, 1965)

Schieffelin, E.L. 'Reciprocity and the Construction of Reality', Man (N.S.), vol. 15, no. 3 (September 1980), pp.502-17

Schlegel, A. (ed.) Sexual Stratification: a Cross-cultural View (Columbia University Press, New York, 1977)

Schneider, J. 'Of Vigilance and Virgins: Honor, Shame and Access to Resources in Mediterranean Societies', Ethnology, vol. 10 (1971), pp.1-24

Schneider, J. and Schneider, P. Culture and Political Economy in Western Sicily (Academic Press, New York, 1976)

Scholte, B. 'Critical Anthropology Since its Reinvention', in J. Kahn and J. Llobera (eds.) The Anthropology of Pre-Capitalist Societies (Macmillan, London, 1981)

Schwimmer, E. Exchange in the Social Structure of the Orokaiva (C. Hurst, London, 1973)

_____ 'Objects of Mediation: Myth and Praxis', in I. Rossi (ed.) The Unconscious in Culture: the Structuralism of Claude Levi-Strauss in Perspective (E.P. Dutton, New York, 1974)

_____ 'The Self and the Product: Concepts of Work in Comparative Perspective', in S. Wallman (ed.) Social Anthropology of Work (Academic Press, London, 1979)

Serrão, J. A Emigraçao Portuguesa (Horizonte, Lisbon, 1974)
_____ (ed.) Dicionario da Historia de Portugal (Inciativas Editoriais, 1965)
Sexton, L.D. 'From Pigs and Pearlshells to Coffee and Cash', paper presented to A.S.A.O. conference 1980 (to be published in D. O'Brien and S. Tiffany (eds.) Rethinking Women's Roles: Perspectives from the Pacific (University of California Press, California)
_____ 'Wok Meri: a Women's Savings and Exchange System in Highland Papua New Guinea', Oceania, vol. 52, no. 3 (1982), pp.167-98
Sharma, U.M. Women, Work and Property in Northwest India (Tavistock Press, London, 1980)
Sillitoe, P. Give and Take: Exchange in Wola Society (Australian National University Press, Canberra, 1979)
Simkins, C.E.W. The Distribution of the African Population of South Africa by Age, Sex and Region - Type, 1960, 1970 and 1980 (Saldru Working Paper no. 32, Cape Town, mimeo, 1981)
Simons, H.J. African Women: Their Legal Status in South Africa (C. Hurst, London, 1968)
Skouteri-Didaskalou, E. 'On Greek Dowry: Spatiotemporal Transformations', Postgraduate Diploma Thesis in Social Anthropology, University of London, 1976
SOPEMI, Continuous Reporting System on Migration (Organization for Economic Co-operation and Development, Paris, 1982)
Soteriadis, G. An Ethnological Map Illustrating Hellenism in the Balkans Peninsula and Asia Minor (Edward Stanford Ltd., London, 1918)
Starr, J. 'Adliye, The Ethnography of a Rural Turkish Court', 35 minute colour Super-8 film and film-script (on file with the author, 1968)
_____ Dispute and Settlement in Rural Turkey: an Ethnography of Law (E.J. Brill, Leiden, 1978)
_____ 'Folk Law in Official Courts of Turkey', in T. Allott (ed.) Folk Law in State Courts (in press)
Starr, J. and Pool, J. 'The Impact of a Legal Revolution in Rural Turkey', Law and Society Review, vol. 8, no. 4 (1974), pp.533-66
Stirling, P. 'Land, Marriage and the Law in Turkish Villages' in 'The Reception of Foreign Law in Turkey', International Social Science Bulletin, vol. 9 (1957), pp.21-33
_____ Turkish Village (Weidenfeld and Nicolson, London, 1965)
_____ 'Cause, Knowledge and Change: Turkish Village Revisited' in J. Davis (ed.) Choice and Change: Essays in Honour of Lucy Mair (Athlone Press, London, 1974)
Stolcke, V. 'Women's Labours: the Naturalisation of Social Inequality and Women's Subordination' in K. Young, C. Wolkowitz and R. McCullagh (eds.) Of Marriage and the Market (CSE Books, London, 1981)
Strathern, A. 'Wiru and Daribi Matrilineal Payments', Journal of Polynesian Society, vol. 80, no. 4 (December 1971),

pp.449-62

_____ '"Finance and Production" Revisited: in Pursuit of a Comparison', in G. Dalton (ed.) Research in Economic Anthropology, vol. 1, 1978

_____ 'Gender, Ideology and Money in Mount Hagen', Man (N.S.), vol. 14, no. 3 (September 1979), pp.530-48

_____ 'The Central and the Contingent: Bridewealth Among the Melpa and the Wiru', in J. Comaroff (ed.) The Meaning of Marriage Payments (Academic Press, London, 1980)

_____ '"Noman": Representations of Identity in Mount Hagen', in L. Holy and M. Stuchlik (eds.) The Structure of Folk Models (Academic Press, London, 1981)

_____ 'Death as Exchange: Two Melanesian Cases', in S.C. Humphreys and H. King (eds.) Mortality and Immortality: the Anthropology and Archaeology of Death (Academic Press, London, 1982)

_____ 'Work Processes and Social Change in Mount Hagen', American Ethnologist (in press)

Strathern, M. Women Between: Female Roles in a Male World (Seminar (Academic) Press, London, 1972)

_____ 'The Self in Self-decoration', Oceania, vol. 49, no. 4 (June 1979), pp.241-57

_____ 'No Nature, No Culture: the Hagen Case', in C. MacCormack and M. Strathern (eds.) Nature, Culture and Gender (Cambridge University Press, Cambridge, 1980)

_____ 'Self-interest and the Social Good: Some Implications of Hagen Gender Imagery', in S. Ortner and H. Whitehead (eds.) Sexual Meanings (Cambridge University Press, New York, 1981)

_____ 'Culture in a Netbag: The Manufacture of a Subdiscipline in Anthropology', Man (N.S.), vol. 16, no. 4 (December 1981), pp.665-88

_____ 'Domesticity and the Denigration of Women', in D. O'Brien and S. Tiffany (eds.) The Value of the Devalued (University of California Press, California, 1982)

Symeonidou-Alatopoulou, X. 'The Development of the Institution of Dowry in Greece, 1956-1974', (in Greek), Greek Review of Social Research (1979), pp.322-40

Tambiah, S.J. 'Dowry and Bridewealth and the Property Rights of Women in South Asia', in J. Goody and S.J. Tambiah Bridewealth and Dowry (Cambridge University Press, London, 1973)

Tanner, R.E.S. 'The Relationships Between the Sexes in a Coastal Islamic Community', African Studies, vol. 21 (1962)

Taylor, L. A Portuguese - English Dictionary (Harrap, London, 1973)

Tapper, R. Pasture and Politics: Economics, Conflict and Ritual Among the Shahsevan Nomads of North-Western Iran (Academic Press, London, 1979)

The 1960 Population Census of Ghana (Census Office, Accra, 1964)

The 1970 Population Census of Ghana, vol. 2 (Census Office, Accra, 1972)

Van Baal, J. Reciprocity and the Position of Women (Van Gorcum, Amsterdam, 1975)

Van der Veen, K. I Give Thee My Daughter (Van Gorcum, Assen, 1972)

Vatuk, S. Kinship and Urbanisation (University of California Press, Berkeley, 1972)

Velidedeoğlu, H.V. 'The Reception of the Swiss Civil Code in Turkey', International Social Science Bulletin, vol. 9 (1957), pp.60-5

Verdon, M. 'Shaking off the Domestic Yoke, or the Sociological Significance of Residence', Comparative Studies in Society and History, vol. 22 (1980) pp.109-32

Wagner, R. 'Analogic Kinship: a Daribi Example', American Ethnologist (1977), pp.623-42

____ Lethal Speech (Cornell University Press, Ithaca, 1978)

Weiner, A.B. Women of Value, Men of Renown: New Perspectives in Trobriand Exchange (University of Texas Press, Austin, 1976)

____ 'The Reproductive Model in Trobriand Society', Mankind, vol. 2, no. 3 (1978)

____ 'Trobriand Kinship from Another View: the Reproductive Power of Women and Men', Man (N.S.), vol. 14, no. 2 (June 1979), pp.328-48

____ 'Reproduction: a Replacement for Reciprocity', American Ethnologist, vol. 7, no. 1 (February 1980), pp.71-85

West, M. 'From Pass Court to Deportation: Changing Patterns of Influx Control in Cape Town, South Africa', Anthropology Seminar Paper (University of Cape Town, mimeo, 1982)

Westwood, S. 'Class Formation in Urban Ghana: a Study of the Ga of James Town, Accra', Unpublished Ph.D. thesis, University of Cambridge, 1978

White, E.H. 'Legal Reform as an Indicator of Women's Status in Muslim Nations', in L. Beck and N. Keddie (eds.) Women in the Muslim World (Harvard University Press, 1978)

Whitehead, A. 'Review of J. Goody, Production and Reproduction', Critique of Anthropology, vol. 3, no. 9-10 (1977) pp.151-9

____ '"I'm Hungry, Mum" - the Politics of Domestic Budgeting', in K. Young, C. Wolkowitz and R. McCullagh (eds.) Of Marriage and the Market (CSE Books, London, 1981)

Widjeyewardene, G. 'Some Aspects of Village Solidarity Among Kiswahili-speaking Communities of Kenya and Tanganyika', Unpublished Ph.D. thesis, University of Cambridge, 1961

Wilden, A. System and Structure: Essays in Communication and Exchange (Tavistock Publications, London, 1972)

Wilson, M. and Mafeje, A. Langa (Oxford University Press, Cape Town, 1963)

Woddis, J. 'Is there an African National Bourgeoisie?', in P. Gutkind and P. Waterman (eds.), African Social Studies: A Radical Reader (Heinemann, London, 1977)

Wolpe, H. (ed.) The Articulation of Modes of Production: Essays from Economy and Society (Routledge, London, 1980)

Women of China, 'Woman's Right to Inherit Property Protected',

March 1980

    _____ 'Marriage Law Revised', December 1980

Xuexi yu Pipan (Study and Criticism) Sun Luoying and Lu Lifen, 'On Confucian Persecution of Women in History', 10 January 1975

Yanagisako, S. 'Family and Household: the Analysis of Domestic Groups', Annual Review of Anthropology, no. 8 (1979)

Yang, M. A Chinese Village: Taitou Shantung Province (Columbia University Press, New York, 1945)

Young, G. Corps de Droit Ottoman, 7 vols. (Clarendon Press, Oxford, 1905)

Zatz, E. 'The Implications of Housing for Kinship Relations in Exarchia', in A. Mackrakis and P. Allen (eds.) Women and Men in Greece: a Society in Transition (in press)

Zhongguo Funu (Women in China) Letter on 'What is the Criterion in Choosing a Spouse?', 1 May 1964

    _____ Ning Mingye, 'The Party Supports Me in My Struggle for Self-determination in Marriage'; Liu Kuihua 'Marriage by Purchase Really Harms People'; 'If You Don't Want Betrothal Gifts, Your Thought is Red', 1 February 1966

Zhongguo Quingnian (Youth of China) 'New Ways of Handling New Things'; 'What Things Should be Emphasised in Handling a Wedding Well?', 24 April 1962

    _____ Cheng Shuizhi 'Is My Objection to an Arranged Marriage Unfilial?' 15 February 1963

    _____ 'Young People Should Take the Lead in Ending the Practice of Betrothal Gifts', 19 November 1964

    _____ 'Changing Undesirable Wedding Customs and Practices', 16 January 1966

CONTRIBUTORS

Sandra Burman

Socio-Legal Centre,
Wolfson College, Oxford

Pat Caplan

Department of Anthropology
Goldsmith's College,
New Cross, London

Elisabeth Croll

Queen Elizabeth House,
St. Giles, Oxford

Renée Hirschon

Department of Social Studies,
Oxford Polytechnic, Oxford

João de Pina-Cabral

ISCTE
University of Lisbon

Ursula Sharma

Department of Sociology,
University of Keele

June Starr

Faculty of Law,
Erasmus University, Rotterdam

Marilyn Strathern

Girton College,
University of Cambridge

Sallie Westwood

Department of Adult Education,
University of Leicester

Ann Whitehead

School of Social Sciences,
University of Sussex

INDEX
Compiled by Jeremy Coote

NAME Index